JEROME

KERSEY

OVERCOMING THE ODDS

KERRY EGGERS

DEMENTI MILESTONE PUBLISHING

Author
Kerry Eggers

Publisher
Wayne Dementi
Dementi Milestone Publishing, Inc.
Manakin-Sabot, VA 23103
www.dementimilestonepublishing.com

Graphic Design
Jayne Hushen

ISBN: 978-1-7368989-3-2

Printed in the USA

Table of contents

About the Author

KERRY EGGERS is a journalist/author who wrote sports for Portland newspapers for 45 years. He worked for the Oregon Journal from 1975-82, at The Oregonian from 1982-2000 and at the Portland Tribune from 2001-2020. Eggers is a six-time the National Sports Media Association's Oregon Sportswriter of the Year, winning in 1981, 1997, 2000, 2003, 2011 and 2018.

Through his career, Eggers covered a variety of major events, including two Summer Olympic Games, four Super Bowls, a World Series, two major-league All-Star Games, five College World Series, two national championship football games, three Davis Cup ties, a golf U.S. Open, a Pro Bowl, six track and field Olympic trials and many NBA Finals and NBA All-Star games.

Eggers is past president of Track & Field Writers of America and recipient of the Jesse Abrahamson Award as the nation's top track and field writer. In 2014, he was honored with the "DNA Award" — recognizing "extraordinary passion and dedication to sport in Oregon" — at the Oregon Sports Awards.

This is Eggers' eighth book. The others: Blazers Profiles (1991), Against the World (1993, with co-author Dwight Jaynes), Wherever You May Be: The Bill Schonely Story (1999), Clyde "The Glide" Drexler: My Life in Basketball (2004), Oregon State University Football Vault (2009), The Civil War Rivalry: Oregon vs. Oregon State (2014) and Jail Blazers: How the Portland Trail Blazers Became the Bad Boys of Basketball (2018).

Dedications

Kerry's dedication:

To two of my friends and greatest sources of inspiration — legendary broadcaster Bill "The Schonz" Schonely, 92 and still kicking tail, and Bud Ossey, who at 101 has more zest for life than many half his age.

To Kiara Kersey, through whom Jerome's spirit lives on.

To Teri Kersey Valentine, whose love and support for this book project provided much inspiration.

To the memory of Jerome Kersey, who was truly one of a kind.

— Kerry Eggers

Hoke's dedication:

Special thanks to the person who made this book project come together. When I first stopped work on a book back in 1998 with it only halfway done, I had no idea it would ever be completed. Thanks to my friend Rohn Brown, it is now complete.

The story it tells is about a man whose exploits are well-documented, but that is only half the story. Rohn has helped us all discover that Jerome Kersey's life was much more than just basketball. He is remembered by thousands of people, mostly as a good human being who cared about others and helped when he could.

— Hoke Currie

(The following is an open letter written in February 1984 by Hoke Currie, then sports information at Longwood College. It was directed to Longwood senior Jerome Kersey as he prepared for the final home game of his college career at Lancer Hall against Mason-Dixon Athletic Conference rival Mount St. Mary's. Ten minutes prior to tip-off, a ceremony took place honoring the Division II All-American.)

Saturday night, you'll step onto the Lancer Hall court for the last time. Here's hoping you go out in a blaze of glory with a typical Jerome Kersey performance that leads to another Longwood victory.

But, no matter what happens Saturday night, I just want to say, "Thanks for the memories, Jerome. It has been a rewarding four years watching you play basketball."

Coach Cal Luther talks about having nightmares thinking about what he'll do without you next season. Well, I just want to say you have been a sports information director's dream the past four years. You were pegged for greatness even when you were a skinny, wide-eyed freshman.

Assistant coach Mo Schoepfer came up with the nickname "The Cobra" because of your quickness. A nickname can't do justice to your style of play, but as nicknames go, I feel it's a pretty good one.

It's gratifying to me that you're finally getting the recognition you deserve. The coach at Pittsburgh-Johnstown said you are the best Division II player he has ever seen. What a lot of people don't realize is that you were a heck of a player even four years ago.

People will remember the leading scorer and rebounder in Longwood history with over 1,700 points and 1,100 rebounds, but I'll remember the other things — the little things.

Things like assists, steals, blocked shots, hustle, teamwork, 101 straight games without a miss.

I'll remember a player with a ton of ability, but with an attitude that more than matched that ability. It's a cliche you hear all the time — "He's not only a great player, but also a great kid."

Well, in your case, Jerome, it's no cliche.

People will ask, "What will we do next season without Jerome?" It will be tough without you. But we all must remember you're leaving behind a lot more than points and rebounds.

With a lot of assistance from several talented players, you're leaving behind a winning tradition and a lesson for excellence gained through honest, old-fashioned work.

I've never seen a player work harder than you, and I doubt I ever will. Whatever the future holds for you — and here's hoping you get a shot at the NBA — don't ever change.

Just keep working.

Foreword

by TERRY PORTER

Jerome Kersey and I were close friends for 30 years. We played together for nine seasons with the Portland Trail Blazers and also one season with the San Antonio Spurs late in our careers. We had a bond and a mutual respect that lasted right up to his death in 2015. It was never broken.

Maybe it was because we had a lot in common. We were both small-school kids — me from Wisconsin-Stevens Point, an NAIA college at the time, Jerome from NCAA Division II Longwood in Farmville, Virginia. We were late draft picks, too — me with the 24th pick in the first round in 1985, he with the 46th overall pick in the second round the year before.

Did we have chips on our shoulders? Probably. We both wound up playing 17 seasons in the NBA.

Not too many guys from North Carolina or Kentucky or Kansas or Duke or anywhere else do that.

Jerome and I met at the first practice my rookie year, I think at the Mittleman Jewish Community Center in Portland. I remember sitting on a bench during a break. We started talking and hit it off right away. I asked him what school he was from and he said Longwood. I said, "What kind of school is that?" I'd never heard of it.

Later on, we'd all kid him about playing at a women's college. Longwood had a few male day students but didn't go fully co-educational until 1976, four years before Jerome started there. We would say he only was there because of the ratio between men and women. He and I would say, "These big-school guys, they don't know what's coming. We're going to come at them with heart and compete hard." That triggered our friendship. From that day on, we always watched out for each other and hung out together.

We had another thing in common. We both got discovered at

the Portsmouth Invitational, predraft camp for college seniors held in Jerome's backyard in Virginia. Off his performance there, Jerome got to go to the Chicago predraft camp. The next year, I got invited to the Aloha Classic, which was the elite predraft camp in those years. They took the projected top 48 players in the draft. All the NBA coaches, GMs and personnel were there.

My rookie year was Jerome's second year in Portland. When he was a rookie, he, Steve Colter and Bernard Thompson hung out together all the time. My rookie year, I sort of replaced Bernard in the group. Steve, Jerome and I were the young guys on the team.

Jerome gave me a nickname — the "Tasmanian Devil." It was about my style of play and the way I got after it. I picked guys up 94 feet. I was relentless. I kept coming after them. If you've ever seen that character in cartoons, you know what he meant.

We called Jerome "Romeo." It was partly because it was a take on Jerome, but mostly because of the women. He liked them and they liked him. He just attracted the ladies. Women and cars were his passions. He loved cars. Always had to get the newest one. Always fantasized about a new car.

He had just about everything through his career. When he was with the Los Angeles Lakers, he had the Magnum P.I. I remember driving in that with him. It's just not the thing you forget.

Jerome was a nice guy, but he was so much more than that. He was always kind, which is a lot harder than being nice. He cared about people who were close to him. He didn't take shit from anyone, though, on or off the court. He was approachable, but he didn't like to be interrupted at dinner, or fans who got a little pushy and interrupted his time. He'd be like, "I'm not doing it right now. If you want to wait 10 minutes, I'll take care of you." That was with fans. He wasn't quite as polite on the court.

Jerome always gave great advice, but he was willing to listen and take advice, too. That was something early in our career that we talked about — how to develop our skills, how to make the NBA into a career.

Terry Porter and Jerome Kersey early in their career with the Trail Blazers. Porter and Kersey were teammates for 11 NBA seasons — 10 with Portland and one with the San Antonio Spurs. *Courtesy Portland Trail Blazers*

We also talked a lot about family stuff. He loved his grandmother, May Kersey, to death. She and her husband, Herman, raised him. Jerome's dad wasn't on the scene. His mother turned over parental duties to her parents, and they did a great job.

I remember when we went to Philadelphia on a road trip one year and he was going to meet his dad for the first time. He was nervous, because his dad wasn't in his life. Jerome wanted to meet him and try to build a relationship with him. They developed a mutual respect for each other, but never in the parameters of a father-son relationship.

Jerome could light up a room. He was easygoing for the most part, very charismatic. He loved interacting with people. He didn't mind being in a big group. Always had jokes. He loved being around friends and hanging out.

On the court, he was one of those rare athletes who could play hard and work hard. When it came time to play ball, he gave it everything he had — every ounce of his body and energy to try to do what was best for the team. He was a great teammate. Always a great team guy, a great locker room guy. I loved him as a friend, but I also loved what he brought to the team. He would run through a wall for you.

He was a bundle of relentless effort and energy. I remember how many times he chased down guys to block their shot at the rim in transition. We called him the 'Rundown Man." He was LeBron James before LeBron in that regard. Jerome would be a game-changer for us. He'd take the charge, sacrifice his body. He was not afraid to give up his body, ever.

Jerome never backed down from anybody. He was always a bruiser type, a banger. He liked to assert his presence on the defensive end. I remember many times when that approach helped us get through games. He played like that and got us all fired up. Even with all the tough guys he matched up with, he didn't back down from anybody. He took on those challenges.

There were scary moments with Jerome. We played a game against Seattle at Memorial Coliseum and Benoit Benjamin undercut him on a dunk and he fell on his neck. But Jerome being Jerome, he bounced back up. He was very durable considering the way he played.

You look at his playoff numbers, he was a better player when it counted most. He was always good in big games and big moments and was able to come up with big-time plays. I remember Game 7 of the Western Conference semifinals series against San Antonio in

1990. He was the one who saved the pass thrown by the Spurs' Rod Strickland and got it to Clyde Drexler, who was streaking downcourt and was fouled. We wouldn't have won that series if Jerome hadn't made that play. Countless times he had a key block or a rebound and put-back to lift us. That's what he brought to that team.

Jerome never made an All-Star Game, but he certainly could have. A couple of years, he was close. During our run in the early '90s, we had three guys make it — me, Clyde and Kevin Duckworth. Even though we were dominant for that three-year period, it was tough to get a fourth. Buck Williams never made it. You had some big names at small forward in the West in those years. But Jerome was well-paid and well-regarded, and we did our best to let him know how important he was to our team.

We were co-captains for three seasons, from 1988-91, but that group didn't have one voice. Everybody at different times would have a voice. Clyde and Buck, first of all, but also me and Jerome and Danny Ainge and Cliff Robinson. There were times when Jerome got in your face with things like, "You have to guard him better," and you knew that he meant it. But really, that group collectively was the voice.

Jerome and I shared a sponsorship of a program with the Boys and Girls Club in Northeast Portland for several years. I grew up in the Boys and Girls Club. It was my life as a kid. When my family moved to the city of Milwaukee, I was always there. I took my first jump shot at a Boys and Girls Club. I swam for the first time there. My freshman and sophomore years in high school, I didn't play high school ball — I played with a Boys and Girls Club team.

When Jerome and I became teammates in Portland, we were asked what we were passionate about in terms of community service, what we wanted to get involved with. Jerome wasn't involved with one particular charity, so we decided to sponsor what we called the "Portland/Phoenix Exchange Club."

We partnered with the Phoenix chapter of the Boys and Girls Club. We'd provide 10 kids and their chaperones a plane ticket to a

Blazers game against the Suns in Phoenix each year. They would stay with Phoenix club members and visit their club or school. They'd come to a Blazers game-day shootaround. We'd take them to lunch, then they'd come to the game and get a chance to meet players. The Suns would do the same thing, sponsoring a group for a trip to Portland to watch them play us and visit our Boys and Girls Club. We'd also take them to visit places like the Oregon Museum of Science and Industry or Niketown. We did it for five or six years. It was really meaningful for both me and Jerome.

After Susie and I got married in 1990, Jerome and I were still close. He'd come over to the house for holidays. We'd do New Year's parties together. Susie loved him. My kids grew up knowing him and loving him.

After I retired from playing and became a head coach for the first time in Milwaukee, I hired Jerome as a member of my coaching staff. We'd had conversations about it when I first got into coaching, so I knew that was my opportunity to bring him on. He was our third assistant with the Bucks, working out guys, doing player development stuff. He taught them what it was like to be a pro. His story resonated with young guys in particular. He related really well to the players. They respected him and his willingness to work with guys and try to make them better.

Through the years, his personality never changed. He was the same Jerome. For several years, he had a mentoring position for the Blazers with their players. Again, he was especially good with kids who were coming into the league at 18, 19 years old without college experience. They didn't have a clue about how to become a pro and how to conduct themselves. Jerome was the perfect guy to teach them that.

When Jerome finally got married in 2013, he was so happy. Teri was great for him. They had a long relationship. I remember talking with Jerome about taking that next step with her. She balanced him out. I really liked her demeanor, and how I saw her interact with Jerome. They were a great match.

I'll never forget the day Jerome died. I was picking up my son, Malcolm, from practice at Jesuit High in Portland, and Jerome's friend, J.R. Harris, called me and said, "He's gone, man. He's gone." I said, "Who you talking about?" He said, "Jerome. I talked to Teri. He's dead." I was in a fog. I got a photo radar ticket driving home. I had no idea how fast I was going. I started calling everybody else, all of our former teammates. It was a really tough day, a punch in the stomach. A lot of the good ones go too soon. We all lost a part of us that day.

Even so, Jerome lived a full life. He lived the best life he could have lived. We often talked about where we came from and what we were able to accomplish, the people we were able to meet, the places we were able to go. He provided a great life for his grandmother and his family. He was a kid who grew up with nothing, but had the ability to rise up and achieve so much because of his work ethic and drive.

He was my closest friend among any teammates. Early in my career, before I got married, we roomed together one summer at his house. We enjoyed life and did a lot of great things together.

I'm honored to write this foreword and happy this book is being written. Jerome was like a brother to me. We grew up as young professionals together, achieved things that we couldn't have imagined as kids growing up. Our paths crossed and it became an unbelievable brotherhood. To be able to honor his life and his legacy is special for me.

Jerome Kersey's story is one from which lessons can be learned. From how he conducted himself in the Portland community, to how its citizens respected him, to what he was about as a person, to what kind of man he grew up to be. Living is about the lives you're able to impact through your journey. Anybody who came into contact with Jerome left that conversation the better for it. He touched your soul.

Introduction

In the Blink of An Eye

The day began in a normal way, though it was far from a normal day.

It was February 18, 2015, the 15th birthday of Madison, Jerome Kersey's stepdaughter by marriage to Teri Donnerberg. Jerome and Teri had taken Maddie to The Original Pancake House in the morning.

After breakfast, Teri headed out to run a few errands. Jerome drove his 2011 Jaguar XJ to the Trail Blazers' offices in Portland's Rose Quarter to take care of some business in his job as the Blazers' director of player programs and alumni.

The former Blazer forward had settled into his position with the team for which he had spent 11 of his 17 NBA seasons. Outgoing and immensely popular with Blazer fans, Kersey was the most visible of the club's ambassadors on game nights at Moda Center. It was a way for him to stay connected to the team and its legions of followers in the City of Roses. He loved what he was doing, and he was beloved in the community.

Six days earlier, Kersey had undergone what was considered minor surgery to repair a meniscus tear in his left knee. Amazingly, it was his first-ever surgery. He had experienced several injuries that had caused him to miss games through his 24 years playing high school, college and NBA basketball, but never one that required surgery.

"The only reason Jerome had his knee scoped was because of golf," close friend Ron Sloy says. "If he played three days in a row, that knee would burn. He wanted to be able to play without any pain."

Kersey's recovery from the procedure seemed routine. The day before, Jerome and fellow former Blazers Terry Porter and Brian Grant had appeared at a celebration of Black History Month at Portland's Madison High. Later in the day, he spent time working the leaf blower in the backyard of his Lake Oswego home.

In the days following the surgery, Jerome had mentioned to Teri that the back of his knee felt tight, which didn't seem unusual. Teri says as far as she knew, the only other person Jerome had talked to about it was former Blazer trainer Jay Jensen.

"Jay had him get on a (stationary) bike," she says. "Jerome could have slammed his hand in the door, and he'd have never complained that anything hurt. He never said anything."

Jerome was a little more revealing to a friend, with whom he confided, "The knee feels fine, but my calf is killing me." Perhaps he didn't want his wife to worry.

Kersey visited his Rose Quarter office on Feb. 18 wearing a sweatsuit. After attending to some duties, he headed downstairs to Rebound clinic, where a physical trainer put him on a stationary bike for 45 minutes. Then he headed home.

Teri returned from a hair appointment and found Jerome on the couch, drinking a Heineken and watching a basketball game on TV. She sat down and joined him. They had reservations for dinner at Benihana's to celebrate Maddie's birthday that evening. Jerome didn't mention anything about pain or discomfort in his leg.

Jerome and Maddie went upstairs to get dressed for dinner. In a few moments, Jerome called out for Teri. Seconds later, he called out again.

Teri rushed upstairs to see Jerome in the bedroom, bent down on one knee.

"I'm having a hard time breathing," he told her.

"Like we should call an ambulance?" she asked.

"Yes."

Maddie called 9-1-1. Very quickly, an ambulance arrived with emergency medical technicians, who immediately administered oxygen as Jerome complained about difficulty in breathing. They hooked him up to an IV. Teri laid next to her husband, holding the IV bag.

"I love you, baby," he kept saying.

"It's OK. They're here. You're going to be OK," she answered.

Six EMTs struggled to carry the 6-7, 260-pound Kersey — perched on a stair chair — out the door and to the ambulance parked in the driveway. When they laid him down, his body started to convulse. The paramedics worked on him en route to Legacy Meridian Park Medical Center in nearby Tualatin, where he was admitted to the emergency room.

Within the hour, the battle was over. He was gone, the result of a blood clot in the leg that traveled to his lungs, causing a fatal pulmonary thromboembolism.

Jerome Kersey was 52.

Life had ended far too soon for the man who became one of the true rags-to-riches stories in the NBA, an inspiring tale of a small-town boy raised by grandparents and his rise to fame and fortune in the game he loved.

But Kersey's story was also about kindness and integrity and the many people whose lives he touched during his time on the planet.

And so it will be told in the pages that follow.

Acknowledgments

It was the spring of 2020, a time of great change in our world due to the advent of COVID-19.

This was true in my personal life as well. In April, I retired after 45 years of writing sports for Portland newspapers.

The question I was frequently being asked, and perhaps was asking of myself: What was I going to do in retirement?

Well, relax a bit, of course. Not have a schedule. Maybe devote a little more time to my middling-at-best golf game. At least that's what I thought.

Then I received an email that changed the course of my life through the next year.

It was from Rohn Brown, a Mechanicsville, Va., resident who had attended Longwood College at the same time as former Trail Blazer Jerome Kersey.

Would I be interested in being involved in a book project about Kersey's life?

That depends, I wrote back. What did he have in mind?

Brown explained that Hoke Currie — the sports information director during Kersey's time at Longwood — had begun writing a book on the school's most famous alum during the 1990s. Would I like to complete it?

My response was no, that's not something in which I would be interested.

But it got me to thinking. I knew Kersey — who died tragically in 2015 after a blood clot in a calf following surgery traveled to his lungs — pretty well from my time covering the Blazers during his heyday in the early '90s. The relationship had continued through the 2000s and into the final years of his life, when we were occasionally on a panel together for a studio show called "Talkin' Ball" on Comcast SportsNet Northwest, which carried Blazer games.

As was the case with just about everyone he'd met, I liked Kersey. He was, in fact, the only athlete I had covered to be invited to my house for a meal.

Shortly after the birth of Jerome's only child, Kiara, we had Jerome, fiancé Anjela Stellato and Kiara over for dinner and an entertaining evening. My three young boys — old enough to be Blazer fans — were thrilled. To this day, they say it was one of the highlights of their childhood.

I had a good deal of respect for the way Jerome carried himself, for the way he had become such a revered and beloved figure in the Portland community through the years. I knew his life story was a compelling one — raised by grandparents in humble surroundings in a small town, a second-round draft pick who defied the odds to forge a very successful 17-year NBA career.

I told Brown I'd be interested in writing my own book on Kersey — using Currie's work for background purposes — but only if there were sufficient funds for an advance payment and a publisher prepared to take the book to print.

All of that is doable, Brown responded.

The results were serendipitous. An agreement was reached with Wayne Dementi, president of Dementi Milestone Publishing in Manakin-Sabot, Va. Rohn would be involved as a "project coordinator." Hoke and his wife, Nancy, would serve as the book's benefactors. It was their dream to see the book finished, and we are indebted to their financial backing.

It would prove to be a true "book team," with regular "Zoom" sessions and the most organized approach to any of the eight books I've written through the years.

Many thanks to Wayne, a wonderful fellow who was most understanding of my methods for putting a book together. His cooperation in terms of use of photos, copy editing, length of manuscript, deadlines and everything else involved in the process of bringing the book home could not have been better.

I knew I would use material from the portion of a book on Kersey that Hoke had written, along with many pages of notes from interviews he had conducted with family, friends, teammates and others involved in Jerome's life. I didn't fully appreciate, however, how much I would lean on him for information I couldn't have gotten elsewhere.

The most difficult part of writing this book was the inability to interview the protagonist. I was able to use quotes from a book I'd written in 1991 (Blazers Profiles) and several interviews we'd had through the years. But Currie's extensive interviews with Jerome in 1998 about his life until then proved invaluable. Hoke did a wonderful job asking the right questions and drawing out thoughtful, informative responses. He also provided interviews from a number of subjects who are no longer with us — notably former teammate Kevin Duckworth, ex-Blazer front office executive Stu Inman and sports psychologist Bruce Ogilvie.

I am most indebted to Rohn, for whom the title "project coordinator" doesn't do justice. He was truly the Swiss Army Knife of the writing process of this book. He patiently answered every question I asked through phone call, text and email diligently and expediently. He went the extra mile to provide every piece of information possible about Jerome's four years at Longwood, including contacts for friends and family members.

When I visited Virginia for four days of research and interviews, Rohn reserved a room in Farmville in which the book team could gather for a two-hour meeting (he even arranged for lunch), set up a confab with Longwood University officials and served as tour guide, showing me the campus while pointing out particular places of interest in terms of Kersey's time there as a student. He even sent me a "Jerome Kersey" bobblehead to add to the collection in my study.

Many thanks to the folks at Longwood, including Trey Eggleston and Chris Cook — and especially athletic director Michelle Meadows and senior associate AD Katie Pate — for their cooperation and support of the book endeavor.

Thanks to Bluestone High and Mecklenburg County Schools, notably superintendent Paul Nichols.

A shout-out to the Portland Trail Blazers, who embraced this book with the fervor of a Jerome Kersey hug. In particular, to director/corporate communications Hilary Gorlin, visual content manager Bruce Ely and president/CEO Chris McGowan.

To Jayne Hushen, our graphic designer. Thanks for your calm demeanor and great work.

To Steve Brandon, my partner in crime through all but one year of my newspaper career, for your work as copy editor of this book. Nobody does it like you do.

To my better half, Stephanie Holladay, for your proof-reading, fact-checking and overall support through the past year. Love you, girl.

—⋙—

OVER THE COURSE of nine months, I interviewed about 80 people for this book.

Thanks to those with NBA and/or Trail Blazer connections who contributed your thoughts, including Rick Adelman, Charles Barkley, Herb Brown, Bucky Buckwalter, P.J. Carlesimo, Rick Carlisle, Dwane Casey, Tom Fletcher, Brian Grant, George Karl, John Lashway, Michael Lewellen, Geoff Petrie, Traci Rose, Bill Schonely, Mike Schuler, Mike Shimensky, John Stockton, Terry Stotts and John Wetzel.

Thanks to those who were coaches, teammates, friends or associates of Jerome during his childhood and time at Longwood, including Bill Bowles, Ira DeGrood, Kenny Ford, Franklin Grant, Ms. Weston Gupton, Tommy Hargrove, Dale Hite, Bryan Kersey, Lonnie Lewis, Troy Littles, Cal Luther, Michael McCroey, Mike Mosely, Ernie Neal, Ron Orr, John Rusevlyan, Mo Schoepfer, Dave Strothers, Doug Toombs, Michael Tucker, Orlando Turner, Mitch Walker and Mike Wills.

A hearty thanks to Jerome's former NBA teammates who offered their observations, including Danny Ainge, Sam Bowie, Mark Bryant, Kenny Carr, Wayne Cooper, Clyde Drexler, Chris Dudley, Sean Elliott, Hersey Hawkins, Michael Holton, Steve Johnson, Steve Kerr, Nate McMillan, Jim Paxson, Will Perdue, Kiki VanDeWeghe, Darnell Valentine and Buck Williams.

Much appreciation to longtime friends and family members, including Eddie Bynum, Doug Gorman, Joe Khorasani, Mary Jones, Tracy Roberts, Anjela Stellato, Andy Stokes and Rick Ziebell.

Also, to John Hargrove, Jerome's birth father. I'm appreciative that you were willing to discuss what I'm sure was a difficult subject.

And to May Kersey, the very first person I interviewed for this book. Bless you, Grandma Kersey.

While writing the book, I made multiple calls to Jerome's close friends J.R. Harris, Ron Sloy and Mitch Walker to fact-check and ask opinions. I appreciate all you guys.

In Virginia, several people went above and beyond to help. In Clarksville, Jerome and Pat Watson offered lunch and a delightful couple of hours of conversation over lunch. After dinner, "Junnie" Kersey took the time to give me a brief tour of the town and showed me the neighborhood in which his late cousin was raised. Kevin "Huggy" Brandon was kind enough to drive from his home in Durham, N.C., rent a hotel room in Farmville and provide an extended in-person interview. Kevin Ricks came to my hotel in Norfolk from his home in Newport News for an interview about his former teammate.

To Terry Porter, you did a superb job in writing the foreword. You did your good friend proud.

To Kiara Kersey, thank you for the support as we pay tribute to your father.

To Teri Kersey Valentine, I can't thank you enough for the time and thought you put into reliving some painful memories. My admiration for you grew through this process. Your reflections were invaluable.

—⚉—

AS WORD GOT OUT about this book project, I received the following email from a Blazer fan named Paul Register:

"I'm so very grateful you are writing Jerome's biography. I can't put into context how important Jerome was to me, and yet he never knew me. When you're a kid, sometimes you need something — a vision of hope — to help you become who you want to be. Jerome was that for me.

"For some unbeknownst reason, when Jerome appeared in his first slam dunk contest, he intrigued me enough to begin following his story. As his playing time increased, I only wanted to emulate him more. So much so that many of my close friends, and occasionally their parents, called me 'Jerome.' Pretty amusing for an under six-foot Caucasian kid.

"My fondest memory of a game Jerome played in wasn't a game the Blazers won. It was a game they lost — badly. In the waning moments of this horrible loss, Jerome did something to force Rip City fans to erupt with pride.

"I don't recall who the opponent was, if we were losing or the player involved, but I'll never forget that moment. We were losing by 20 points or so … a breakaway dunk was about to ensue and the night was going to end in shameful fashion. But Jerome wouldn't have it.

"That night, Jerome Kersey invented the "Chase-down Block," decades before LeBron James became a name. The ball was sent into the second row of the stands. Rip City had an overwhelming moment of pure elation despite the one-sided loss. Those cheers went up not because of one play, but because we had Jerome Kersey, and the rest of the NBA did not. He was that second-round gift from above. It's too bad we had to give him back so soon."

—⁓—

I AM PLEASED that proceeds from sales of the general edition of this book will go to both the Jerome Kersey Foundation in Portland and to the Jerome Kersey '84 Men's Basketball Scholarship at Longwood University in Farmville, Va.

During the interview process, several subjects made mention of just how extraordinary Jerome's life story is.

"Every kid needs to read this book," Jerome's friend Doug Gorman told me.

Kevin and Rhonda Brandon, close friends of Jerome, established a scholarship in his name at Longwood. *Courtesy Longwood University*

"If anybody deserves to have his legacy incorporated in writing, it's Jerome," said Mike McCroey, his college teammate.

Instructed former Blazer teammate Sam Bowie: "Make sure in your book that you let people know: Jerome Kersey was special."

He was. I'm hopeful that Blazer fans will enjoy reading about one of the true greats in the franchise's long history.

During a long, thoughtful phone interview with Buck Williams, he made mention of something I've written about a couple of times. The Trail Blazers need to retire Jerome Kersey's No. 25 jersey. I'm hopeful the powers-that-be in the organization will make that happen sooner rather than later.

In the process of writing this book, I've thought often about Jerome, the life he led and what kind of person he proved to be. It's probably the most difficult book I've done because it's a posthumous endeavor. I tried to do you justice, my friend. I hope I did you right.

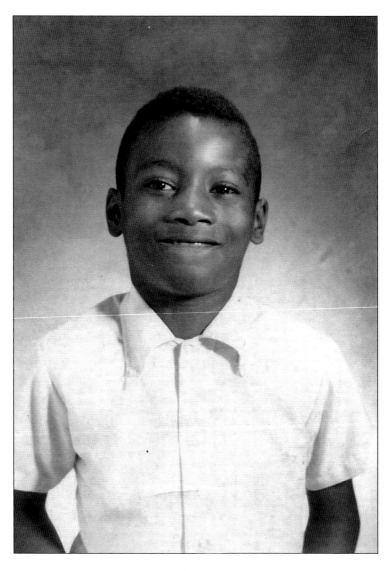

Jerome at six years old. *Courtesy Kersey Family.*

Chapter One

The Beginning

JEROME KERSEY came into the world on June 26, 1962, in the rural town of Clarksville, Va., just a few miles from the North Carolina state line. He was born to Deloris Kersey, the oldest of the seven children of Herman and Mary Kersey.

Deloris had just turned 18 years of age. The father, John Hargrove, was 20. Neither would play a major role in Jerome's life.

Jerome was raised by his maternal grandparents, alongside his aunts and uncles. Deloris is the oldest, followed by Lawrence, Mary, Jean, Joyce, Calvin— known as "Buck" — and Brenda.

Deloris would soon move to Richmond, Va., and would mostly see Jerome for a few weeks each summer until he turned 18. Soon after Jerome's birth, she yielded her parental rights to her own parents. Through his life, Jerome regarded Deloris like an aunt.

John, who had recently been released from the Army when Jerome was born, says he was living in Philadelphia and was married to another woman when he learned he was Jerome's father.

The de facto parents were Herman and Mary, the latter called "May" since her childhood by most of those who knew her. The couple raised Jerome as if he were their son.

"I don't call Jerome my grandson," May Kersey said in an interview with Hoke Currie in 1998. "I feel like Jerome is mine because I raised him from a baby."

Jerome felt the same way.

"I called them 'Mom' and 'Dad,'" Jerome told Currie. "I owe everything to them."

"He called his grandmother 'Mama,'" says a cousin, Clifton Kersey Jr., who was always known as Junnie. "He called his mother 'Deloris.'"

Herman was born on January 3, 1923. He died from a heart condition in May 1993 at the age of 70. May, still alive and living in Clarksville, was born on June 29, 1928. They were married for 49 years.

Until the age of nine, Jerome lived in a two-bedroom house outside of town on a tobacco farm owned by a man named Charlie Parker. Jerome's earliest memory was that "there were five of us living there — my grandparents, me, my aunt Brenda and uncle Calvin."

Brenda, the youngest of the seven offspring of Herman and May, was only three years older than Jerome. Calvin was six years Jerome's senior. He looked at them as if they were a sister and brother.

Along with her parents, a sister and two brothers, May grew up in Soudan, Va., about five miles south of Clarksville. Her father raised hogs, grew vegetables and got milk by tending to a neighbor's cows. Her mother worked cleaning houses for neighbors. They were members of the Second Baptist Church.

May was born during the Great Depression. "My parents never owned a home," May said during an interview with the author in November 2020. "We stayed on different farms."

May has a seventh-grade education. She was 16 when she got married to Herman, who was 21. Through the years, Herman worked at a sawmill, as a truck driver and at a factory. May did domestic work, worked at the Russell Stover Candy factory and at the Burlington

Industries woolen plant. With seven children of their own, money was tight.

"They were very poor," says Jerome Watson, Jerome Kersey's basketball coach for two years at Bluestone High. "But they made it work."

In 1966, when Jerome was four, Deloris married Thomas Florence. They would have three children together.

"My grandfather was my father, but Thomas was like a step-father," Jerome said. "He was always good to me. He treated me like a son."

His grandfather, though, was whom he considered his real dad.

"He was a real solid person," Jerome said in 1998. "He didn't say a lot except on the weekends, when he had a few drinks. He had selective hearing. I didn't really start to enjoy my grandfather until I was in college.

"He liked kids a lot. He wouldn't outwardly show it, but when all the little cousins were born, he'd be like, 'Bring that child over here!' They'd wind up on his lap. It was a side of him most people didn't see. He had a rough, rugged side. Every day he'd come home from work at the sawmill and it was like, 'I'm ready to eat. Then I'll be ready to take a nap.' He had to get up at 5 the next morning to be to work again. It wasn't like he wanted to get into a lot of horseplay in between.

"My grandmother did most of the discipline, and my aunts. Every once in a while he would give you the overflow whipping for being hard-headed with my grandmother. I could never understand it. My grandmother had already whipped me; then she would tell him what I'd done, and he would whip me, too. That only happened once in a while, but the ones he would give you would last."

In an article in the Mecklenburg Sun, Jerome said this about May Kersey:

"She was my hero, my inspiration. She was the rock of the family. She set a great foundation for me. When she was waking up before her 11 p.m. shift at Russell Stover, tired from cleaning the machines the previous night and silently feeling the aches and pains, I would watch her and tell myself there isn't anything I can do to compare to her."

To Currie, Jerome added this: "My grandmother never complained about anything. Even if she didn't feel good or her legs were hurting, she still went to work. She endured all the pain and hardship and continued to, along with my grandfather, provide for the family. I would see that and think, 'Well, if she can do all this, there's nothing I can't endure.' It instilled in me that I can go out there and work hard. I can be the guy who works just a little bit harder. That's something that comes from deep inside, and they can't take that away from you."

For nine years, May also did housecleaning twice a week for a Clarksville resident named Harriet Overstreet. This was while May worked the night shift at Russell Stover.

In 1998, Harriet told Currie that May was "one of the finest people I knew. My children were small then. They loved her. She was 1,000 percent honest and loyal — one of the most pleasant people. One of my friends described her as like having your best friend come to see you, but she cleaned the house while she was there. I attribute Jerome's success and his staying out of trouble to his grandmother's influence."

Jerome recalled going to the Overstreets at times when his grandmother provided housework. At other times, he'd visit his great grandmother, Channie Kersey.

"When my grandmother worked at Russell Stover, (Channie) would keep me during the day," Jerome said. "She loved going fishing every morning. I would go to her house at 8 o'clock. She was probably 60 then. She'd get her straw hat and her bucket, and we would go fishing for perch for two to three hours. She would come back and cook the fish we caught on an old wood stove. I was so bored fishing."

Jerome said he could be difficult as a child.

"I got real hardheaded at times," he said. "I was stubborn. I wanted to do things my way. I bitched and moaned. I cursed. I wasn't a saint. I talked back and sassed. My grandma took it in stride. She knew when to get on me, though."

May was three days short of her 34th birthday when Jerome was born. Though she had her hands full with her own offspring, she was young enough to handle having another one.

"It wasn't hard," she says today. "Jerome was always a lovable person. He was a good student. He mostly behaved himself. He just enjoyed life."

Jerome Watson and his wife, Pat, were members of the Second Baptist Church in downtown Clarksville along with May.

"We were in the same missionary group," Pat says. "Lovely family. She's a sweet person. She dearly loved Jerome."

All of the Kerseys attended Second Baptist Church during Jerome's childhood.

"Jerome and I went to church every Sunday when we were kids," Junnie says. "It wasn't just expected of us. It was expected of the whole community."

Those who knew the Kerseys held Herman and May in high esteem.

"The most loving people in the world," cousin Junnie Kersey says. "I was at their place a lot growing up. Whatever they ate, I ate. They treated me like I was their son. That's the way our families grew up. Everybody took care of everybody else."

"I called them 'Miss May' and 'Mr. Herman,'" says Tracy Roberts, who lived on the same block as the Kerseys. "To this day, Miss May is very sweet. Mr. Herman was quiet, but he was a disciplinarian. He believed in doing the right thing. They were good people."

"I used to see Jerome's granddaddy every morning at the post office," says Dale Hite, who owns a clothing store in town and is the same age as Jerome's uncle Buck. "Herman was a hardworking man, a good person. I knew him pretty well. I knew May better. One of the sweetest ladies you'll ever meet. A lot of Jerome's personality was the result of those two. They were such good family people."

"May instilled a lot in Jerome — the attitude, the work ethic, his general approach to things," says Bill Bowles, who was Jerome's football and basketball coach as a senior at Bluestone High. "In that respect, he had things a lot of other kids didn't have. She did a great job with him. As a coach, you try to bring those things out, if they're already there. She was the one who put them there."

Tommy Hargrove is the nephew of John Hargrove, Jerome's birth father, and was 17 years Jerome's senior. Tommy's mother, Susie, was Herman Kersey's twin.

"Jerome was at our house more than at his own mother's house," Tommy says. "His grandparents were exceptional people. Jerome was a very reserved young man coming up. As an adult, he never forgot where he came from. His upbringing made him what he ended up being — a great individual. His grandparents really nurtured him through his formative years."

Jerome Watson was Kersey's basketball coach at Bluestone when he was a sophomore and junior.

"His grandmother was just super," Watson says today. "She would never worry about him as long as I'd go pick him up. I said, 'Mrs. Kersey, I want to carry Jerome down to Winston-Salem for a clinic.' She said, 'That's fine, as long as he's with you.' She is a beautiful lady. Herman did an excellent job with Jerome, too. He was crazy about Jerome. He talked about Jerome all the time."

DRIVE WEST ON U.S. Route 58 from Norfolk to Clarksville across southern Virginia today and you'll see roads lined with pine trees that wind through small towns and old farmhouses, and dwellings located precariously close to the highway. In March 2021, there were still plenty of "Trump/Pence" signs along the way, and even a Confederate flag or two waving on a pole.

It is conservative country, not unlike it was in the 1960s and '70s when Jerome Kersey was raised there. It is still a rural area. Clarksville's population in 1962 was about 1,500; today it has dipped to about 1,100. In 1962, Mecklenburg County had about 31,000 residents, about the same as it is today.

In one way, Clarksville has changed dramatically since Jerome grew up there.

"We were a blue-collar industrial town," says Dale Hite, whose family has owned a clothing store in town for decades. "Those things are gone. Russell Stover is gone. Burlington Industries is gone. It's all

6

about tourism and outdoor activities now. The lake sucks people in from everywhere."

"Those were two huge employers," says Mike Mosely, sports editor of the Mecklenburg Sun and a Bluestone High grad. "When Clarksville didn't bring in any businesses to replace them, people just could not stay here. They had to pull up stakes and move to live somewhere else."

Clarksville sits just above the North Carolina state line, located along the Roanoke River and along Buggs Island Lake, the state's largest aquatic playground. Kerr Reservoir straddles the North Carolina/Virginia border and is home to Occoneechee State Park.

"The lake was about five or 10 minutes from our houses," Junnie Kersey says. "Us kids could walk through the woods to get there. We'd play cowboys and Indians, run around the edge of the water, fish just about every day."

"We'd go there to have picnic and family reunions," says Jerome's cousin, Mary Jones. "My dad would go fishing. We'd walk down the hill to the lake. Jerome would come sometimes. It's still a popular place for people to go."

Jones, who is Tommy Hargrove's sister, was almost a year older than Jerome.

"We grew up together," says Mary, who everyone called "Meme" (as in Mimi). "I have very good memories of our childhood. Jerome and Junnie came to our house every morning to catch the school bus. My grandmother, who is their great grandmother (Channie Kersey), would fix us hot biscuits. My mother raised Junnie's father, Clifton, from the time he was three months old. My brother, Kenny Christmas, taught Jerome how to play basketball.

"We played together every day. We'd eat together. We'd run up and down the court. We played baseball, softball, basketball — all kinds of sports. Jerome was such a kind, sweet, loving, good-hearted person. We got along very well — all of us."

Mary says blacks experienced "a lot of racism" in Clarksville during those years.

"Sometimes you'd go in stores, they'd follow you around because you were African-American," she says. "But the kids — we got along good with the ones we went to school with. We became good friends with a lot of them."

In the early 1960s, schools were integrated in Clarksville. By the late '70s and '80s, race relations had changed considerably there.

"Sports helped that," says Jerome Watson, who coached the Kerseys at Bluestone High. "When I got over there, the athletes banded together, black and white. They walked to class together. They were just real close. That carried over to the rest of the kids in school. When West End kids started going to the high school at Bluestone, that's when things changed. Sports was a big factor in all of that."

"It wasn't as bad for us coming up as it had been for the previous generation," Junnie Kersey says. "Things were breaking by the time we got into our childhood. We were fortunate that way. We grew up with a lot of white friends. We had a lot of support from the community, both white and black people. It was a good place to grow up."

Dale Hite, who is white, was six years older than Jerome.

"I'm not saying we didn't have race issues, but it was probably not as bad as it was in the cities," Hite says. "With the kids, we all knew each other. We grew up together. We played sports together. White guys had black friends and black guys had white friends. I lived on a farm. I worked with black kids my age picking tobacco. We rode bicycles together. We went to the creek together. Everybody got along.

"And I can tell you, Jerome was so easygoing and well-liked. If you couldn't get along with Jerome Kersey, something was wrong."

Says Mosely, who is black: "You knew (racism) was out there, but Jerome never let it affect him. He had as many white friends as he did black friends."

Today, Clarksville's racial makeup is 71 percent white and 27 percent black.

"It's been a good place to live," says Mosely. "I know white people who can't stand black people. I know black people who can't stand white people. But the majority of people around here now do try to respect each other."

JEROME ENJOYED outdoor pursuits as a child, especially after his family moved into town and onto Eighth Street, a few houses down from relatives. The Kerseys moved from the Parker farm, May Kersey says, because "the landlord said they wanted the house."

The home they rented on Eighth Street was bigger, with six rooms. There were fewer of the Kersey kids still at home, so there was more space for Jerome to maneuver. Cousin Junnie — seven months older and in the same grade in school — provided companionship and competition. Junnie lived on the same block with his parents, Clifton Sr. and Jo-ann Kersey. Clifton — the son of Fannie Mitchell, who was the sister of Herman Kersey — ran his upholstery shop next door to the house.

"We started fighting more," Jerome said. "I fought everybody. I was stubborn and always wanted to do things everybody else was doing. I wanted to stay out longer. I wanted to stay on the court longer. Sometimes you'd fight the kid two years older than you just to prove yourself. Me and Junnie fought more than anybody. I guess we were alike in certain aspects. But we were probably closer than both of us realized."

At the time, it was a fair fight. They were roughly the same size. That wasn't the case later. Jerome grew to 6 foot, 7 inches tall. Junnie topped out at 5-6.

"We fought every day," Junnie says of the childhood years. "Fistfights. Kids would egg us on and we'd fight. I'd say it was pretty even. We were competitive in everything. We were competitive in sports. We were competitive in school, too."

Even before that, though, the boys were competing.

"When we were four or five, we'd put a clothes hamper in the corner of a room and make it a hoop, and make a basketball out of socks," Junnie says. "That's when it started."

The fights ended in their teenage years, though a competition between the two continued on the athletic fields.

"They'd fight some, but they were just being kids, both of them trying to be the best in the sport that they were playing," says Jones. "They loved each other. We were all tight. We couldn't go a day without seeing each other — none of us."

"Jerome and Junnie were cousins," Mike Mosely says. "But really, they were like brothers."

While May and Herman were Jerome's parents, they didn't have to go it alone.

Junnie's father, Clifton Kersey Sr., "was like a father to me, too," Jerome said. "Clifton was one of my heroes. He was very influential in my life. I was a little jealous of Junnie because his dad owned an upholstery shop. Junnie used to get just about anything he wanted. But really, anything he gave Junnie, he gave me."

Says Junnie: "If Jerome was jealous, it was probably that I had a father in my life. But Dad helped him, too."

"Jerome had some good mentors growing up," says Jerome Watson, who coached Jerome in basketball during his sophomore and junior seasons at Bluestone. "Clifton Kersey was one. He took the boys around to basketball camps and games when they were small."

It wasn't just Jerome whom Clifton Kersey looked after.

"My dad took care of a lot of family members," Junnie says. "A lot of them didn't have their own father. He rented out tobacco fields and helped support the rest of the family by giving them all summer work. All us kids worked in them."

When Jerome and Junnie were six or seven they started picking tobacco for Clifton Sr., along with Jerome's uncles, Buck and Lawrence. Jerome and Junnie continued working in the fields every summer through high school.

"We'd start about 6 in the morning," Junnie says. "We'd come home for lunch and Dad would work in his upholstery shop from about noon to four o'clock. We'd go back and work from maybe 5 to 8 p.m. through high school. It was hard work. Sometimes I didn't want to get up in the mornings, but Dad kept on calling me.

"My mom went to work at 4 p.m. We'd go to my aunt's house and walk all the way from there to the farm about a mile away. As soon as we got there, we'd get pails of water from the well in back of the house. Jerome and I would each get two buckets of water. We'd see who could take it longer before he had to set it down."

IN HIS 1998 interview with Hoke Currie, Jerome recalled his years attending Hillcrest Elementary School in first grade, then Clarksville Elementary from second to sixth grade.

"Mrs. King was my first-grade teacher," he said. "She would spank us on the hand with a ruler if we were chewing gum, talking, acting up. She would tell you to put your hand out and spank you on the palm. If you jerked back, you got another one. Some days she used two rulers. She would get you early morning, too. We didn't want to get the ruler from Mrs. King.

"Me and a kid named Ricky Crow used to get in a fight all the time in fourth grade. I went to the office so many times for fighting that guy. He was a white kid. He was just nuts. I guess he thought I was nuts, too. One morning, I pushed him into the closet and locked the door and he couldn't get out while the teacher was out of the room. She sent both of us to the office when she came back."

As he got into junior high, Jerome had a bit of puppy love with a neighbor two houses down.

"We were kind of childhood crushes," Tracy Roberts says today. "He was two years older than me. We lived so close. Junnie was right down the street. Mary was around the corner. It was a close-knit neighborhood. Everybody looked out for each other. That's how we were as a community."

Tracy says the Roberts' house was a gathering place for her friends.

"We'd play records and dance around," she says. "We watched sports together. Normal stuff. Fun stuff. Innocent stuff. My mom would load us kids up in the car out in the country to collect soda bottles, and take that money to buy hot dogs and hamburgers for a cookout. Or we'd pick blackberries and she'd make pies. Or we'd all go to the drive-in together.

"He was very quiet, very shy, but he was very competitive. We'd all play games. It didn't matter whether you were a girl or a boy, if you did something, he'd defend himself. He didn't let anybody take advantage of him. One time I hit him and I turned around and ran. He chased me and knocked the breath out of me. I remember telling his grandfather, 'Mr. Herman, he hit me.' Jerome got in trouble. He was punished for it. It didn't happen again."

Tracy's mother called Jerome "Jeremiah."

"I don't know why," says Tracy, chuckling. "He'd come to my home and do things to help her. We had a Saint Bernard. He was the only one my mom could find to walk the dog. All the guys would tease him about it, but he didn't care. He did it anyway, just to be helpful. He was just good that way.

"My brother is much younger. One time all of us went to see the movie 'Friday the 13th.' On the way home, Jerome had my brother in his lap. I don't know if it was because the movie was scary or not, but he threw up all over Jerome. He just laughed it off.

"He had a simplicity about him, a purity. An innocence about him. He was kind. In my life, there will never be a person who views me the same way he did when we were teenagers. It was an innocent, pure feeling. I can't tell you how good of a person he was."

ONCE THE KERSEYS moved to the house on Eighth Street, Jerome began playing basketball. There was a court in a park across the street from where the Kerseys lived, next door to where Junnie lived. Clifton Sr. erected a hoop there. "We played on what was a dirt court, with roots on the ground," Junnie says.

"Jerome spent endless hours on that court, a lot of times alone just shooting and shooting," neighbor Tracy Roberts says.

"One time when we were 12 or 13, it snowed," Junnie Kersey recalls. "Jerome came knocking on the door and said, 'Junnie, let's play some basketball.' I said, 'I ain't playing no basketball in that damn snow.' I looked outside, you know what he was doing? He had a shovel out there digging the snow."

It became a ritual whenever it snowed in Clarksville.

"He'd work for a long time just to get the snow out of the way; then he'd play basketball the rest of the day," says his grandmother, May Kersey.

Clifton Kersey Sr. and Perry Penn coached the youth basketball teams of Jerome and Junnie from fifth to seventh grade. They would practice on the outside asphalt court at the elementary school. Games were scheduled against school teams from neighboring towns, against YMCA teams and Boy Scout troops.

"Cliff would drive us in his truck to games, and sometimes Perry, too," Jerome said. "You'd get some money from your parents, but they basically paid the way for all of us. We got to play our games in high school gyms. It was my first taste of organized basketball."

Junnie recalls an English assignment in sixth grade. Each student had to write a paper on lifetime aspirations.

Says Junnie: "Jerome wrote, 'One day I'm going to play against Dr. J in the NBA.' And everybody laughed at him. I know I did."

Even at 11 years of age, Jerome was all about setting goals — and reaching them.

Jerome, wearing a bow tie and a smile, at four years old. *Courtesy Kersey family*

Jerome at 10 years old, as a fifth-grader at Clarksville Elementary School. *Courtesy Kersey family*

Jerome with an Afro at 12 years old, as a seventh-grader at Clarksville Junior High. *Courtesy Kersey family*

Bluestone High School in Skipwith Virginia, Jerome's alma mater. Bluestone will be replaced with a new county-wide high school in fall 2022. *Courtesy Wayne Dementi*

Jerome (holding trophy with his left hand and pointing with his right, not wearing glasses) celebrates Bluestone's Southside district championship that Bluestone earned as a junior in 1979 with a 62-55 win over Brunswick High. Cousin "Junnie" Kersey (left) was hurt and did not suit up the second half of the season. Head coach Jerome Watson stands next to Junnie. *Courtesy Jerome Watson/taken by Bob Howerton, formerly of Mecklenburg Sun*

Jerome Watson and wife Pat are now retired and live in Clarksville, Va. Watson coached Jerome Kersey during his sophomore and junior seasons at Bluestone High. *Courtesy Kerry Eggers*

Jerome and fellow senior William Park were co-captains for Bluestone High during the 1979-80 season. Jerome's No. 12 hangs in the Barons' gymnasium along with No. 6 — the baseball jersey of Michael Tucker, former Bluestone, Longwood and major league baseball stalwart. *Courtesy 1980 "Golden Link," Bluestone High's yearbook*

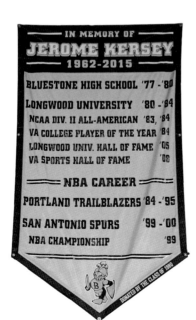

The Bluestone High class of 1980 donated this banner shortly after Jerome's death in 2015. The banner hangs in the Barons' gymnasium and commemorates Kersey's career from high school to the NBA. *Courtesy Patrick Love, Bluestone High/Mecklenburg County Public Schools*

Jerome is joined by Longwood teammate Kevin Ricks (front row with sunglasses) and Jerome's grandparents, Herman and May Kersey, at "Jerome Kersey Day" in Clarksville, Va., in 1985. *Courtesy News-Progress, Mecklenburg County, Va., taken by Rick Magann*

Jerome is flanked by grandparents May and Herman Kersey at "Jerome Kersey Day." *Courtesy News Progress, Mecklenburg County, Va., taken by Rick Magann*

Clifton Kersey, Sr., and wife Jo-ann in 1986. Clifton, Jerome's uncle, was a father figure to him during his formative years. *Courtesy Clifton "Junnie" Kersey, Jr.*

Jerome (in background) made a surprise visit to Clarksville for the 20-year reunion of the Bluestone High class of 1980 in 2000. From left are Rita Marrow, Marcellette Foster-Rice and Jerome's cousins, Junnie Kersey and Mary Jones. *Contributed by Junnie Kersey/Courtesy Tracy Y. Roberts*

Jerome displays his Virginia Sports Hall of Fame plaque with grandmother May Kersey at his induction in April 2008. Later that year, Kersey was inducted into the Oregon Sports Hall of Fame. *Courtesy Teri Kersey Valentine*

Jerome with Bill Bowles, his football and basketball coach as a Bluestone High senior, at the Virginia Sports Hall of Fame induction in 2008. *Courtesy Bill Bowles*

Junnie Kersey and Kevin "Huggy" Brandon stand in front of the former Clarksville Elementary School. Junnie was Jerome's cousin, Huggy one of Jerome's closest friends. *Courtesy Wayne Dementi*

The town of Clarksville is in Mecklenburg County, Va., just north of the North Carolina state line. Known as Virginia's only lakeside town, it is a popular fishing and boating destination and hosts an annual balloon festival each July. *Courtesy Justin Eubank Photography*

Jerome (far right) wasn't yet a physical specimen during his junior
year at Bluestone High. Here he trails play as teammate Chris Watkins
shoots against Gloucester (Va.) in the Class AA Regionals. *Courtesy
Jerome Watson. Photo by Bob Howerton/Mecklenburg Sun*

Chapter Two

From 'Daffy' to Dominant

A MILE AND A HALF from downtown Clarksville, Va., and across Highway 58, about a half-mile from Buggs Island Lake, Jerome Watson's home of 30 years sits on a two-acre plot of land on rural Wild Life Road.

It's the perfect spot for an outdoorsman like Watson.

"Love to fish," says Watson, 77, the man who coached Jerome Kersey his first two seasons at Bluestone High. "For years, I hunted. Now, there's so much land posted. (Deer hunters) started using four-wheelers and the high-powered rifles and took all the fun out of hunting. The deer don't have a chance when it's like that. Plus, I don't trust hunters now, with some of the guns they use in the woods.

"I used to hunt deer and small game — rabbits and squirrels. I would bring my older neighbor some meat to barbecue. He'd say, 'What did you bring me today?' Lots of times it would be half a deer. He'd say, 'I'm going to grind it up and make hamburger out of it and freeze some of it. That's what I'm going to eat the whole month.'

"Sometimes I'd say, 'I brought you some squirrels.' He'd be happy to get them, too. He'd say, 'I'm going to clean them and cook them.' I love rabbit myself. I'm not that crazy about squirrels. I will eat them, though. I don't hunt much anymore. I love to shoot, though."

So did the most famous basketball player Watson coached, though Jerome Kersey didn't get to shoot as often as he'd have liked during his 17-year NBA career.

The man they call "Wat" is retired after a long career as a coach and educator in Clarksville. The former junior high principal worked in Mecklenburg County for 31 years, then went across the border for more duty in North Carolina before retiring in 2008 after 43 years in education. He coached high school basketball for 11 years in Clarksville — four at West End High and the final seven at Bluestone.

"We had some excellent teachers, some good mentors for the kids during my time," says Watson as he enjoys a lunch of barbecued pork and coleslaw prepared by his wife of 52 years, Pat, with a visitor. "We tried to instill in those kids that just because you're rural — a lot of them worked on the tobacco farms — it doesn't mean they couldn't achieve things in school and go further in life."

Back in the day, Watson was a 6-3, 210-pound center/linebacker at Division II Winston-Salem State, captain of the Rams' defense. Hall of Fame basketball coach Clarence "Big House" Gaines was an assistant coach in football during that time, when Earl "The Pearl" Monroe was dazzling fans at the school and destroying opposing defenses on the hardcourts.

"Earl is a good friend of mine," says Watson in a voice that reminds of Lou Rawls, with a look not unlike that of Morgan Freeman. "And I learned a whole lot of basketball from Big House.

"When I first started coaching at West End High, I drove down to Winston-Salem and said, 'Coach Gaines, I have these little, short ballplayers. They can shoot, but I don't know what to do with them.' He asked, 'Can they run?' I said, 'Yeah.' He said, 'Run the fast break and keep the ball off the floor. You can move the basketball faster than the players can move their feet. Go to the passing game.' So that's what we did."

Watson became acquainted with Kersey when he was a ninth-grader at Bluestone Junior High.

"His coordination was completely off," Watson says. "He was as clumsy and awkward as could be."

Kersey had played with his cousin, Junnie Kersey, on youth teams coached by his uncle, Clifton Kersey Sr., and Perry Penn from fifth to seventh grade. The next year, Jerome Kersey approached Bill Bowles, who coached the junior varsity team at Bluestone High.

Recalls Bowles today: "I remember a little kid came up to me — it was either at the grocery store or the post office — and said, 'You're the JV (high school) basketball coach?' I said, 'Yeah.' He said, 'I want to play basketball for you.' I said, 'OK.' He was in eighth grade. Next time I saw him might have been a year and a half later. He'd grown quite a bit. I didn't even recognize him. I just couldn't believe it was the same kid. He had played with the older kids all the time on the asphalt at Clarksville. That helped him a lot."

Dale Hite was one of the "older kids."

"I had a nickname for Jerome during that time — Shorty," Hite says. "I was 19 or 20 and he was 13 or 14. He was still pretty small. There were several of us who played basketball with him at the town courts. At that time, Jerome got abused on the courts by the older kids. He just wasn't that good. But all of a sudden, he blossomed."

"I played basketball every day at the elementary school outdoor courts," Kersey told Hoke Currie in 1998. "At first, the older kids wouldn't let me play. Then one day I was playing against a guy named Kurt Bowers. Things were going good and I was making plays. All the guys were talking junk to him because he couldn't stop me. After that, they accepted me playing. We would have four-on-four or five-on-five games just about year-round."

Jerome and Junnie played together as seventh- and eighth-graders at Bluestone Junior High. As ninth-graders, they were called up to play on the high school JV team for the last five games of the season when some players were declared scholastically ineligible.

"Jerome, who was maybe 5-9, stepped in at guard along with Junnie," Bowles says. "Jerome showed me some stuff then, more than we expected. He had to handle the ball a lot. That helped him in the long run. He always had a knack for getting rebounds and driving to the basket. He worked so hard on his jump shot."

IT TOOK AWHILE, though, for Kersey to get his bearings on a basketball court.

"My first year playing with him, everybody was calling him 'Daffy Duck,' " says Mike Mosely, who was a year behind Jerome and played two seasons of basketball with him at Bluestone. "He was growing and couldn't get into a rhythm."

Before the start of Kersey's sophomore season, head varsity coach Jerome Watson had a talk with him.

"I told him, 'Jerome, we have work to do if you're going to be a basketball player,' " Watson says. "He said, 'Yeah, I agree.' I said, 'You're going straight to varsity. We're going to work on your agility skills.'

"He had the best attitude. He was so coachable. He would always listen. He ran 10 extra laps after every practice. The other kids would go to the shower room. He'd be running. Then we would do 20 agility drills. No other kids were doing it. He needed to improve the coordination. And he kept on improving every week."

Kersey would sometimes catch a ride home after practice with Watson.

"One day he got real quiet," Watson says. "I said, 'Jerome, tell me what's wrong.' He said, 'Coach, why do I have to do all this extra stuff and others don't?' I said, 'My name is Jerome and your name is Jerome. They say you're my son. If you're gonna be my son, you gotta be good. You have to practice hard. Do you have a problem with that?' He said, 'No I don't. I know I need it.' He never questioned me about it again."

After playing guard as a freshman, Kersey played power forward as a sophomore on varsity. He averaged only 3.9 points that season. As a junior, he switched back to guard.

"I told him, 'You'll never play in college unless you learn how to dribble,'" Watson says. "And he did."

During that junior season, the Barons won the Southside District championship. By then, Kersey was becoming a force.

"I don't recall who we beat to clinch the championship, but I remember it was a road game," Mosely says. "Jerome came out of his sheet that night — rebounding, shooting, scoring. He'd improved so much, he didn't look like he should be on the court with the rest of us. He was Daffy Duck no more."

"Jerome may not have been the best player on the team at the time, but no one could match his discipline, desire or drive," Hite says. "And as he grew, his skills got better."

Through their junior year at Bluestone, Junnie Kersey had the upper hand on his cousin athletically.

"Junnie had always been the big name, the star," says Tracy Roberts, a neighbor and classmate.

"Growing up, Junnie was quick and a stocky kid — a good athlete, too," Bowles says. "He used to beat Jerome. Junnie would get in his head. They would push and go back and forth at each other. They were pretty competitive, regardless of what they were doing. But they were a good team together, I can tell you that."

"I was better all the way through until (their junior year)," Junnie says. "Everybody knew that. But Jerome took over his senior year. He was the man. He shot up that summer to about 6-4 by the time we got back to school (in September). He grew and I didn't. The other thing was, he put in the extra amount of work. He did more than I did to make himself better."

Jerome Watson smiles when the subject is broached.

"Junnie was a good basketball player, but he didn't have the work ethic Jerome did," he says. "Junnie was the better player when they were younger. He could shoot and handle the ball. Once they got to high school, though, Junnie thought he was better than Jerome, but Jerome was the better player by far."

Jerome Kersey led the Barons to a 17-8 record and a league championship as a junior. By then, Junnie had turned his attention primarily to football. He was also a star on the gridiron at Bluestone and soon accepted a scholarship to North Carolina Central, where he would become a four-year starter at running back and punt return specialist and an all-league selection as a senior.

Clifton Sr. called Jerome and Junnie into his upholstery shop before their senior basketball season.

"You could be the best combination of cousins who ever came through this county if you'll just play together," Clifton Sr. told them.

"That brought us closer together," Junnie says today. "I told Jerome, 'I got my scholarship; now I have to help you get yours.' That senior season, I'd push the ball upcourt, get it to him, get out of the way and let him go dunk."

After the 1978-79 school year, Watson — who had been teaching U.S. history at Bluestone High — was asked to be principal at the junior high. When he accepted that position, it meant he had to give up coaching at the high school. It turned out to be the end of his coaching career.

"I was disappointed not to get to coach Jerome his senior year," Watson says, "but I knew I could help some other kids in another way."

Watson doesn't consider Kersey his greatest player.

"Carnell Goode was the best player I ever coached," Watson says. "Had some good ones at West End, too. Carnell played at Bluestone. Had a scholarship to Hampton, but he didn't stay in school. He never worked as hard as Jerome, but he had the ability. Jerome was the hardest-working player I ever had."

BILL BOWLES, who had been Watson's assistant, took over the head coaching reins in basketball in 1979-80. But first, there was a football season to play. And Bowles — head coach of the Barons on the gridiron, too — enlisted the services of Kersey.

"Jerome played 'Midget' football from fifth to eighth grade, then stopped playing," Junnie Kersey recalls. "He was good. I was the quarterback. He was a receiver. I threw it to him all the time."

"My grandmother didn't want me playing football," Kersey told Hoke Currie in 1998. "Junnie's dad talked to her. Football was my first love as a sport. I had no big aspiration for playing, but I went out my senior year and played.

"Actually, I started as manager and then decided I wanted to play. I was getting all the water (for the players); then I thought, 'The heck with this, let somebody else bring me water.' I got better toward the end of the season. Scored one touchdown. It turned out to be one of the best things I did."

The Barons' offense was built around Junnie and the ground game.

"Jerome could catch the ball," Bowles says. "Problem was, we had to get it to him. But I think football was good for Jerome. The contact helped him in basketball."

Kersey entered his senior basketball season at about 6-4 and 175.

"By that time, if I were picking a team (for a pick-up game), I was going to try to get him on my side," Dale Hite says. "He played with all the adults. He was a beast. All of a sudden, he was not 5-10 anymore."

Bowles moved Kersey inside to power forward.

"But he helped us break the press that season," Bowles says. "The time he spent at guard helped him. That season was when he took off. He was an excellent defensive player. I remember the defense more than the offense. He was a great hustler. He was tremendous on the press, and we pressed a lot because we played in a lot of small gyms. He was always the middle man, because he could cover a lot of ground. His hustle would put him in places where you wouldn't expect him to be."

"That senior season, it was over with," teammate Mike Mosely says. "Put the ball in his hands and if you got up to guard him, he was going to feed you dinner. He was also going to feed you some knowledge. It wasn't just his taking command of the game. Whatever you needed at that moment, he was going to get it for you. "He was one of the most humble, unselfish players I ever met. He was going to feed you some knowledge. He worked for everything he got. Sometimes that's a cliché, but it wasn't with Jerome. And that's the way he was raised."

Even at that tender age, Kersey wasn't to be messed with.

"He had a certain amount of mean streak in him," Bowles says. "He wasn't going to back down to anybody, but he always maintained his poise. Jerome would get in his share of cheap shots, too, but you wouldn't see him do it."

Mosely recalls a game at Greenville High that season.

"We were on the bus ready to go and Jerome looked at me and said, 'What goals have you set tonight?' " he says. "I was like, 'I haven't set any goals for tonight.' He looked at me with surprise on his face. I asked him what goal he had set. He said, 'To get six dunks.' "

Kersey got them.

"I'll never forget it," Mosely says. "He had two in the first half. In the second half, he took two dunks from the foul line. If Jerome ever got that step on you, you were dust. He was going to the rim regardless of what was in his way. If you were in his way, you were in trouble. After he got the second dunk, the other team called timeout. It was so powerful that the whole crowd went crazy over it.

"The reason Jerome made it (to the NBA), he came to the gym every day with a goal in mind. When he came to practice or a game, he had a goal he wanted to accomplish."

In their first playoff game that season, Bluestone played Clover Hill in a tight game.

"We had split with them (in the regular season), then went overtime in the playoff game," Bowles says. "Jerome hit a shot from the same place on the floor at critical times in all three games (against Clover Hill). He'd go around the baseline and curl up on the elbow on the left side. He knocked one down to get it to overtime and shot one there to win the playoff game.

"If he missed a shot that meant something in a game, that's what he would work on after practice was over the next day. He was a very coachable kid. You could get on him and it wouldn't get him down. He wouldn't take things personally. He could accept the criticism. He worked very hard to get better."

Bowles liked another thing about Kersey.

"He didn't run with the regular crowd," the coach says. "He was personable, but he was kind of to himself, a loner. He separated himself from some of the problems that existed. He wouldn't go along with some of the things kids wanted him to go along with — drinking and that type of thing. At least if he did, he kept it to himself."

Kersey averaged 19.4 points and 14 rebounds that season, leading Bluestone to a 13-9 record. He tied the school single-game scoring record with 38 points in a 92-80 win over Randolph-Henry in the district tournament and was named to the All-Southside District team.

Bowles coached high school basketball for 15 years.

"Jerome was the best player I ever coached," he says. "Never had one make the impact that he did."

Shortly after his senior season, Kersey wrote this letter:

"To Myself.

"My high school basketball days are over. Now it's time for bigger and better things. I will always remember my high school days, especially the coaches, my teammates and the people we played against. The guys I played with were a great bunch of fellows. I enjoyed every one of them. Even though we had our differences, which were few, we still got along well together. I will miss my teammates and my coaches, who I love with all my heart, but I know they want to see me excel in life, so that's what I'm going to do. I hope my college days (will) be just as memorable as my high school days were, and more. I expect a lot from myself and therefore I'm going to push myself to the limits to achieve this status in life.

To The #1 person,
Myself"

THERE WAS one more basketball game to be played during his

final spring at Bluestone. Dale Hite put together a team to play in a local adult tournament.

"I asked Jerome to play with us," he says. "Our first game was against a team of Longwood guys. There were two Longwood assistant coaches at the game. Jerome put on a show. He scored 38 points and just dominated that game. I used to tease him, he owed that scholarship to me."

Kersey hadn't seriously considered the possibility of even going to college until his senior year.

"I never dreamed he would want to go to college," says his grandmother, May Kersey. He was the first from his family to consider it.

When Bowles brought up the possibility before his senior season, "you could tell he didn't really think it was a possibility," the coach said. "A lot of the kids from the area during that time were that way."

Once Kersey began to see it as a possibility, he knew his grandparents couldn't afford putting him through college. He would have to get a scholarship.

There was no recruiting battle for Jerome, though some schools were beginning to show some interest.

"There was talk of a package deal at (Division II) Saint Paul's College — me for football, Jerome for basketball," Junnie Kersey says. "But neither of us wanted to go there."

Longwood, about an hour's drive from Clarksville, was on Jerome's radar in part because of his friendship with Doug Toombs, who had been a year ahead of him at Bluestone and was at Longwood. A catcher, Toombs became Longwood's first baseball All-American as a freshman that spring. Kersey stayed with Toombs during his recruiting visit during the spring of Jerome's senior year at Bluestone and would room with him at Cox Dorm as a freshman in 1980-81.

"We became close my junior year in high school," Toombs recalls. "He was a sophomore and was like 5-11 and 160. We got into a fight. In those days, guys would get into a fight, get up off the floor, shake hands and become friends.

"We were a lot alike. We were both raised in the country. Our parents instilled certain values. He wasn't the best basketball player to start with. I went down that same road. It was the work ethic that allowed both of us to achieve what we achieved in life. And he grew. By the time he got to Longwood, he became a man real quick."

During Kersey's recruiting visit to Longwood, coach Ron Bash had him spend time with 6-6 center Mike Wills at Frazer Hall for the weekend.

"Jerome and I sneaked into French Gym and played some one-on-one and H-O-R-S-E into the night," Wills recalls today. "He was a handful on the court in every way. Just an incredible talent and a super nice kid."

Toombs says Kersey's generous spirit and positive attitude were his greatest assets.

"He would give the shirt off his back to anybody," Toombs says. "He could be having the worst day, but Jerome always had a smile on his face."

Toombs says during the 1979-80 basketball season, he sought out Bash and suggested he take a look at a kid from his high school. Bowles says he had already reached out to Longwood assistant coach Mo Schoepfer.

"Jerome was kind of a late bloomer, but I felt he could play somewhere," Bowles says. "Somehow I got Mo's name. I called probably around Christmas his senior year and said, 'This is a kid you might want to take a look at.' He came and liked what he saw."

Schoepfer says he first heard about Kersey on a list provided by a scouting service.

"I would go through those lists and find middle-of-the-road kind of players, because you weren't going to get superstars in our area," Schoepfer says. "One of the people I came across was Jerome."

In the first Bluestone game Schoepfer scouted that season, "Jerome did everything. He rebounded, dribbled down the court … he was the whole team. We wanted to have a big guard who could post up. Jerome really couldn't shoot, but he handled it well for a guy about 6-4, ran the floor like crazy and never got tired. I thought he would be the perfect two-guard for what we were trying to do."

Schoepfer says he watched Kersey play "at least twice, maybe more than that" as a senior.

"I wrote him a letter," Schoepfer says. "He sent back a question-naire. I stayed in contact with him. Through phone calls and working with (Bowles), he became interested in Longwood. We arranged for him to visit several times and a relationship grew. We were on Jerome early, he liked the place and it worked out."

Schoepfer worried that he might lose Kersey if a bigger school made a scholarship offer.

"Jerome got better through his senior year," says Schoepfer, who after coaching basketball for about 20 years became an attorney, prac-ticing criminal and family law in Connecticut. "It became one of those deals where you're afraid some Division I school is going to step in at the last second. I heard Richmond was on him for a while.

"But he really didn't have a position, and he didn't shoot well enough to be a scoring forward. There was no place (for a D-I pro-gram) to put him. Richmond decided not to recruit him, and he wound up coming to Longwood."

There was another possibility. The spring after Kersey's senior season, Jerome Watson — who had been the Bluestone head coach his sopho-more and junior years — took Jerome to Winston-Salem for a recruiting visit one weekend. He met with legendary coach "Big House" Gaines and got to play a pickup game with several of the team's best players.

"On the way back, we rode about 20 miles and Jerome got real quiet," Watson says. "I said, 'Jerome, tell me what's on your mind.' "

"I would love to go to Winston-Salem, but you won't get mad at me if I go to Longwood, will you?" Kersey asked.

"Tell me why you want to go to Longwood," Watson said.

"I want to be closer to my grandmother," Kersey said.

"Jerome, you go where you're going to be happy," Watson said.

"Whew," Kersey said. "I sure feel better now.' "

Winston-Salem State offered a partial ride, but Kersey needed more financial help, which made the decision easier. No other college extended a full scholarship offer other than Longwood. Many schools would come to regret that over the next four years.

A postscript is offered by Bowles:

"The next year, I got a call from a college coach — can't remember who it was — and he asked, 'You got any more Jerome Kerseys?' That ticked me off. I hung up on him."

By Jerome's sophomore year at Longwood, he had learned how to convert steals into dunks. *Courtesy Longwood University*

Chapter Three

Sir Lancer-Lot

SUNSHINE BEAMS DOWN from blue skies to warm the chill in the air on a brisk morning at Longwood University in Farmville, Va., in early March 2021. School is in session, though COVID-19 has placed limits on classroom participation by students.

Those students on hand traverse the charming campus are wearing masks but still kibitzing as they walk along Brock Commons, a pedestrian promenade that opened in 2004.

Longwood is the third-oldest public university in Virginia. It began as Farmville Seminary in 1839, became State Normal School in 1884, turned into Longwood College in 1949 and gained its university status in 2002.

Today, Farmville is a college town of about 7,800 located near the headwaters of the Appomattox River in the central part of the state. Longwood's enrollment is about 5,000, more than double what it was when Jerome Kersey was a student there from 1980-84. Red brick buildings are the norm through campus, with the centerpiece edifice the historic, iconic "Rotunda" along High Street, just across from the legendary Hotel Weyanoke.

Cox, Frazer and Curry halls — dormitories where Jerome Kersey resided some four decades ago — still house students at Longwood, though two have different names. The basketball team plays at Willett Hall, which opened during Kersey's freshman season with the Lancers in 1980-81 as Lancer Hall. Change is in the offing, though; the $40 million Joan Perry Brock Center will open in time for the 2023-24 season. The Lancers are now a Division I team participating in the Big South Conference.

Kersey arrived at Longwood in a period of transition for the athletic program. Not only was Lancer Hall making its debut, but the Lancers were moving up from NCAA Division III to Division II. Until 1976, Longwood was a women's college, so the men's basketball program was in only its fourth year when it reached the Division III Final Four in 1980.

While a senior at Bluestone High in March of 1980, Kersey was in the stands at nearby Hampden-Sydney College with Barons coach Bill Bowles to watch Longwood put away favored Potsdam (N.Y.) State 78-61 in the national quarterfinals. Kersey saw 6-2 junior Kenny Ford, a transfer from Shaw University in Raleigh, N.C., go for 21 points, and told Bowles, "Man, I'd love to play with that guy right there. I could complement him. He's so smooth."

The Lancers, who went 25-1 in the regular season and finished 28-3, would lose 57-55 to defending national champion North Park of Chicago — led by future Portland Trail Blazers forward Michael Harper — in the semifinals.

The coach was Ron Bash, who was in his second season at the helm in Farmville. He arrived at Longwood in 1978 after the Lancers had gone 2-12 and 8-16 in their first two seasons. Bash, a native of Trenton, N.J., with a New York pedigree, had turned around the program at Stony Brook (N.Y.). before he arrived in Virginia. The brash Bash — "that's what people mean when they say, 'A guy from New York,' " Kersey would joke — had recruited heavily to Longwood in his home area; seven of the 12 squad members on the 1979-80 Lancers were from the New York/New Jersey region.

With the move up to Division II, Longwood was able to offer

athletic scholarships for the first time. The first two male athletes to receive full rides were basketball players — Kersey and Mike McCroey, a transfer from Allegheny (Md.) JC.

"That was my guy," says McCroey, who now works as a middle-school teacher in Baltimore. "I looked at Jerome as my little brother, like I was responsible for him.

"Jerome is one of the reasons I went to Longwood. I had 15 D-I scholarship offers. I had made (recruiting) visits to three other schools before I went to Longwood with a friend of mine. The night I met Jerome, we played some pickup games. The talent in Longwood's gym was far superior to the talent I saw in Division I gyms. Part of that was Jerome. He was 6-4 (as a high school senior), but he grew to 6-7. You could see the raw talent. Me being from Baltimore, where pros were coming out of my area, I could tell that this kid was going to be special."

McCroey says Bash was a strong recruiter who "got Division I players at the Division II level."

"People underestimated the quality of play at the D-II level at the time," says McCroey, a 6-1 guard who started his two seasons at Longwood, setting a school single-season steals record his junior year and serving as the No. 2 scorer behind Kersey as a senior.

During Kersey's career, the Lancers played against D-II programs Virginia Union, led by Charles Oakley; West Virginia Tech, which boasted Sedale Threatt, and District of Columbia, with a roster that included 7-footer Earl Jones. Oakley played 19 NBA seasons, Threatt 14. Jones, a first-round draft pick of the Los Angeles Lakers, would play two NBA campaigns.

"Add Kenny Ford, who came from the same high school as David Thompson (Crest in Shelby, N.C.) — you could take that team and play against the Big East," McCroey says. "Including Jerome, four NBA guys from one small cul-de-sac."

The Lancers played an at-large schedule through Kersey's first three seasons before joining the Mason-Dixon Athletic Conference for his senior campaign.

WHEN THE PLAYERS gathered at Lancer Hall for pickup games prior to the start of formal practice during the fall of 1980, the talent was substantial. Ford, a third-team All-American for the Final Four team the previous season, could score, jump and play defense.

"Kenny was always blocking my shot," Kersey told Hoke Currie in 1998. "It was the first time anybody had done that. Kenny was explosive. Once I got past that, after about a week and a half, then everything came together. I said, 'I have to go at guys and try to dunk this thing,' and everything got better."

Not for Bash, though. Ford and Randy Johnson, a 6-4 forward who led the Lancers in rebounding in 1979-80, were academically ineligible and would not join the team until late December. Two other players, 6-3 Wilbert Hall and 6-5 Tony Ellison, left school.

The latter two "were missing their girlfriends," Kersey said. "I don't know if I would have started if Wilbert were there. "If those guys had stayed, we'd have gone to the (Division II) tournament that year."

Kersey would grow to appreciate Bash.

"He treated me very fairly," Kersey said. "He didn't always do things by the book, but he got it done. He always stayed calm, cool and collected no matter what. You never saw him get riled up or bent out of shape.

"Well, he used to get mad at (center) Ronnie Orr. I think Ronnie's whole job as a basketball player was to get Bash upset with him. He'd do something stupid. Once he got mad at Ronnie, then everyone else would get it, too."

Then there were Bash's battles with gymnastics coach Ruth Budd over use of the gym. The gymnasts were scheduled for workouts just prior to the men's basketball practice sessions on most days.

"It was like an everyday deal: 'Get that damn chalk up!' " Kersey recalled with a laugh. "They would never be out in time when we came in. The poor lady would be half in tears."

McCroey liked Kersey from the start.

"We instantly bonded," McCroey says. "He was deeply rooted in being a good person, a humble kid, a sponge who was always willing to work to get better. He continued to strive to match the competitive level, and he continued to grow."

The other freshman in Kersey's recruiting class was Mitch Walker, a 6-2 guard out of Hollis, N.Y. They would become life-long friends, close enough that Walker was a member of Kersey's wedding party in 2013.

"We came in for recruiting visits during the same weekend the spring of our senior year," says Walker, now a financial investor in New York City. "Jerome was about 6-4. When we came back in August, he had grown two, almost three inches. That changed the trajectory of his career dramatically.

"We couldn't have had more different backgrounds. I was inner city. He grew up in a rural environment. We became friends around the game of basketball. We both played hard and had fun together. He wasn't super skilled at that point, but he was a tremendous athlete who ran the court extremely well and could finish. He played strictly around the basket."

Like McCroey, Walker noticed Kersey's humility.

"Early on, he didn't realize how good he was," Walker says. "I had played against guys like Chris Mullin and Jerry Reynolds in New York City. I said, 'Jerome, I'm telling you, you can play at the highest level.' He was confident but not cocky. Extremely modest, really. The traits that took him to an NBA career were the same things that got him through an extremely competitive environment at Longwood."

IT TOOK LITTLE TIME for Kersey to make an impression on his coaches. Before his freshman season in 1980-81, he scored 33 points in an intrasquad scrimmage.

"Jerome has a chance to be the best player I've ever coached," Bash told a reporter. "He's like lightning. By midseason, he could be one of the best players in the state, regardless of level."

Kersey would start every game he played at Longwood — 103 in all. Wearing No. 34 as a freshman — he would be adorned by No. 54 the rest of his career at Longwood — he scored nine points and grabbed a team-high 12 rebounds as the Lancers beat Maryland-Eastern Shore 62-54 in their opener.

Listed at 6-5 and 180 in Hoke Currie's press guide, Kersey would lead the Lancers in scoring in four of the first six games, in rebounds five times over that span.

"Jerome was very good right away," says Mo Schoepfer, who recruited Kersey and would serve as a Longwood assistant coach his first two seasons there. "He had some deficiencies in his game. He had very small hands. At times, he didn't have great control of the ball. He didn't shoot well. But the things he did well, he did very well. He ran the lanes. He rebounded strongly, and the bigger he got, the better he got at it.

"And he got more of a mental grasp of the game. He started to become a basketball player. He could get by on pure talent in high school. In college, you have guys who are strong and quick and your game has to step up."

Kersey would go the first nine games without Kenny Ford, the star of the 1979-80 Lancers who was academically ineligible until December. Ford, a Division III All-American and the first Longwood player to score 1,000 career points, had grown close to Kersey during informal preseason workouts on campus.

"I was like a big brother, him listening to what I had to say," Ford says today. "He was very malleable. He had the qualities of being a good player and he had the desire. You could tell he was raised in a small area. He was very polite, very soft-spoken. He was a nice, mannerly, down-to-earth person, eager to learn. I took to him quickly because he worked so hard."

The Lancers were 10-4 — with three of the losses coming by one point — when they flew cross-country to Alaska for four games, two each against Alaska-Fairbanks and Alaska-Anchorage. Because of limited funding, Longwood took only nine players and Bash — no assistant coaches, no managers, no trainers.

It was the first airplane flight of Kersey's life. He left a big impression in the Last Frontier, leading the team in rebounds each game and scoring 27, 24 and 20 points in the final three contests. In the finale,

Kersey's 20-foot jump shot with three seconds left gave Longwood a 67-66 victory over Alaska-Anchorage, its third win of the trip.

"That was big," Mitch Walker says. "Jerome played really well. He was aggressive. He was always looking to smash guys between those four lines."

"Alaska-Anchorage had a couple of NBA-caliber bigs," Mike McCroey recalls. "With the game going down to the wire, I throw Jerome an inbound pass. He's facing me, with (one defender) under the basket and (the other) guarding Jerome on the block. Jerome catches the ball, takes one dribble and hook-dunks it over the bigger guy for a basket. I'm saying to myself, 'This kid is going to be a pro.' He had arrived at the point where competitively, that dog in you comes out."

Ford recalls a play against Fairbanks.

"I went up for a layup and got undercut," he says. "I looked back and saw Jerome's body twisting in the air, dunking the (rebound) backward. When we were playing against that Anchorage crew, I saw him doing things against those players, too. That's when I first knew he was on that level.

"I told one of my friends, 'This is an NBA player.' Not because of his great talent, but because he had something inside that a lot of players with talent don't have. Jerome had more heart and desire than most players I knew. If a fast-break started, he was going to be in on it. Most guys his size didn't think with the mentality that I can get out there just as good as a 6-foot player. He didn't think like a guy 6-5 or 6-6; he thought like a guard."

In a newspaper interview after the tournament, Bash called Kersey "the best freshman in the state of Virginia. We lucked out. Here's a kid who could play anywhere and we got him." Larger schools didn't take the time to sniff him out, Bash said. "Why should a college send someone to Clarksville to see a Jerome Kersey when they can go to Washington (D.C.) and see four or five good players play in the same game? They play the percentages."

Longwood finished the season 19-9, with five one-point losses on the road and a 95-77 win over Division I Howard. In that one, Kersey had 21 points going against 6-7 Larry Spriggs, who would play five seasons in the NBA.

Kersey had 31 points and nine rebounds against Virginia State, 27 points and 15 boards against Alaska-Fairbanks and 26 points and 13 rebounds vs. Quinnipiac. He topped the Lancers in scoring 15 times and in rebounds 20 times. He was named to the all-tournament team in four of the five tourneys in which the Lancers participated.

The freshman shot .629 from the field, ranking 11th in the Division II ranks. He led the team in scoring (16.9 points), set school single-season records for rebounds (249, an 8.9 average) and field goals made (197) and was named to Eastern Basketball's Division II All-East Freshman team.

The good thing was, Jerome was only getting started.

Melvin Jones, Lincoln (PA) University Coach

"He (Kersey) is in a class by himself. If you guard him with a small player he'll kill you inside and he's too quick for most big men to cover. He gives us a lot of problems."

Jim O'Hara, THE FARMVILLE HERALD

"Kersey, LC's leading scorer and rebounder, continued to show his remarkable abilities (in 92-65 win over Pembroke State) as the power forward sank nine of 13 shots, two of three free throws, led the team in rebounds with nine and added six assists and seven steals in an all-around performance."

Fred Jeter, THE RICHMOND NEWS LEADER

"Kersey, . . . is a coach's dream. He shoots with accuracy (better than 60 per cent for career). He rebounds with vengeance (20 in one game this year). He's a non-stop hustler who leads the team in floor burns.

Kersey had 23 points, 20 rebounds and seven assists in the final against Armstrong (87-83 Longwood vistory).

And Jerome Kersey, who had 22 points and 11 rebounds at Navy, is a heckuva player . . . ."

Cal Luther, Longwood College Coach

"I've never had a big guy that hustles like Jerome. He moves around like he has a motor in his behind. You expect that from 5-8 guys, but not from players the size of Jerome.

He probably hustles more than any player I've ever coached."

The Cobra Strikes

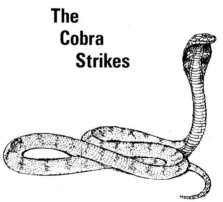

The campaign to promote Jerome for All-American honors was in full throttle by his sophomore season. *Courtesy Longwood University*

Chapter Four

The Cobra Strikes

TO HIS LONGWOOD TEAMMATES, Jerome Kersey's nickname was always "Gee," as in the first syllable of his name.

But Hoke Currie, the school's sports information director, wanted more.

Currie wanted to embark on an All-America campaign for Longwood's star pivot as he began his sophomore season in 1981-82. Now listed at 6-7 and 220 — two inches and 40 pounds more than the previous campaign — Kersey was becoming a force to reckon with, and Currie wanted a nickname.

"We sat in my kitchen one night and thought for a long time," assistant coach Mo Schoepfer says today. "Hoke was trying to pump him up for All-American. Finally 'Cobra' came up. It was a PR thing for Hoke."

It was a catchy sobriquet, one based on Kersey's long, lean frame and his ability to strike quickly on the court like the cobra, the king of snakes.

Schoepfer would coach "the Cobra" for only one more year before becoming head coach at D-III Connecticut College, where he spent 11 seasons.

Ron Bash's contract as athletic director and basketball coach, meanwhile, would not be renewed, ending his tenure with a 66-20 record over three years at Longwood. Administrative officials at the school were less than enamored of the way he ran his program, with outside allegations of NCAA violations on a number of counts. A subsequent investigation by the NCAA after Bash's departure determined there was no wrongdoing. "Alienation of others" was the only explanation offered publicly by Longwood for Bash's dismissal.

In his place came Cal Luther, who had previously been a head coach at Division I Murray State for 16 years (1958-74), taking the Racers to three Ohio Valley Conference championships and two NCAA Tournament appearances. Luther was out of coaching for seven years, serving a stint as Murray State's athletic director before moving into teaching for a couple of years. Schoepfer, who had applied to get the head job, stayed on to serve as his assistant for the 1981-82 season at Longwood.

Kersey had no big dreams, at least at this point. He told Currie in 1998 that some people recommended after his freshman year at Longwood that he transfer to a larger school to give himself more opportunity to prove himself to NBA scouts.

"I would tell them, 'I'd rather be a big fish in a small pond than a little fish in a big pond,' " he said. "Not that I was a BMOC (Big Man on Campus) or anything like that. I just said, 'If it was meant for me to be in the pros, then something good will come along. If not, I'll get an education.' I thought I would get a four-year education, and the atmosphere was good. Longwood gave me a positive outlook about myself that really helped me.

"That gave me an even better work ethic than I already had. I studied hard and kept my head in the books. I figured I'd get my degree and probably work at Burlington (Industries), or maybe in probation or parole work — adult supervision."

A friend and classmate says Jerome is wrong about the "BMOC" reference.

"He was definitely the BMOC, and not only for his size," says Bryan Kersey (no relation), the son of longtime NBA referee Jess Kersey and a tennis player at Longwood. Bryan, a year behind Kersey in school, is today supervisor of basketball officials for the Atlantic Coast Conference. Jerome lived in the room directly above Bryan's for a year at Frazer Hall.

"We hung out all the time," Bryan says. "Everybody liked Jerome. Everybody wanted to get close to him. He was nice to everybody, but he let only a few into his inner circle — his teammates and some others who were living near him on campus. I was fortunate to be one of those, and it lasted a lifetime.

"He was genuine. What you saw is what you got. We all knew he was going to be somebody. He worked on his fitness every day. He was a fitness freak. He'd come to my parents' house during spring break or in the summer and sprint a mile."

Jerome was an usher in Bryan's wedding in the summer after Jerome's last season at Longwood.

"We had to get him a suit," recalls Bryan. "He had a sport coat but no dress pants. In those days, the NBA gave referees those God-awful Sansabelt pants with jagged bottoms. Dad's pants fit Jerome lengthwise. That's what he wore to my wedding.

"Jerome gave me $10 for my wedding gift. That was a lot of money for him in those days. Things changed soon, though; my wedding was the week before the NBA draft."

UNDER CAL LUTHER, Kersey had an outstanding sophomore campaign, leading the Lancers to a 15-8 record against at-large competition.

"He is in a class by himself," said Lincoln (Pa.) coach Melvin Jones after Kersey collected 21 points and 17 rebounds in a 94-77 romp over the Lions. "If you guard him with a small player, he'll kill you inside, and he's too quick for the big men to cover."

Kersey shot .584 from the field and led the team in scoring (17.0), rebounds (11.8) and steals (2.0) and had 26 of the team's 40 blocked shots.

Midway through the season, Hoke Currie issued a pamphlet to media around the state entitled "The Cobra Strikes," extolling Kersey's virtues.

"He became a very good shooter, much better than when he first came in," Mo Schoepfer says. "He learned the ins and outs of playing basketball, of offense and defense and how you play as a team. He embraced the role of a leader. He was clearly our best player. Cal did a great job with him.

"Jerome was a very nice guy, very quiet, the kind of personality I would expect coming from a small, rural town. He made up for that in terms of talent and the way he played the game. Some people assert leadership by being rah-rah or taking control. He was just a nice guy to have on the team. He complemented our other players. He never demanded the ball, but he scored his points. He made shots by scoring off rebounds, by running the floor, by doing the kind of things you can't teach. His effort was always outstanding."

Kersey was beginning to make it a practice of bringing his best when playing the best. In a late-season 99-70 road loss to eventual national Division II champion District of Columbia — led by All-Americans Earl Jones and Michael Britt — Kersey scored 28 points with seven rebounds. "Transfer! Transfer!" the Firebirds' student section chanted late in the game. They could only wish. Jerome also totaled 26 points, 13 rebounds, seven assists and three steals in a 94-86 win over West Virginia Tech and Sedale Threatt.

Luther appreciated the way Kersey worked on improving his body.

"Weight programs were not too organized when Jerome was here," says Luther, 93, shortly before his death in May 2021. "We did have our guys go in regularly, and Jerome would come by and see me on the weekends and get the key to the weight room. He enjoyed it."

Orlando Turner, a 6-3 guard, was a year ahead of Kersey at Longwood and played with him for his first two seasons in Farmville.

"I saw his growth from high school to the end of his sophomore year," says Turner, now loan specialist for the U.S. Small Business

Administration living in Fredericksburg, Va. "In just that time frame, he grew leaps and bounds — literally. He was a great raw talent when he came in, but we had players on the team who challenged him and helped groom him.

"Jerome was one of those people who maximized his potential. He got every ounce out of his ability. He'd have been great at anything. He committed 100 percent to whatever he was doing or whoever he was with. It was like you were the only person there."

Kersey set the tone in workouts.

"I had to guard him in practice," says 6-6 center Ron Orr, who played with Kersey from 1980-83. "I didn't like doing that. You had to work, and work hard. He never loafed. We didn't hang out. He was a country boy. I was a city guy from New York. But we were cool. Awesome personality. Awesome athlete. And his game was coming together."

Turner and several of his teammates — Mitch Walker, Dalany Brown, Mike McCroey, Kenny Ford and Troy Littles — were members of a black fraternity on campus, Omega Psi Phi.

Another member was Kevin Brandon, who would become one of Jerome's closest friends. They met during Jerome's freshman year. Soon, Luther strongly advised his players not to join a fraternity after an incident involving Walker. It was the result of a hazing incident during pledge process during the fall of Walker's junior year. He tore a quad muscle and never played a game of college ball again.

Kersey never sought membership to Omega Psi Phi. Part of that was Luther's prohibition.

"But part of it was he was so dedicated to getting better as a player," McCroey says. "He was focused. We would have conversations about it. I kind of wanted him to pledge, but kind of didn't want him to, because I thought it might knock him off his square.

"We wanted to nurture him. I didn't want him to go through all the drama of pledging a fraternity. There was a lot of physical hazing going on then. I don't think he wanted to go through that, but he would have if he wasn't so focused on getting better as a player. And he wasn't ready for the social aspects, like the partying and drinking. We wanted to protect him from that."

But Kersey was definitely one of the boys.

"We were all very close," Turner says. "It was like a brotherhood. We adopted Jerome, anyway, as an honorary member."

Says McCroey: "Jerome was as close to that fraternity as you could be without actually pledging."

There was nothing condescending about Kersey, Turner says, despite his status on campus as a star athlete. That continued in the years after college.

"Jerome was just a normal guy," Turner says. "We fought like brothers. At the end of it, we'd have a drink and laugh and drink and argue some more.

"He was always good-natured, very personable. I can't think of anybody who didn't like him. He's the kind of person who would be a mayor. He just had that personality. He had friends of all races. He was very approachable, even when he got to the NBA level. He would always remember the little things about people he went to college with. He'd always ask about my wife. He remembered the people who were with him along the way."

There was no big city in Kersey, either, even after his time in the NBA.

"His personality was Clarksville, from the day he signed with Longwood until the day he died," McCroey says. "He continued to grow as he played against players better than him. That became his benchmark. He played his way into being a pro. That's what I love about him. He earned it. And he never changed."

WITH MO SCHOEPFER gone, Cal Luther hired Ernie Neal as his assistant coach and strength and conditioning coach in 1982. Neal, who had been a high school assistant coach in Gaithersburg, Md., for two years, wound up staying in Farmville through 1990. He found the city "two-sided," "segregated" and "hostile."

"Whites and blacks lived on different sides of town," says Neal, now an assistant principal at an alternative school in Louisville. "The whites lived on one side that had better homes, better schools. They lived on the 'avenues' where they had sidewalks, streetlights and curbs. The blacks lived on the other side. They lived on the 'streets.' No sidewalks. No streetlights.

"The whites didn't have a whole lot to do with the blacks. They were trying to separate themselves. They didn't want to have anything to do with the blacks. (Blacks) had to fight to get anything."

At the time, Neal says, Longwood wanted to expand its campus to a largely black area. Longwood officials reached out to homeowners in the area to try to acquire land.

"Some of the black families were willing to sell; others weren't," Neal says. "The ones who did were moved miles outside the city. (Longwood) used eminent domain (the right for a government or a public agency to expropriate private property for public use, with payment for compensation) to get the others out."

Things were different for those on the Longwood campus, however.

"It was a separate entity," Neal says. "The college was different from the community. Nearly every team had black athletes. Most of them had a black coach. Blacks and whites got along well. There wasn't any in-fighting on campus. I don't know any situation where there was race-baiting or name-calling, or where blacks and whites did not party together or get along well."

Kevin Brandon — Jerome's close friend and a Longwood student at the time — confirms Neal's account.

"I took a class in assertiveness training," Brandon says. "One assignment was to do something you would typically not do — go out of your comfort zone, so to speak. A (white) classmate of mine and I decided we'd go to a jewelry store in town and pretend we were looking for a ring because we were going to get married. Our professor would not allow us to do that because he did not feel it would be safe, did not know how it would turn out and didn't want to put us in danger.

"But things on campus were very cool racially. I was a member of the campus police and remember no incidents happening or being reported. I didn't experience racism at all during my time there. Longwood (officials) intentionally made the campus comfortable for all of the students. They went out of their way and should be applauded for it."

BEFORE THE 1982-83 SEASON, Neal set about getting his players in shape.

"We didn't have a track," Neal says. "I had the players run up and down hills. I put down markers on the streets."

Neal never had to worry about Kersey.

"Jerome didn't need anybody to help him get ready to play basketball," Neal says. "He was always ready to play. He made everybody on the team accountable. He lived in the gym. He left a legacy with how he played. He was a superbly conditioned athlete. Every rebound belonged to him. He always seemed to play as if it were his last game. He wanted to prove himself in the NBA as a way to thank his grandmother for raising him.

"He faced a lot of adversity, but he stayed focused. He was always hopeful and ready — that was Jerome. He stayed on a mission and played with his heart. He never wanted to lose or be outdone, especially in terms of effort, hustle, desire or conditioning. He had a mindset that was focused and driven to be great. He never took a day off."

Kersey maximized his strengths and worked on his weaknesses.

"Jerome wasn't flashy," Neal says. "He was a straight-on, stay-on-a-path player from baseline to baseline.

He didn't shoot well from the perimeter. He wasn't going to be a triple-double guy, but you could count on him to get 13, 14 rebounds. He was a consummate team player who defended, was aggressive and gave more effort than anybody."

Neal says he expected a lot from Kersey, "but he expected a lot from himself."

"Jerome was never one to seek credit or glory, but he always wanted to be the best," Neal says. "He held his teammates accountable. He had a quest for learning. He could change a game with his energy.

I called him an 'overworker.' He was a warrior. He'd dive for a ball like Dennis Rodman — full tilt ahead. He wouldn't stop for nothing."

Kersey's stats dipped a bit as a junior in 1982-83, in part due to an early-season foot injury. He was the third-leading scorer on a team that went 15-10 in an at-large schedule, behind guard Joe Remar (18.7) and center Ron Orr (16.4). Kersey led the Lancers in rebounds (10.8), steals (3.1), blocks (1.7) and dunks (22 in 25 games) and was honored as a third-team All-American by the National Association of Basketball Coaches.

Things changed for Kersey's senior season. Longwood joined the Mason-Dixon Athletic Conference and finished in second place in the regular season with a 7-3 league mark. The Lancers were 15-12 overall, winning their final six contests.

Kersey was sensational from start to finish. In Longwood's opener, he collected 30 points and 14 rebounds in a 65-61 victory over Saint Paul's. In the final regular-season game of his career — before a packed house of 2,200 at Lancer Hall — he scored 27 points, matched his school record with 26 rebounds and dished out nine assists in an 86-77 triumph over Mount St. Mary's.

As Longwood's captain and lone senior, Kersey led the Lancers in scoring (19.6 points) and topped Division II players with a 14.2 rebound average. He also led the team in assists (3.7), steals (2.9), blocks (1.6) and dunks (28 of the team's 40). Kersey was a first-team NABC Division II All-American, Virginia college division Player of the Year and conference Player of the Year. He left Longwood with dozens of school records, including career scoring (1,796), rebounds (1,162), steals (248), blocks (142) and dunks (93).

Teammates won't forget an early-season matchup at home against Virginia Union and 6-8 junior Charles Oakley, won by the Panthers 55-48. Kersey did his part with 16 points and 10 rebounds against the player who would be named NABC Division II Player of the Year the following season. Oakley finished with 16 points and 12 boards.

"Those two were going at it, battling each other, and it was certainly above the rest of the game," forward Dave Strothers says today. "The intensity was ratcheted up another level. You could feel something special, with a high level of competitiveness and physical play. I knew how good Oakley was — I'd played against him in high school. That made me feel like Jerome had a legitimate shot at making it to the NBA."

"Oakley was the biggest man I'd seen in my life," forward John Rusevlyan says. "Watching those two titans go at each other was unbelievable."

KEVIN RICKS remembers a 78-64 victory at Liberty Baptist (now Liberty) during Kersey's senior season.

"Liberty had a 6-8 kid who was tough, and Jerome handled him pretty well," says Ricks, a freshman who started at point guard that season. "The Reverend Jerry Falwell came into our locker room afterward to congratulate us. He was president of the university. He couldn't wait to get over to Jerome. I was standing there when he shook Jerome's hand and said, 'Awesome job.' And pretty soon I realized I was the only one who knew who he was.

"After he left, I got up and said, 'Do y'all know who just left the room?' The guys just looked at me. Nobody said anything. I said, 'That is the Reverend Jerry Falwell!' Then the guys started cheering."

When Ricks, a Newport News, Va., native, was being recruited, he says Luther "talked up" Kersey. Ricks decided to do some research on the Lancers program.

"I was all but signed, sealed and delivered to (Division I) Richmond," says Ricks, who would start for four years at Longwood. "After I read about Jerome I thought, 'Sure, I want to play with this guy.'"

Ricks says he learned a lot from watching Kersey.

"From the first time we had pickup games, he set the tone of intensity for what it meant to be a college basketball player and how to compete," Ricks says. "He didn't take any plays off, and he did not want to lose. He was hard-nosed. No matter who you were, he went right after you. Once we started preseason conditioning, we'd do sprints. Jerome ran with the guards. I was trying to win every sprint, and so were those long legs of Jerome. We competed hard.

"Once we began formal practices, our relationship started to bloom. He was taking a young buck under his wing. I saw it as an opportunity for a freshman to hang out with the big dog. We partied and had a good time, but he would always stress academics. He'd say, 'Don't get in trouble with the books. Stay on top of it.' He was giving me true mentorship — guidance of what it took to be successful in college."

Ricks studied Kersey's game in order to maximize his teammate's talents.

"Jerome was solid shooting mid-range in, and anything going to the basket, it was, 'Look out below,' he was dunking on you," Ricks says. "Jerome had small hands — he couldn't palm a basketball — but he had serious leap. I loved it on the fast-break. He'd fill the lane, and I knew when I'd throw it to him, he would finish.

"I understood where his shots were in the offense. I tried to determine where I could get him the ball. He could hit that little elbow shot. Anything from that in, he had the green light. And that's where I'd look to get him the ball."

Though Kersey was the Lancers' star, he wasn't above taking a ribbing.

"When Jerome came back from Thanksgiving break that season, he had a Jheri curl in his hair," Ricks recalls with a laugh. "Let me tell you, that lasted a day and a half. We couldn't even sleep that night. We joked him so bad, he went back home and took it out."

Ricks grew to appreciate Kersey as a person.

"Jerome was so kindhearted," he says. "He had great interpersonal skills. He talked to everybody. He never acted like an All-American. After he came into the pros, he signed autographs and spent time with fans. I never saw him mad about anything or upset. He always seemed to keep his cool; he knew just how far to go and then peel it back."

Ricks and Kersey hung out in the summertime through Ricks' career at Longwood. The summer after Ricks' junior year, Kersey came back to take some classes to work toward completing graduation requirements. "We stayed in the same house off of Third Street in Farmville," Ricks says. "You talk about intense workouts. He was bringing back what he'd been doing at the pro level."

Ricks and teammate Lonnie Lewis drove to Clarksville to take part in "Jerome Kersey Day" in 1985.

"I rode in the convertible with Jerome in the parade," Ricks says. "I met the grandparents. Nice, humble people."

Ms. Weston Gupton organized "Jerome Kersey Day" in Clarksville after Kersey's rookie season with the Trail Blazers. Residents were trying to get a local YMCA built, so Gupton — a 1958 Longwood graduate — put together a fundraiser.

"Jerome was the only person of notoriety in Mecklenburg County at that time," says Gupton, now 85 and still living in Clarksville. "We featured him to draw a crowd of people. We had a parade and a meal at Bluestone High. We charged admission and sold memberships to the Y. Jerome was nice enough to come back and speak. That was my earliest recollection of him as an adult."

Gupton's son, Randy, was a classmate of Kersey in elementary school and played "Midget" football with him. Her daughter, Amy, was a cheerleader.

"Jerome was a very likable and well-raised kid," Gupton says. "He was a bit bashful but always very friendly. He was a tall kid, a little awkward at that age. Everybody knew he loved basketball and everybody recognized him."

LONNIE LEWIS was another Lancer who loved giving Kersey a hard time.

"Jerome had this favorite pair of dress shoes," says Lewis, a 6-3 forward who started on the front line alongside Kersey as a freshman and sophomore from 1982-84. "They were more red than burgundy. Everybody on the team thought they were the ugliest shoes ever, but Jerome loved those shoes.

"My sophomore year, we were playing at Virginia State. All the players gave our valuables to a manager for safekeeping. Somebody broke into our locker room during the game and stole everything, including those shoes. It was the angriest I've ever seen Jerome. I was like, 'You shouldn't be mad, Jerome; you should thank the guy who took them.' "

(To compound matters, the Lancers lost that game 76-73 despite 24 points and 23 rebounds from Kersey.)

Early in his freshman season, when he was yet to become a starter, Lewis learned what it was like to play against Kersey.

"The toughest player I was ever on the floor with," says Lewis, a retired fire captain and paramedic now living in Midlothian, Va. "Going against him in practice was tougher than going against 99 percent of the players we faced — different than anyone else we experienced in Division II. He was a beast.

"His goal was to be really good at whatever he did. You put him in a basketball combine, he probably wouldn't have graded very high. But on the floor, he was so strong — country strong. He very rarely lifted weights, but my goodness, he was strong."

After his first two NBA seasons, Kersey stayed with Lewis for several weeks while they played summer league ball at Virginia Commonwealth.

"I didn't see any differences in him than before he left Longwood," Lewis says. "He was still the same person. He was always jolly, enjoyed having fun."

The first summer back, Lewis asked him how it felt to be rich.

"I drive a little bit better car and have a nice house now, but the true meaning of being rich is to have a place to live, a car, your health and to be able to put food on the table," Kersey said. "You may not drive a Mercedes or Porsche, but if you have those things, you're rich."

"It hit me and made me think about the question I asked," Lewis says today. "There are not many things that stick with you that you still pass on to people 35 years later. That characterizes who he was even after he made it."

TROY LITTLES was part of the same freshman class as Jerome Kersey at Longwood and played two years of varsity ball with him.

"The growth from his freshman to senior years was extraordinary," says Littles, now retired from the military, living in Woodbridge, Va., and working as chief operating officer for an agency within the U.S. government.

" 'Gee' separated himself from us. We were just basketball players. He was an NBA player."

Littles says Kersey was "sort of quiet, sort of shy, not as outgoing as people saw him later on."

"He was always very generous," says Littles, a 6-3 forward. "Coaches gave the players meal money on a road trip to Atlantic City. Some of the guys gambled it all away. At our hotel, Jerome was playing the slot machines. I walked by and noticed he was doing pretty well. He had a stack of money. He said, 'You want some money?' And he gave me some."

Through his college career, Kersey had little disposable money.

"I was on a monthly ROTC stipend," Littles says. "Jerome would ask, 'Troy, can you lend me some money?' I often did and he always paid me back. I trusted him. After he got into the NBA, he'd take me places, trips and cruises, and he'd pay for it."

In summer 1985, Kersey invited Littles to accompany him on a Carnival Cruise Line trip to the Caribbean.

"We docked at St. Martin, rented a car and drove to a nude beach," Littles recalls. "Jerome was not going to take his clothes off. I said, 'No one out here knows you,' and convinced him to do it. Just as we both stripped down, about 30 people from our ship showed up. He ran way out into the water so it covered him up. He was embarrassed. He said, 'I can't believe you got me to do it.' He was angry at me the rest of the trip."

Soon after Littles married his college sweetheart, she began student teaching.

"She needed some help coloring pictures for the kids in her class," Littles says. "Jerome and I helped out. I have a picture of a 6-7 guy lying on the floor, coloring pictures to support my wife."

Through the years, Kersey and Littles often got together when they were in the same part of the country.

"When I was in the Army at Fort Huachuca (in Sierra Vista, Ariz.), he was in Phoenix for a charity event (early in his NBA career)," says Littles, who made the three-hour drive to meet his friend. Kersey reserved a hotel room for him.

"I get there, and Jerome has an envelope with money for me," Littles says. "He had a heart of gold. Through the years, he gave me a lot of stuff. I have a Blazers sweatsuit with his name embroidered on it that he gave me. I'm going to donate it to the university."

DAVE STROTHERS, a 6-6 forward who came to Longwood as a junior transfer during Jerome Kersey's senior year, arrived on campus a month before fall term began. They would wind up rooming together on the road that season. While training with Kersey and All-America soccer player Darryl Case, the Cleveland native got an early lesson in how seriously his new teammate took conditioning.

"Jerome bought this little plastic stopwatch that he put around his wrist," says Strothers, a middle school principal who now lives in Ellicott City, Md. "We teased him about the cheap watch. We did some long runs around Farmville. He timed our runs so we could try to keep getting better. He would start that thing and we had to beat our best time.

"In the last part of our run, there was an incline. He'd kick it into gear going into the last stretch. I'd let him go. 'OK, Jerome, go get 'em.' It stuck in my mind: 'This guy is hungry!' He was very serious about it. He had a commitment."

On the first day of school in the fall, players had gathered for a pickup game at Lancer Hall. A crowd of students watched the action. Strothers wound up matched up against Kersey.

"Jerome is coming downcourt on a fast- break with an angle to the basket," Strothers recalls. "I'm thinking, 'I got this guy.' I'm going to go up with him. I could usually jump off one foot and block a guy's shot. But he goes up a little sooner than I thought. He goes up high and makes a thunderous slam right over me — in my face. All the girls are going, 'Oooh!' Everybody is high-fiving. That's my baptism into Jerome Kersey and what he could do — my first experience getting 'Kerseyed.' "

Kersey was the Lancers' franchise player. It gave the team's trainer, Hollis "Doc" Powers, an opportunity to pull a joke on coach Cal Luther.

"Over winter break, Jerome hurt his foot in practice," Strothers says. "Doc takes Jerome to the training room, then comes out with a grim face, looking bad. He pulls Coach Luther aside and says, 'Coach, his ankle is broken.' Coach says, 'Goddamnit!' He is crestfallen. He is pacing around, thinking, 'there goes our season.' And then Hollis says, 'I'm just kidding, Coach. It's not broken. It will be fine.' And Coach is like, 'You son of a bitch!' He got Coach on that one."

For a couple of weeks over winter break, dorm rooms were closed on campus, so the players were housed together in Lancer Hall. One night, they were preparing for bed.

"Jerome had just bought a pair of black sneakers," Strothers says. "They looked like referee shoes or football place-kicker shoes. Jerome was really proud of them. We're teasing him mercilessly about them. Jerome rarely got mad, but finally he says, 'The next person who talks about these shoes is going to have a problem.'

"We're all kind of settling in and it's quiet. Then one of the players — Tim Wilson, who had been drinking — comes in. He has no idea Jerome has laid down the law. He sees the shoes, sets up a pillow and boots it like a field goal. Jerome hops up out of bed, grabs Tim and takes him down. He doesn't hurt him and lets him go after a minute, but he's mad. Tim is like, 'What was that?' "

Once during that season, Kersey caught a cold or flu bug the day before a game and missed practice. Later, Strothers and a couple of teammates dropped by his dorm to see how he was doing.

"I'm feeling a lot better," Kersey said.

There was a school dance that night. Several of the Lancer players went — including Kersey.

"Meanwhile, Coach Luther grabs his wife (Linda) and says, 'Let's go to Jerome's dorm room and see how he's doing,' " Strothers says. "He figures he'll find Jerome lying there with a thermometer in his mouth, on his death bed. Jerome is nowhere to be found. So Coach does a little investigating. He finds out about the dance. He goes to investigate and there's Jerome out there on the middle of the floor, doing the boogaloo.

"Coach told the story to the team the next day, and I don't think Jerome got disciplined or anything. But Coach wasn't happy about it for a while."

Strothers says Kersey was friends with everyone on the team.

"Whites, blacks — he got along with everyone," says Strothers, who is white. 'We all hung out. You name the group or crowd, he was part of it. Never in any kind of a conflict with anybody. A class act all the way."

Several times through the years, Strothers attended games in which the Blazers played the Bullets in Washington, D.C. Once, he met Kersey in the office of his agent.

"I sat there waiting for him for a while," Strothers says. "Jerome was on top of his finances. He was very wise. He wasn't going to blow his money and spend it frivolously. When he came out of the meeting, he said, 'Sorry, Dave, but these guys come first. I have to make sure they have everything on the financial side straight.' I was impressed."

Strothers marvels at the long NBA career his former teammate would fashion.

"I was proud of him, how focused and dedicated he was," he says. "He lasted so long because he was a great model to follow, a locker-room kind of player. It was how he carried himself. Why wouldn't you want a guy like Jerome around your other players? He was going to work his tail off. Organizations saw a lot of value in having Jerome as part of the team culture."

JOHN RUSEVLYAN was a 6-3 sophomore forward during Jerome Kersey's senior year. They had met the previous year, became roommates at mid-semester and roomed together the next school year, too. Rusevlyan got to know Kersey well on a personal level.

"Jerome came from very modest means," says Rusevlyan, who now owns a real estate firm in Florence, Ala. "He had nothing. But he got love and care from his grandmother.

"She would come up to games (from Clarksville) periodically, which was a big deal for her. It wasn't easy. She'd come up and after the game would give him $20. He'd take that money to McDonald's and get $20 worth of food and come back to the dorm and say, 'Anyone who wants to have at it, have at it.' I was like, 'Jerome, save some of that money.' He was like, 'No, this is my treat, and I want everybody to enjoy it.' That was Jerome. That burned so deeply in my mind. It was like, 'I'm going to give when I can give, and this is my opportunity to give.' "

As a little-used reserve, Rusevlyan would sometimes get matched up against Kersey during practice.

"He was 110 percent full blast," he says. "Never stopped. That carried over to the games. It was the only speed he knew. We'd be doing one-on-one drills. Somebody's going to have to guard Jerome. He was just so strong and fast, you couldn't deal with him. He would just pound you. He was nonstop until the horn sounded. Jerome was truly a silent assassin."

Like his Longwood teammates, Rusevlyan grew to appreciate their leader's style.

"Non-pretentious," he says. "Friendly. Happy-go-lucky. Unassuming. Always thinking not of himself but of others. There was nobody in college that he crossed. And that smile — that big, wide smile. It summarized who he was."

ABOVE ALL, Kersey's Longwood friends and teammates appreciated that the money and success didn't spoil him.

"He didn't change a whole lot," Orlando Turner says. "He had the same personality at 50 that he did at 21. He was busier and became a little more guarded of his time, but to us, he was the same guy. "

"I used to go to Madison Square Garden to watch Jerome and the Blazers beat my Knicks on a regular basis," Mike Wills says. "One time early in his career, I yelled out to him when he was returning to the floor from halftime. He turned around with that smile and greeted me. He came over and we embraced. What a wonderful man and teammate he was!"

Jerome shoots a free throw during his second NBA season. *Courtesy Portland Trail Blazers*

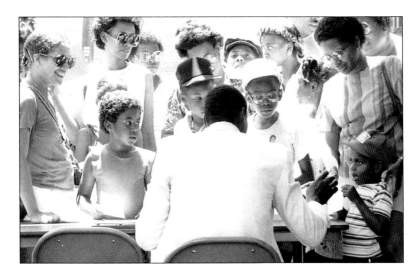

Jerome was already a big deal in Clarksville (Va.) when he signed autographis on "Jerome Kersey Day" in his hometown after his rookie season with the Blazers in 1985. *Courtesy News-Progress, Mecklenburg County, Va., photo by Rick Magann*

Chapter Five

Making the League

HIS COLLEGE CAREER was over, and Jerome Kersey wasn't sure about the future. He hoped he'd get an opportunity to try out for an NBA team, but had little indication that would happen.

NBA scouting operations in 1984 weren't nearly as sophisticated as today. NBA teams did a reasonably thorough job in evaluation of the Division I ranks, but the lower divisions were much more hit and miss.

Marty Blake was considered the "human database" of NBA scouting. A former NBA general manager, he founded his own scouting service in 1971 in an era before videotape existed and teams set aside a budget for scouting. In 1976, the league named Blake as its director of scouting services. He served in that position for 30 years, gathering information on prospects that he funneled to every team in the league. Teams would do their own scouting, but they would also rely on Blake and his service for both data and opinions that would factor into their selections in the draft.

In the 1980s, Blake's duties included helping to line up players for pre-draft camps, including the Portsmouth (Va.) Invitational Tournament and what became known as the NBA Combine in Chicago.

Portsmouth, which had existed since 1953, was first on the calendar each year. In 1984, the PIT featured 64 seniors, divided into eight teams of eight players, who spent four days in tournament play as NBA scouts watched. Players expected to go in the first round of the draft generally skipped the PIT. There were 10 rounds to the draft that year, and those invited to Portsmouth were mostly players in the middle rounds. Still, Kersey wasn't on anyone's radar.

"We didn't get any kind of letters or inquiries from NBA teams — not one," said Cal Luther, Kersey's coach his final three seasons at Longwood. "Nobody showed any interest at all. I don't think many pro scouts had seen him. So we had to generate interest."

At least one scout had heard about Kersey.

"I had gotten a call from a friend who was a high school coach in South Carolina," says Bucky Buckwalter, then the Portland Trail Blazers' chief scout. "He had seen Jerome play. I started checking on him. I found out he was a raw talent but very athletic."

During Kersey's senior season, Luther began to lobby for his inclusion at Portsmouth. The coach was friends with Blake. During his time at Murray State, Luther had coached Dick Cunningham, who played seven years in the NBA, and Stew Johnson, who played nine ABA seasons.

"The PIT was going to be the one chance for Jerome, the only chance to showcase him in any way," Luther says. "I felt like I had to get him into that thing. Late in his senior year, Marty called me about some players and I said, 'I've got a kid who's really good.' I thought Jerome had a real chance to make it. If he got on the right team, he'd have a great chance to make it. I told Marty, 'He'll make a better pro than a college player.'

"Jerome could go to the goal with the ball great. He could rebound great. He was great defensively. He ran the floor just super. He played aggressively. He did a great job in our press and our running game. He was not a great perimeter shooter. When people zoned us, they surrounded him and cut down on his effectiveness. But I could see he was going to get bigger and stronger, because he was a worker. He worked hard in the weight room and in what he was doing on the court."

In April, as the PIT loomed, Kersey was not among the players scheduled to be invited to participate. Luther called selection committee head Yale Dolsey in an 11th-hour lobbying bid.

"There's no way we can get that kid in here," Dolsey told Luther. "We're taking only one local guy — David Pope (from Norfolk State). He's the only kid we're even considering."

"He just turned me off in a heartbeat," Luther said. "Wouldn't give me the time of day."

Luther called Blake for help.

"You know I've never called you before (to lobby for a player)," Luther told Blake. "I know this kid has a legitimate shot to make it (to the NBA)."

Says Luther: "Marty hemmed and hawed for a while, then said, 'Cal, tell you what I'll do. Bring the kid to Portsmouth. Every year we have somebody who doesn't show up at the last minute. I'll make sure he gets in if you get him there.' "

At least one other person had advocated for Kersey. Bryan Kersey — no relation to Jerome — was the son of NBA referee Jess Kersey. Bryan, a member of the tennis team at Longwood, lived in a dorm room next to Jerome for a spell. They became good friends. During Jerome's senior season, Bryan called his father said, 'Dad, there's a guy at Longwood y'all need to see.' "

"We knew Marty Blake very well," says Bryan Kersey, now supervisor of basketball officials for the Atlantic Coast Conference after a long career as a referee. "My dad talked to Marty about Jerome. I know Cal called him, too."

After Luther's first call to Blake, he asked one of his scouts, Chick Craig, to watch him play for Longwood.

"The game Chick watched, he got 28 rebounds or something," Blake told Hoke Currie. "Chick said, 'I'd bring him to the PIT.' "

The night before the tournament, Cal and his wife Linda picked up Kersey and set out for the 2 1/2-hour drive from Farmville to Portsmouth.

"We had a small car," Luther recalls. "With his long legs, Jerome took up the whole back seat. We talked on the way. Guys like (Matt) Doherty from North Carolina were in (the tournament). Jerome said, 'Gosh, the only time I've ever seen some of these guys is on TV.' I said, 'Hell, Jerome, you're damn good. You'll eat Doherty alive. He doesn't have anywhere near the athletic ability you do. It doesn't matter if they've been on TV or not. This is your chance. Just play all out.' "

The Luthers and Kersey arrived in Portsmouth about 5 p.m. They went to dinner, then headed for the hotel in which the players were being housed. Blake was there. About 10 p.m., he called Luther over.

"Cal, the kid from Oregon State (Charlie Sitton) had a death in the family and he's not coming," Blake told him. "Get your kid."

The PIT provided meal money and took care of hotel expenses for the players. Not, initially, for Kersey, however.

"Jerome wasn't on the list," Luther says. "So I gave him $30 — I think everybody else was getting $40 — got him a room and told him, 'The rest is up to you.' "

After the first day, Kersey received the same $40 daily stipend as did his fellow participants. It was as if he'd hit the lottery.

"That was the first time I'd had that much money in my pocket," Kersey told Hoke Currie in 1998. "While the other guys were going out eating nabs (sandwich crackers) and Cokes and gambling with their money, I saved most of mine. I was out of rural Virginia."

AFTER A DAY of practice, the players at Portsmouth began playing games. Scouts from every NBA club were represented. Buckwalter was in the stands. So were the likes of Dave Cowens, Red Auerbach and Jerry West, among others.

Most of the players were lesser-knowns, including Gonzaga point guard John Stockton.

"I paid my way there," Stockton says.

Only three players who participated in the '84 PIT would be chosen in the first two rounds of the draft — Stockton, Kersey and Boston College forward Gary Plummer. Tournament MVP Curtis Green of Southern Mississippi was taken in the third round. He never played in the NBA.

Kersey's team was matched up with that of Doherty in their first game.

"I was nervous," Kersey said. "I mean, you had big names there. You had Doherty there. A lot of guys you'd seen play on TV."

Kersey collected 14 points, 10 rebounds and two blocks. Doherty — who would never play in an NBA game — scored 10 points but had 10 turnovers.

"Jerome was a little tight and didn't play that well but showed some flashes of things," Luther recalled. "He played really good defense on Doherty. Doherty couldn't do anything against him."

Others critiqued Kersey more harshly.

"He just went through the motions," Blake said. "He had a terrible first game. He was a little out of shape, and we told him if he didn't feel like playing we'd send him home now."

Longwood assistant coach Ernie Neal had driven to Portsmouth to watch the tournament.

"The first game, Jerome looked like a baby fish in a large pond," Neal says. "He was sleep-walking or something. But the next game he got better, and the next game better, and then it was, 'Who is this guy?' "

Kersey hadn't been on the top of his game, but after facing Doherty, he knew he belonged.

"After the first night, I was like, 'I can play with these guys,' " Kersey said.

One of Kersey's teammates that week was Phillip "Doom" Haynes, a 6-3 guard from Memphis State.

"One play helped Jerome's career," Luther says. "A rebound comes off and Jerome is going down the left side of the floor. Doom gets an outlet pass and he's dribbling up the right side of the floor. He gets over the half-court line and throws a long lob pass to Jerome right at the goal. When he threw the ball, you could see Jerome accelerate. He put it into another gear, took off, caught it and stuffed that thing in. It was just a big-time play that you very seldom see in any game. There may not have been a play like that in the entire tournament.

"I turned my head to look at the (NBA) scouts and coaches who were sitting in chairs on the end line. Every single guy was writing down a note. It was like in unison. They were all turning pages and writing as fast as they could. When I saw Marty after the game, he said, 'Yeah, the kid's not bad. He has some possibilities.'"

Buckwalter thought so, too.

"Jerome was terrific athletically," the long-time Blazer scout and front-office executive says. "He could get to every ball, he would pursue every rebound, he was always a factor on the floor. He had incredible energy. He was very strong and quick and had quick feet.

"He was a very poor shooter, though. His range was about four feet, but he could get to four feet. He did not handle the ball well. It was in subsequent years that he made himself into a decent ballhandler. And he worked very hard and made himself into a shooter."

Kersey was named to the 11-player all-tournament team along with Stockton. There was only one disappointment for Kersey. The Aloha Classic — featuring many of the top 48 players in the nation — was the following week. He didn't get selected.

"After we won, it was like, 'I'm going to get to go to Hawaii on this deal,'" Kersey said years later.

It didn't happen, but with a recommendation from Blake, Kersey earned a bid to the Chicago pre-draft camp two weeks later.

Says Luther: "When the final night (at Portsmouth) was over, Marty said, 'I'm going to take your kid to Chicago. He's got a shot (at the NBA).'"

NONE OF THE top 15 players in the draft participated in the games at Chicago, but there was ample talent. As luck would have it, Kersey was placed on a team with Stockton and 7-footer Kevin Willis from Michigan State. The team with Kersey, Stockton and Willis — coached by Fred Carter, then an assistant with the Chicago Bulls — went undefeated and won the tournament.

"We all played pretty well together," recalls Stockton, who would go on to a Hall of Fame career with the Utah Jazz. "It wasn't disjointed. We were a bit of a well-oiled machine in very short notice. It was a ton of fun.

"I always felt that was a big reason both Jerome and I got a chance to make it in the league. That experience exposed our abilities. It was a really good coming-out party for both of us. I went to Chicago with no expectations of being drafted. After the tournament, Marty Blake mentioned both Jerome and me in the same sentence. He held a lot of sway during that time. That was kind of cool."

The experience forged a bond between Stockton and Kersey.

"We became pretty good friends under the circumstances," Stockton says. "We stayed connected for a couple of years after that. We'd see each other when we played in Portland or when they played in Salt Lake City, find a way to hook up over dinner for a few years. I always considered him a friend."

Buckwalter was in Chicago. So, too, was Portland general manager Stu Inman, who ran the camp with big man guru Pete Newell. Newell, who coached the 1960 U.S. Olympic team to the gold medal, later served as general manager of the San Diego Rockets and Los Angeles Lakers.

"I was on the floor, so I could chat briefly with kids from time to time," Inman told Hoke Currie in 1998. "I stopped Jerome on the court one day and said, 'Where in the world is that school you went to? Longwood — what is that?'" And he looked at me as only Jerome can and said — not in an apologetic way — 'Well, it used to be a girls' school.' I got home and back to the office and looked up Longwood, and there was my friend Cal Luther."

Luther and Inman had coached against each other when Luther

was at Murray State and Inman at San Jose State.

"Stu calls me and says, 'Give me the scoop on this kid,' " Luther says. "He starts talking about his work habits, says the sucker gets out there and works hard every day. 'It's yes sir and no sir.' "

"I don't know if this is an act or not," Inman told Luther. "I've never had a kid do this before. Jerome told me, 'We're getting too much meal money.' I asked him why. He said, 'Because the guys are going out and buying crackers and a hamburger and Coke, then taking the money and playing poker and gambling and staying up half the night.' "

"Is this guy conning me?" Inman asked Luther. "In all my years of working, I've never had a player tell me something like that."

"I told him he was right about Jerome," Luther said, "that he was an honest, hardworking kid who doesn't have a car or any extra stuff at all." He said, 'Cal, we're going to draft him.' I didn't know who else might have been interested, but no one else called me."

Said Inman: "Jerome performed quite well. You had to be taken by him. The kid didn't shoot it very well, but he was so active and paid attention to defense. There was something special about this kid. Naive, yes, but there was a purpose to his game. The rebound was an important thing to him. Defending — though maybe his technique wasn't the best — was important to him. We would say he was a kid who didn't have a ceiling. He can grow, get better. He may never be a great shooter, but he'll find ways to influence a game.

"The bottom line is: Can he find a way to make an eight- or nine-man rotation and help you win a game on some kind of a consistent basis? Can he identify with a loose ball, with a rebound? Place a significance on the defensive end? Understand what his strengths and limitations are? Play within himself? All these things go into the making of a good role player on a good team."

Inman offered another observation: "Jerome was lucky to meet up with Cal at that stage of his career. Cal was a very knowledgeable guy. His evaluation of Jerome was right on the button. He didn't oversell."

Unfortunately, in the years ahead, the Kersey-Luther relationship would sour, at least in the coach's perspective. That is according to both Neal and to Luther's wife, Linda.

"We were proud to have something to do with Jerome getting a shot at the NBA," Linda Luther says today. "As much as we loved him and thought a lot of him, there was a disappointment he didn't do more for the community and college and didn't do any more in terms of keeping up with my husband. I was surprised he didn't. My husband was hurt about that — he really was. Not that he wanted anything from Jerome, but it's like he never acknowledged the main reason he got to the NBA was that my husband pushed Marty Blake to take a look at him."

Neal feels the same way.

"After Jerome left Longwood, he did not have a lot to say to Coach Luther," Neal says. "Jerome never said a 'thank you.' (Luther) was always waiting for it. It never came. I can't tell you why. For Jerome to turn it off like that made no sense. It devastated Coach Luther. Coach never did anything to hurt him or said anything demeaning to him. There was never any kind of an issue. Coach doesn't know why to this day. We just know (Kersey) stopped talking. He never invited us to Portland. He never invited us to a game."

Neal says he saw Kersey once, at a preseason game in Indianapolis.

"I drove there, and he gave me a sweatsuit and one for Coach Luther," Neal says. "That's the only thing he ever gave Coach Luther or me. I spoke to Jerome about that and asked him to let the man know he appreciated what he did for him. Jerome never did. (Luther) is so hurt by that. Coach Luther did everything for Jerome."

As is detailed later in the book, Kersey actually did quite a bit for his alma mater after leaving in 1984. And, at least in the short term, he kept in close touch with Luther and sought his advice, especially before and during his rookie season.

AS THE NBA DRAFT APPROACHED, Kersey needed to hire an agent.

"The thing that concerned me most was I wanted him to get a

reputable organization to represent him," Cal Luther said. "After Portsmouth, people were calling him at the dorm — bypassing me — and trying to talk him into playing in Italy and other places."

Luther asked Ernie Neal to take Kersey on the three-hour drive to Washington D.C., to the office of super-agent Donald Dell. Dell's ProServ marketing group represented such sports names as Arthur Ashe, Jimmy Connors and Michael Jordan. Kersey arrived decked from head to toe in a white outfit, paid for by Luther.

"He looked like Jerry Butler, the 'Ice Man,' " Neal says today with a laugh.

"Jerome didn't know what to expect, how it would take place, what would be said or what they would offer," Neal says. "We go in and they have these Playboy Bunny-looking girls running around. The offices are real plush. White carpet everywhere and the best furniture.

"When Jerome walked in the front door, everybody migrated toward him, asking him questions, laying out a welcome mat to him. It was something to behold."

Kersey and Neal met with one of Dell's agents, Bill Strickland.

"Bill did most of the selling on Donald Dell's program," Neal recalls. "He told Jerome how his money would be invested and what opportunities he would have by going with Pro-Serv. He talked about other clients, showed him portfolios and flyers, talked about other opportunities they had for him, how they would pay his bills. All the money would be sent to the agency; then they would earmark the money to be paid to the different companies.

"Before we got through the presentation, Jerome had decided he would sign with Pro-Serv. He was really happy. It was his dream."

THE 1984 NBA DRAFT was held at the Felt Forum inside New York City's Madison Square Garden on June 19 — a week before Kersey's 22nd birthday. He rented a room at the Lighthouse Motel in Clarksville to watch the draft on TV with cousin Jesse Kersey and his friend Leroy Bacon.

The announcing crew included Al Albert, Lou Carnesecca and a pair of broadcasting names who became familiar to Trail Blazer fans — Steve "Snapper" Jones and Eddie Doucette. Jones was an analyst and Doucette a play-by-play man for Portland games in the 1990s.

The 1984 draft was top-heavy with greatness, with Hakeem Olajuwon, Michael Jordan, Sam Perkins, Charles Barkley, Kevin Willis, Otis Thorpe and John Stockton going among the first 16 picks. They all wound up playing at least 15 NBA seasons. Olajuwon, Jordan, Barkley and Stockton made it to the Hall of Fame.

Nobody else drafted below the first round played more than 10 years in the NBA except Kersey, who lasted 17 years. He was the Blazers' fifth pick of that draft, behind Kentucky center Sam Bowie (No. 2), Fresno State swing man Bernard Thompson (No. 19) in the first round and Xavier guard Victor Fleming (No. 26) and New Mexico State guard Steve Colter (33) in the second round. Kersey went at No. 46, the next-to-last pick of the round.

(There were 24 picks in the first round. The Cleveland Cavaliers were awarded an extra first-round selection to compensate for the picks traded away by previous owner Ted Stepien.)

Were those in the Blazers' "war room" concerned a team might take Kersey before they did?

"I was concerned more than the rest of them," Buckwalter says. "I felt we needed to get Jerome, a good athlete who had a desire to improve. By the time he came to us, it was great relief.

"In those years, we were a pretty good team but not great. I felt we had to go for the athletes and make basketball players out of them. Oftentimes that manifested itself into being a player from a small school or an unknown player — one who wasn't that highly touted. We had great success with second-round players."

The selection surprised Kersey.

"I had no idea Portland was interested in me until they drafted me," he said. "I'd heard the Atlanta Hawks were interested. They said after the draft they had me on their board for a third-round pick.

"I was like, 'Where in the heck is Portland, Oregon?' I was looking at it on a map. I was like, 'It's way up there at the top and Clarksville, Va., is way down here at the bottom. It seemed like a world away. Then I got out there, and it was just beautiful."

Kersey's selection created little stir in Portland. It merited one paragraph of mention in The Oregonian: "With their third pick in the second round, the 46th choice overall, the Blazers rolled the dice. They decided upon Jerome Kersey, a 6-7 center at Longwood College in Virginia."

In late June, the group converged on Portland for a week-long rookie camp. Among the 22 players participating were Thompson, Fleming, Colter and Kersey, along with veteran free-agent center Tom Scheffler. Running the camp were head coach Jack Ramsay and Rick Adelman, the latter beginning his second year as a Blazer assistant. Inman and Buckwalter were also in observance, along with sports psychologist Bruce Ogilvie, who would eventually work with nine NBA teams. Ogilvie was there to develop psychological profiles on each of the athletes as he had done with Ramsay teams of the past. He would continue working with the Blazers until Paul Allen bought the team in 1988.

"I'm one of the pioneers in the application of psychology and working with elite and Olympic athletes," Ogilvie told Hoke Currie in 1998. "I'm a clinician by training, but my interest is in creating the most ideal environment to develop talent. That's what my specialty has been. We wanted to understand and have many insights that would enable the coaching staff to provide what we call the ideal teaching and learning environment for each player."

Kersey, said Ogilvie, had "an outstanding profile."

"Jerome had very strong leadership qualities and characteristics — more than most," the sports psychologist said. "It's a quality that is so important. He was a very tough-minded young man. We weren't worried about him being fragile if the coaches lit into him and came at him hard. That's an issue for rookies coming in. He was very driven. He had very high standards and performance goals for himself. He was unusually self-confident. He came in feeling very good about the coaching he had received in the past, so he had a trusting feeling regarding the coaching he was going to be exposed to."

Ogilvie administered what he called an "Athletic Motivation Inventory" test, designed to critique 11 sports-oriented characteristics such as drive, aggressiveness, mental toughness and coachability. The year before, rookie Clyde Drexler had tested out in the first percentile.

"Jerome would be in the upper five percent," Ogilvie said. "He was a superb-looking man on the inside. He came close to setting the standard for what we would like to see. I told both Jerome and Clyde, 'God, I sure hope you can play basketball, because you have everything (mentally) I would look for.' "

When Ogilvie later made a film about his studies, he used Kersey as one of two athletes for an example.

"I used him because he's a very articulate guy, just as sharp as could be," Ogilvie said. "He was fun, had a good sense of humor. He was very comfortable to be with. I think of him as one of the great young men I've met in the sports world.

"He had a great team attitude. We picked up on that in the first three days of camp. That's the most hellish evaluation process any kid can be subjected to, and he handled it. He knew it would start Monday and (the roster) would be whittled down by Wednesday and probably only four of them would be brought back for summer league. After the third day, some of the (camp) coaches were in the coffee room talking about him. They said, 'This kid can play in the NBA right away.' "

There was a difference of opinion on that, however.

Portland's summer league team — featuring Thompson, Fleming, Colter, Kersey, Scheffler and third-year forward Audie Norris — began play the following week in San Diego. The Blazers stayed at the Bahia Resort Hotel and practiced at La Jolla High. After summer league, all but Norris returned to Portland and worked out for three days under Ramsay and Adelman.

Ramsay then brought in Kersey for a talk that would become legend.

"You've got some raw talent," Ramsay said. "I think you should go over to Europe, play one or two seasons and then come back and we'll take another look. We'll retain your rights."

"I go, 'What?' " Kersey would later say. "I thought I had done pretty well. I had to make a decision after that. Do I go home? Do I go to Europe? If I come back to training camp, I'll miss Europe. If I didn't make the team, I would have to go to the (Continental Basketball Association) or go home."

Kersey returned to Farmville and spoke a couple of times with his Longwood coach, Cal Luther.

"If you think you can make it, go back (to Portland) for training camp," Luther said.

"So I did," Kersey said. "(The Blazers) were a little surprised I came back. I was stubborn."

Luther gave him a pep talk.

"I don't give a damn what Ramsay or anybody else says," he said. "You stay with them 'til they tell you that you're cut. Work your butt off. Something will happen. Somebody will get hurt, somebody will be traded, something will take place. You don't want to miss out on an opportunity if you're a good enough player, and you are."

KERSEY RETURNED to Portland in early October for his first training camp. The Blazers were stacked with forwards, including veterans Kiki Vandeweghe, Mychal Thompson, Kenny Carr and Audie Norris along with fellow rookie Bernard Thompson, who could also play shooting guard. Kersey wound up battling Pete Verhoeven — who had been with the team the previous year — for the final roster spot.

"Jack (Ramsay) and Stu (Inman) were still talking about trying to send Jerome to Europe to play," Portland coach Rick Adelman said. "They didn't think he was ready to play in the NBA. But Jerome wouldn't accept it. And he made the team. He forced his way in, and he deserved it, and got better and better. He played so hard. God, he played hard. It was unbelievable the stuff he did. He had such a belief in himself."

Clyde Drexler, entering his second season with the Blazers, saw that, too.

"Bucky (Buckwalter) loved Jerome and thought he was a diamond in the rough, and he was absolutely right," Drexler says. "That was Kiki's first year with the team, too, and they were looking for a backup for Kiki. Pete was with the team the year before. He was well-liked, a hard worker, just a great guy. But Jerome sheer-hustled himself into a spot on the team, and he continued to work himself into bigger roles through those first few years."

Even so, it wasn't a cinch Kersey was going to make the team.

"He was very close to getting cut," recalls Sam Bowie, the oft-injured center who came in as a rookie with Kersey in 1984. "Pete rolled his ankle late in training camp; Jerome was on the bubble. I remember him coming into my room late one night, concerned he might not make the squad.

"And look at the way things turned out. I retired in 1995 and there was Jerome, still playing six years later."

Kersey was tough-minded from the jump.

"I laid it all out there," he said. "(The veterans) were all buddy/ buddy and I was a little rookie. But I said to myself, 'Nobody is going to outwork me. I'll stand up for myself. I'm not backing down.' "

Kersey recalled one incident during camp involving free-agent guard Danny Tarkanian, son of then-UNLV coach Jerry Tarkanian.

"I set a pick on him one day and put him out for the rest of practice," Kersey said. "That may have gotten (the coaches') attention."

"His determination impressed all of us," Buckwalter says. "He made it strictly on his athleticism because he was not yet a basketball player. He was a great athlete who became a basketball player. He was a tenacious defender. His footwork wasn't good and he wasn't fundamentally sound, but if you were going to score on him, you had to go through him, and he would fight you."

Kersey played superbly in the preseason. His 15.4-point scoring average led Blazer rookies. He shot .523 from the field and grabbed 50 rebounds in seven games.

In a 105-97 exhibition win over the L.A. Clippers, Kersey had 19 points, eight rebounds and two steals in 30 minutes off the bench. In a 119-112 loss to Utah, he had 20 points and nine boards in 33 minutes. Mychal Thompson was calling him a "young Bernard King."

Late in the preseason, the night before the team's final cuts, Kersey went to dinner with sports psychologist Bruce Ogilvie, Colter and Thompson, then returned to his motel room. About 10:30 p.m., Ogilvie knocked on his door.

"You're going to make the team,' " he said.

"Get the hell out of here," Kersey said.

"I thought he was joking at first," Kersey would say later. "I was overwhelmed. I was going to be on the team. I didn't sleep at all that night. The adrenaline was too high. I called everybody I knew. I stayed up all night and watched TV."

Jerome goes up for a layup during his freshman season at Longwood, the only year he wore No. 34. He led the Lancers in scoring (16.9 points per game) and rebounds (8.9) his first season in Farmville.
Courtesy Longwood University

A team picture of the 1980-81 Longwood Lancers. Kersey is top row, second from left.
Courtesy Longwood University

Cal Luther coached Jerome his final three seasons at Longwood. Luther was instrumental in getting him a spot in the Portsmouth Invitational pre-draft tournament, which proved to be a springboard to Jerome's NBA career. Luther, 93, passed away on May 8, 2021. *Courtesy Longwood University*

Jerome dunks against a rare Division I opponent — Navy — as a sophomore in December 1981. He still holds Longwood's career records in rebounds, steals and blocked shots and is third on the school's career scoring list. *Courtesy Longwood University*

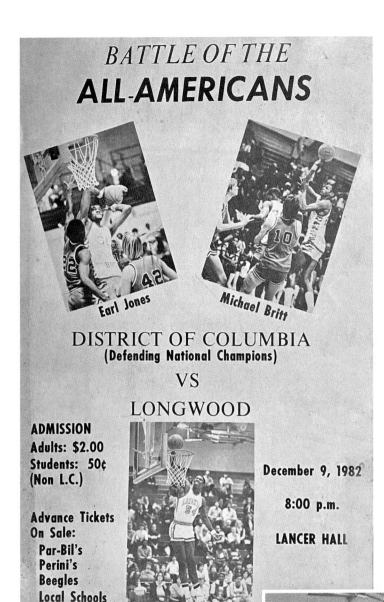

BATTLE OF THE
ALL-AMERICANS

Earl Jones

Michael Britt

DISTRICT OF COLUMBIA
(Defending National Champions)

VS

LONGWOOD

ADMISSION
Adults: $2.00
Students: 50¢
(Non L.C.)

Advance Tickets
On Sale:
  Par-Bil's
  Perini's
  Beegles
  Local Schools

December 9, 1982

8:00 p.m.

LANCER HALL

Jerome Kersey

Jerome shoots a floater over 7-1 Earl
Jones of District of Columbia in front of a
packed house at Lancer (now Willett) Hall
in the "Battle of All-Americans." Kersey
collected 17 points, five rebounds and
six steals but Longwood came up on the
short end of a 65-64 loss to the Firebirds.
Courtesy Longwood University

1,567 POINTS, 1,009 REBOUNDS, 59 VICTORIES

AND COUNTING

JEROME KERSEY

Remember "THE COBRA!" It's a sure bet that Longwood opponents from the past four years will remember him for a long time. The Cobra is Jerome Kersey, a 6-7, 220-pound cager, who scores (1,567 points), rebounds (1,009), plays defense (223 steals, 124 blocked shots) and sets up his teammates (225 assists). A third team NABC All-American last season, Kersey is currently in the midst of his best season ever.

Division II's leading rebounder (13.5 as of January 30), Kersey has averaged 20 points per game as well, leading a young Longwood team to eight wins in its last 10 games. He leads the Lancers in steals (50), assists (64), blocked shots (24) and slams (17). A senior captain and social work major, Kersey plans to become a probation officer for young offenders.

Led by his hustle and consistency, Longwood has compiled a record of 59-34 during his career.

ACCOMPLISHMENTS

THIRD TEAM NABC DIVISION II ALL-AMERICAN (1982-83)
SECOND TEAM ALL-SOUTH ATLANTIC REGION (1982-83)
College Division All-State (1982-83)
Mansfield State Tip-Off All-Tournament
PRE-SEASON SMALL COLLEGE ALL-AMERICA (Street & Smith's) 1982-83
Fourth Team All-East (Eastern Basketball) 1981-82
FIRST TEAM ALL-SOUTH ATLANTIC REGION (1981-82)
Armstrong State Holiday Classic All-Tournament
Pocono Classic All-Tournament
Yellow Jacket Classic All-Tournament
Longwood Invitational All-Tournament
Augusta Tip-Off All-Tournament
Eastern Basketball Division II All-Freshman Team (All-East) 1980-81

COMMENTS ON THE COBRA

HAL NUNNALLY, Randolph-Macon Coach
(after Kersey scored 21 points and grabbed 18 rebounds)
". . . if he's (Kersey) not an All-American again, the people who pick them don't know what one is."

"I don't think we've ever given up 11 offensive boards to someone else before. He's (Kersey) playing much harder than I remember him playing."

TOM SOUTHERLAND, West Virginia Tech Coach
(college coach of 76ers' Sedale Threatt)
"I think his chances are good at making a team in the NBA. He passes the ball well, goes to the boards, moves away from the ball and gets in there and scraps with anyone. He does need to improve on his ball-handling a little. But he's the kind of player that teams are looking for to play a power forward in the NBA."

FRED JETER, Sports Writer with the Richmond (VA) News Leader
"Jerome Kersey, the Lancers' all-time scorer, rebounder, sh blocker, and dunker, is a 6-7 athlete who'd look right at home on tl centerfold of *FLEX* magazine. . . . On one occasion, he (Kerse grabbed a defensive rebound and dribbled the length of the floc weaving in and out of traffic, before converting a three point play . . .'

JIM O'HARA, Sports Editor with the Farmville Herald
"Kersey hasn't disappointed anyone. In fact, as he enters his fin season wearing the Blue and White for Longwood, the 6-7 senior h probably become THE best forward in the state barring none. And he continues to play like he did this past weekend in the Par-Bi Tournament, he could become Longwood's first cager to be draft into the NBA ranks.

"He is, ladies and gentlemen, that good."

CAL LUTHER, Longwood College Coach
"Jerome's a bona fide pro prospect. He plays all out all the time." "He probably hustles more than any player I've ever coached."

SHOOTING PERCENTAGES

	Career	PCT.	This Season	PCT.
FIELD GOALS	633-1106	.572	136-268	.507
FREE THROWS	283- 606	.601	67-115	.583

STATISTICS

CAREER

Category	Number	Career Rank	Average (per game)
POINTS	1,567	First	16.8
REBOUNDS	1,009	First	10.8
ASSISTS	225	Third	2.4
BLOCKED SHOTS	124	First	1.3
STEALS	223	First	2.4
SLAMS	80	First	.9

THIS SEASON

Category	Number	Season Rank	Average (per gam
POINTS	339	First	19.9
REBOUNDS	230	First	13.5
ASSISTS	64	First	3.8
BLOCKED SHOTS	24	First	1.4
STEALS	50	First	2.9
SLAMS	17	First	1.0

Longwood SID Hoke Currie's campaign flyer pushing Jerome for All-American honors. Assistant coach Martin "Mo" Schoepfer coined Kersey as "The Cobra," the nickname based on the 6-7 post's long frame and athletic instincts. *Courtesy Longwood University*

Jerome is honored before his final home game at Longwood in February 1984 as his No. 54 (which he wore his final three seasons) was retired. Jerome is congratulated by athletic director Dr. Carolyn Hodges Crosby during the ceremony as his teammates and coaches Cal Luther and Ernie Neal look on. *Courtesy Longwood University*

Jerome being interviewed by broadcaster Don Lemish after his last game at Longwood. Kersey accounted for 27 points, 26 rebounds, nine assists and three steals in an 86-77 victory over rival Mount St. Mary's (MD). *Courtesy Longwood University*

Jerome works for position against former North Carolina standout Matt Doherty at the 1984 Portsmouth Invitational Tournament. Kersey averaged 15.3 points and 12.7 rebounds in three games and joined Gonzaga's John Stockton on the all-tournament team.
Courtesy Farmville, Va., Herald/ taken by former employee Jim O'Hara

Jerome (second row, far left with scarf) is joined by other ex-Longwood players at "Jerome Kersey Bobblehead and Reunion Day" in 2013. The day was highlighted by the Lancers' 76-61 win over Big South Conference rival Radford. *Courtesy Longwood University*

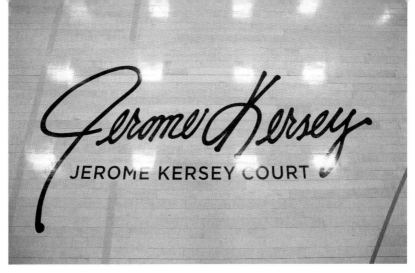

The basketball court in Longwood's Willett Hall was named in Jerome's honor in 2016. *Courtesy Longwood University*

Mitch Walker (right, with cap) reminisces as he looks at a Jerome Kersey mural and memorabilia in the Longwood men's basketball locker room before "Jerome Kersey Day" in 2020. Jerome's former teammate and close friend is joined by Longwood staffers. *Courtesy Longwood University*

Jerome delivered the keynote address during the commencement ceremony for the Longwood class of 2009. Kersey noted that hard work was
the "secret sauce" for success. *Courtesy Longwood University*

The Rotunda is the signature building on the Longwood campus. Originally founded in
1839 as a women's seminary, Longwood College became fully co-educational in 1976 and
became Longwood University in 2002. Longwood is in Farmville, Va., 64 miles west of
Richmond and 47 miles east of Lynchburg. *Courtesy Longwood University*

Chapter Six

The Rookie

SHORTLY AFTER signing his first contract with the Trail Blazers in the summer of 1984, Jerome Kersey placed a down payment on a new house for his grandparents, Herman and May Kersey. It was a modest three-bedroom home in a quiet area on the outskirts of Clarksville, Va.

Then Kersey settled into living in a townhouse at Oswego Summit in Lake Oswego, Ore.

"Other players on the team were living (in the complex), too," Kersey told Hoke Currie in a 1998 interview. "My rent was something like $700 a month. My rookie contract was for $92,000. Beats working in a factory back home.

"Me and (fellow rookies) Bernard Thompson and Steve Colter would hang around each other all the time. Me and 'Bernardo' were always getting together to do stuff."

Kersey didn't pal around with Clyde "the Glide" Drexler, the Blazers' second-year swing man and budding superstar. Drexler was closer to the team's other small forward, Kiki Vandeweghe. But Clyde developed a good relationship with Kersey, too.

"I took a liking to him and was like a big brother to him from Day One," Drexler says. "Jerome didn't know anything about Portland. He asked me every day for some help on something. I took him around, told him where to get an apartment, told him where to get his clothes and restaurants to visit.

"I liked the way he played. He was a hard-nosed effort guy, a hustler. He was a guy who loved the game. He loved to win, too."

Kersey imported some additional emotional support from back in Virginia. Longwood friends Kevin "Huggy" Brandon and Mitch Walker flew out and spent a good deal of time with him in Portland during his rookie season in 1984-85.

"Huggy and I were there for the entire ride, from getting drafted to the end of the season," Walker says. "Jerome didn't know anybody. We wound up hanging out and being there for him as he transitioned from little Farmville (Va.) to a decent-sized city. We were doing what 22-year-olds do, but we were also very protective of him from outsiders. Once you make it, there are a lot of people around you. We built a barrier around him."

Brandon guesses he and Walker spent a week or so with Kersey in Portland a half-dozen times during that rookie season, and it continued for several years.

"Typically, it was both of us, but there were times it was just me or just Mitch, depending on our schedules," Brandon says. "We were just looking out for Jerome, being another set of eyes in almost every environment we went into."

Kersey loved having his friends there. He also embraced the idea of being on his own, so far away from home. There were some mixed emotions about it, though.

"That year went by really fast," Kersey told Currie. "I got to know myself a little bit more. All of a sudden, I had a responsibility. It was the first time I had my own car. First time living by myself. I had the responsibility of a household and just being responsible for my schedule and everyday life. It was all so new. I'd never been in an NBA gym until my rookie year. Never saw a game in person.

"I would think, 'This is great. I get to come and do what I want, and I have some money in my pocket.' But I would also think, 'God, I miss home!' "

Instead of playing 27 games, as he had done as a senior at Longwood, Kersey was now looking at an 82-game regular-season schedule, plus eight exhibition games, plus the playoffs if the Blazers were fortunate enough to participate. And he was flying all across the country.

"I couldn't believe how hectic the schedule was," he said. "Going here and there to places I'd never been before. We were flying commercial then. You would play at night and have to get up at 5:30 or 6 and get on the bus and leave for another flight. You'd get on the plane and everybody's heads are laid-back. Everybody is sleeping — especially if you've had a few beers after the game the night before."

There was also the adjustment to a new position and playing against bigger, better players.

"During the last couple of years at Longwood I played mostly center, so I wasn't going out on the floor (away from the basket) guarding people," Kersey said. "I was having trouble with that. Sometimes I'd go out to guard somebody and he'd blow right by me."

Assistant coach Bucky Buckwalter, also the team's chief scout, worked with Kersey at the defensive end.

"I knew I had the quickness," Jerome said. "Bucky used to remind me that you run out fast, but on your last couple of steps, you have to get down lower into position to control the guy. He would demonstrate it. I figured if an old guy could do it, then I could do it."

JACK RAMSAY was in the ninth season of a 10-year run as the Blazers' head coach. In his first season at the helm, he had coached the Blazers to their first — and to date, only — NBA championship. Since then, Portland had made the playoffs every year but one but had yet to again advance past the Western Conference semifinals. In 1983-84, the Blazers had gone 48-34 in the regular season but lost 3-2 in a best-of-five first-round series with Phoenix.

"(Ramsay) wasn't a young players' coach," Kersey said of the man who would one day be inducted into the Naismith Basketball Hall of Fame. "He liked veterans who think the game when they're out there. Jack was fair. He's the one who taught me to work hard and keep myself in condition. He was a conditioning nut. He wanted his players to be in the top physical condition they could be in. He had a real business sense toward the game. His approach was very organized."

If Ramsay seemed distant at times, Kersey enjoyed a warm relationship with assistant coaches Bucky Buckwalter and Rick Adelman.

"When you see Bucky, the first thing you notice is the gold — the bracelets on his wrist, the watch, the rings," Kersey would say years later. "He looked like a guy out of Vegas. He was smooth, well-groomed. He had the open collar shirt, too. Diamonds and stuff."

Adelman had been an original Blazer, the team's first point guard during its inaugural 1970-71 season. He was in his first year as an assistant coach after several years as head coach at nearby Chemeketa Community College in Salem.

"Rick was always the guy helping me out," Kersey said. "Rick was your friend, your confidante, your coach. We were close. He could talk to you more on a one-on-one level."

Years later, Kersey would recollect that Ramsay gave him little playing time that season.

"He didn't believe in playing rookies a lot — or at all, unless you're a first-rounder," Kersey said. "I got time mostly when the game was over."

Kersey stayed in close touch with his coach at Longwood College, Cal Luther, as a rookie.

"The first year was really tough on him," Luther would recall. "He would call me from the airports, from hotel lobbies, from his room. He was despondent about the amount of playing time he was getting."

"Don't feel sorry for yourself," Luther told Kersey. "Do some extra laps, hit the weight room, keep yourself in great shape. Don't go out drinking beer afterward with the guys who already have it made. You have to be in a different mold. Something will happen. You'll get a chance."

Truth be told, Ramsay gave Kersey ample opportunities right from the start. But Portland returned most of its roster from the previous season, led by forwards Vandeweghe and Mychal Thompson, All-Star shooting guard Jim Paxson and Drexler. Kersey had moved ahead of fellow rookie Bernard Thompson in the battle for minutes at small forward, but still was behind Vandeweghe — in his first year with the club after averaging 29.4 points for Denver the previous season — and the emerging Drexler, who was splitting his time backing up Kiki at the "3" and Paxson at the "2."

But Kersey wouldn't settle for an entirely bench role. Fellow rookie Sam Bowie noticed that right away.

"The first thing that comes to mind is 'relentless,' " says Bowie, the 7-1 center whom the Blazers famously made the No. 2 pick of the 1984 draft, just ahead of Michael Jordan. "He refused to be outworked. You know the term 'heart of a lion?' That was Jerome.

"We were kids when we came in together. He was the type who loved to play hard. It's as simple as that. I wish I had the motor he had. He was extremely raw. He was hyper. Mychal said he was like the Energizer Bunny. He'd say, 'Get out of fourth gear, Romeo — come back into neutral.' If Jerome was going for a walk, it was at full speed. Going to lunch, going to dinner — same thing. He couldn't relax."

Bowie took it upon himself to be a frequent dinner partner with Kersey.

"I was the second pick in the draft, and got compensated for that," Bowie says. "Jerome was making minimum wage. I looked forward to picking up the tabs for us on the road, knowing I was a little more fortunate than him. I remember how appreciative he was that I was showing that kind of love."

Kersey didn't mind spending his own money on one of his passions — cars.

Early in his rookie season, he visited a Volkswagen/Porsche/Audi dealership in Northeast Portland. Sales manager Joe Khorasani greeted him.

"He pulled up in this ugly black Volvo," Khorasani says today. "I didn't know who he was. He said, 'I play for the Blazers. I'm looking for a new car. I might want to buy a Porsche.' "

Khorasani showed Kersey some choices.

"I let him take the Porsche he liked the best for a night and said, 'Enjoy your date,' " Khorasani says. "He couldn't believe it. We became friends after that."

Khorasani got to know Kersey well over the next three decades. In the mid-2000s, he founded a sports agency for which Kersey worked as a player agent for a short time.

"At one point I owned 11 dealerships," Khorasani says. "I lost everything in 2008. That didn't stop him from being my friend. It wasn't about that I had money. He was a true friend — loyal, someone you could trust. I trusted him with my family. Never heard him talk bad about anyone."

IT DIDN'T TAKE Kersey long to make an impression on the court. In the home opener and second game of the regular season, a 115-83 blowout win over Seattle, he entered the game with four minutes left in the second quarter and the score tied at 42-42. He provided an immediate lift, first stripping Ricky Sobers of the ball and feeding Kiki VanDeWeghe for a fast-break layup. Kersey then picked up a loose ball and again got the ball to Kiki, who was fouled. Kersey picked Sobers' pocket again and soloed for a dunk. Playing almost the entire fourth period before a sellout throng of 12,666, Kersey finished with 11 points, six rebounds, three assists and three steals.

"It was the biggest crowd I've ever played before," Kersey said. "I've never played in a crowded gym even."

"I like Jerome Kersey's game," Portland coach Jack Ramsay told reporters. "He gave us a little extra energy."

On November 12, Ramsay went to him in the third quarter to cool Golden State's Purvis Short, who had scored 29 points in the first half. Short wound up with 48 but the Blazers won comfortably, and Kersey gave his team's best defensive effort against the Warriors' high-scoring forward.

"I like to be known as a defensive player," Kersey said. "I'm glad the coach had the confidence to put me in to guard him."

Two nights later, Ramsay again showed confidence in the rookie. He was in at the end of a 101-94 loss to Dallas, sinking two free throws with 20 seconds remaining to pull the Blazers to within 96-94.

On November 15, Kersey came off the bench for 19 points and nine rebounds, hitting 7 of 12 shots from the field, to help the Blazers beat Utah 129-120.

"It was my biggest thrill since I made the team," Kersey said. "I was really pumped up."

Portland ran off a 15-4 spurt that effectively closed out Utah. It was a spree capped by an explosive play by Kersey.

Portland's Audie Norris blocked an Adrian Dantley shot and Kersey did a tightrope walk along the baseline to gain possession. He wheeled and took off for the other end and climaxed the end-to-end dash with a flying slam dunk. The play was even more spectacular because Kersey — already being kidded by teammates about his small hands — lost control of the ball while going for the dunk, then regained it.

"The ball was way down my arm," he said. "I can't palm the ball. Somehow, I don't know how I did it, I got the ball back in my hand."

The next night, with the Blazers trailing Seattle by one point with 30 seconds left, Kersey threw up a 17-foot jumper that missed badly, and the Sonics rebounded. Portland never got another shot at the lead in a 91-89 loss.

"It came from a lack of experience," Kersey said. "I thought the shot was there, but it wasn't the best one to take. I should have looked for one of the veteran players. I will learn from my mistakes. The next time I'll know how to react in that situation."

Kersey was off to a great start, the only rookie to play in all 12 games, averaging 7.3 points and 3.8 rebounds in 15.7 minutes per game.

"I'm pleased with the way I'm playing," he said. "I've played more minutes than I thought I would — probably the result of all the injuries we've had. I think I've proved I can play in this league. There was a little doubt in my mind. I had never played against players like this before. But now that doubt is erased."

Already, Kersey was a fan favorite. Wrote The Oregonian's Dwight Jaynes, "When Kersey enters a game at Memorial Coliseum, Portland fans buzz in anticipation."

"I kind of feel the fans," he said. "It's not something I can explain, but it gives you a boost."

Playing in a smaller NBA market was a good fit for Kersey.

"Portland had the perfect type of environment for him," Paxson says. "He was a little naive when he came in. If he'd have gone to a New York or Chicago, that would have been a little tougher for him. In Portland, fans related to him as a small-town guy, and he related to the fans. They loved his work ethic and he appreciated their love for him.

"Portland is a place where they find one rookie each year who they really pull for. Jerome was the guy that year, and he gave them a lot to pull for."

Paxson was a star and Kersey an unheralded rookie, but they got along fine right away.

"The biggest thing about Jerome was his intensity and level of effort all the time," says Paxson, an All-Star in each of the two seasons before Kersey arrived in Portland. "He came in as an athletic, hard-working kid who wasn't that skilled of a basketball player. He worked on those things and made himself into a good player. With hard work combined with his physical tools, he had a great career.

"Everybody loved him. He was a great teammate. Always had a smile on his face on and off the floor. He enjoyed being around his teammates. He brought a certain level of optimism and charisma that the fans fell in love with as well. He was a fun-loving person. He got along with people. He enjoyed life — not just the game, but all the things that surrounded it."

Though he wasn't playing as much as he'd like, Kersey was living the dream. In a 126-116 loss at Philadelphia, he got to play against one of his heroes, Julius "Dr. J" Erving.

"He came onto the court and said, 'Hey, what's up, young fella?' " said Kersey, who scored eight points in the game on 4-for-4 shooting in a 10-minute appearance. "I was like, 'Man, he spoke to me. He really spoke to me!' I scored one basket on him."

One way to get Kersey on the floor was with a young group to apply change-of-pace defensive pressure on the opposition. On November 27, it paid off against the Cleveland Cavaliers.

"The Cavs led 92-85 with nine minutes to go," Ramsay wrote in a weekly column he contributed to The Oregonian. "I called for the Blazer trappers — Darnell Valentine, Clyde Drexler, Jerome Kersey, Kenny Carr and Sam Bowie. They caused some turnovers, got the fast-break going and in six minutes we outscored Cleveland 19-4 and won 115-106."

On December 4, Ramsay employed a different group in a 112-104 win over Phoenix. Wrote Jaynes: "Trailing 33-29 going into the second quarter, Ramsay used Sam Bowie, Bernard Thompson, Steve Colter, Jerome Kersey and Audie Norris (all rookies but Norris). The youngsters, employing a scrambling half-court press, held their own. Ramsay rested his starters as a group again in the second half and when he brought the first team back in, the fresh troops outscored the Suns 14-3 to break the game open in the final period."

John Wetzel, who would later serve as an assistant in Portland during Rick Adelman's reign as head coach, was an assistant for the Suns that season.

"Six minutes into the game, Jack would bring Jerome in and all hell broke loose," recalls Wetzel, who was head coach in Phoenix for the 1987-88 season. "They had a zone press they would use and Jerome was all over the floor. He was a wild man. He changed the tenor of the game with his energy.

"That was my initial exposure to Jerome. Kiki (Vandeweghe) was docile in his attitude, his movements and mannerisms. And here comes Jerome — he was like a pit bull. The game might be tied and four minutes later they might be up by eight or 10. He'd get out in the open court, steal the ball and dunk."

Kersey had already gained the fans' attention with his high-flying dunks. At times, it could get dangerous. Wrote Jaynes: "Portland's Wednesday practice was punctuated by a flying dunk by rookie Jerome Kersey that broke a glass backboard. The backboard was equipped with a breakaway rim, but the only thing that broke was glass. No one was hurt."

With VanDeWeghe and Drexler ahead of him at small forward, Kersey's minutes were still difficult to come by. But Ramsay had him in the lineup in one critical moment in late January, a game the Blazers lost 128-127 at Boston on a 22-foot Larry Bird shot at the buzzer.

With three seconds left and the Celtics trailing 127-126, Coach K.C. Jones called timeout and grabbed a chalkboard to draw up a play. "Forget about it," Bird said, wiping the chalkboard clean. "Just get me the ball."

Dennis Johnson inbounded Bird the ball with Kersey overplaying him. "I don't know how he even caught the ball," Kersey said. "It was a great catch and a great shot. I was right up on him, as close as you could be without fouling him."

Kersey had helped out at the offensive end down the stretch, hitting back-to-back baskets on a 19-foot jumper and a dunk, the latter drawing the Blazers to within 124-122 with 55 seconds left. It took an epic Bird shot to save the Celtics, who would finish 63-19 in the regular season and go on to lose to the Lakers in the NBA Finals.

That Kersey was in at the end said something. That he was used to defend Bird said even more.

"I feel good when (Ramsay) shows that kind of confidence in me,"

Kersey said. "I did all I could without fouling him."

There were some who thought Kersey should get more playing time. Ramsay was not the easiest of coaches on young players.

"His game has to get more together," the veteran coach said. "That's not meant as a criticism. You can't expect a guy out of Longwood College to come into this league and play a lot right away. He still needs experience. He's going to help us, and he's going to get his minutes."

Ramsay was using Jerome some at power forward, too.

"Jerome gives us some activity around the basket, and with this team, that's important," the coach said. "He takes the ball to the basket strong, and he's active around the hoop. We are sorely in need of people who work hard at the basket."

"A lot of times, I'll sit on the bench and wish I were out there playing," Kersey said. "You always think you can help. But when the game's over, I'm not upset about not playing much. I understand the situation here. I just try to be ready when I'm called upon to play."

On January 18, in a 127-122 loss to Utah, Jazz center Mark Eaton gave one of the all-time individual performances by a Blazer opponent, even while going 1 for 12 from the field. Eaton, who made 10 of 12 attempts from the foul line, totaled 12 points, 20 rebounds and 14 blocked shots. The 7-4 giant already had 10 blocks when Kersey dared to challenge him, throwing down a monster jam to the wonderment of his teammates.

Said Kersey afterward: "It flew through my mind, 'Should I do this?' He's the best shot-blocker in the league. Plus he's big. I figured the only way to find out was to take it right to him. I did. It worked."

At the end of Kersey's rookie season, broadcaster Bill Schonely and his wife joined other Blazer players and employees on a Carnival cruise to the Caribbean.

"Jerome had his grandmother with him," Schonely says. "She was delightful. We spent some time together aboard the ship, and then we'd stop someplace and play golf. Jerome always brought life to the moment."

THERE SIMPLY weren't many minutes available for Kersey that season, though. VanDeWeghe was a superb offensive player, 6-9, ambidextrous and equally adept scoring from long range and driving to the basket. The five-year veteran shot .534 from the field, averaged 22.4 points through the regular season and was more than willing to share accumulated wisdom with his rookie teammate.

"We spent a fair amount of time together talking," VanDeWeghe says now. "Jerome was very inquisitive and curious. He wanted to be a great player and worked hard on his game. He asked me endless questions, and we spent a lot of time talking about footwork, how to look at the game, how to size up an opponent.

"Basketball is a game that a lot of people play, but very few people are cerebral about it. Jerome not only improved his skills, but his basketball IQ, too. He became a student of the game."

VanDeWeghe grew to appreciate Kersey the person, too.

"Jerome played with such energy and a joy for playing, a joy for learning," says VanDeWeghe, who now serves as the NBA's executive vice president/basketball operations. "You never saw him in a bad mood. He was a unique individual. He wanted the best for everybody.

"He was a tough competitor. It wasn't a fun night for anybody who played against him. I certainly didn't enjoy playing against him many days in practice. He played so hard every single second. He'd fight you tooth and nail, but he was impossible not to like. He was happy if you did well; he was happy if he did well. He always had a great smile and a good word for everybody. The best way to describe him would be, just a joyous individual."

Kersey was happiest, of course, when he was playing basketball. That wasn't happening much in the playoffs his rookie season. He played a total of 12 minutes in Portland's first-round playoff series with Dallas, with VanDeWeghe and Kenny Carr — the latter starting instead of Thompson — drawing most of the time at the forward spots and Drexler and Paxson getting the minutes at shooting guard. The Blazers dropped the opener 139-131, then swept the next three to advance to a Western Conference semifinal series against the eventual NBA champion Lakers.

The Lakers rolled to a 125-101 win in the opener. Rookie guard Steve Colter was the lone bright spot for Portland, coming off the bench to hit 11 of 15 shots and collect 26 points and eight assists. Kersey contributed two points and three rebounds in 12 reserve minutes.

Kersey played four total minutes as the Blazers dropped the next two to fall behind in the best-of-seven series 3-0.

He finally made a contribution in Game 4, with Ramsay employing the trap with his second unit. Jerome had six points, three steals and two rebounds in an 11-minute first-half stretch when Blazers outscored Lakers 36-19 to take a 10-point halftime lead. Kersey finished with 10 points, three rebounds and three steals in 15 minutes of a 115-107 victory.

"Given the chance, he went wild," Thompson said afterward. "That's why we call him 'Jerome Crazy.' When he does that in practice, we just get out of the way."

The Lakers were impressed, too.

Byron Scott: "When Kersey came in, it gave them a big boost."

Michael Cooper: "Kersey got his hands on a lot of passes and filled the gaps. And once we turned it over, he was out quick on the break."

James Worthy: "Kersey is part of the most positive energy on that team. He's full of fire out there."

Coach Pat Riley: "He plays the game above the rim. He's a tremendous athlete."

The Lakers would wrap up the series with a 139-120 romp in Game 5. Kersey played four minutes in the first half, then finished with 18 points in 17 minutes, hitting 6 of 8 from the field and 6 of 8 from the line. Afterward, Ramsay was asked why Kersey didn't play more in the first half.

"In the second quarter, Jerome was having trouble on defense," the coach said. "He's not a good perimeter shooter — and they were giving us perimeter shots.

"Jerome has some raw skills that are almost unique — even in the NBA. But he is unpredictable. If he's good, you want to go with him. If not, you have to find other ways."

In his first regular season, Kersey wound up shooting a solid .478 from the field and averaging 6.1 points and 2.7 rebounds in only 12.4 minutes a game.

Already, the question was being asked: Is Kersey the team's small forward of the future?

The man who drafted him — general manager Stu Inman — wouldn't be around to experience it. Inman fell out of favor with owner Larry Weinberg and would leave the team later that year to become director of player personnel in Milwaukee. Inman, though, was appreciative of what Kersey achieved while he was still in Portland.

"Jerome was infectious with his attitude, with his enthusiasm, with his devotion to the team," Inman would say later. "His willingness to accept a role played a big part in his success. And he was always a delight, fun to be around. He brought such a positive influence to the locker room."

Chapter Seven

"Larry Bird, I Want You"

AS HE ENTERED his second season with the Blazers, Jerome Kersey was a man on a mission. He had proved himself as an NBA-caliber player, but he wanted more. He wanted to be a starter or at least a major contributor, and he was willing to work hard for it.

Kersey spent a few weeks during the summer of '85 visiting family and friends in Virginia, but he was in Oregon much of the time, too, honing his skills. He participated with a Portland team in the Northwest Summer League, playing games in Washington, Oregon and Northern California against other NBA summer league teams.

"I'm here to work on my defense, and I want to work on my outside shot," Kersey said at the onset of summer league.

Coach Jack Ramsay wanted him to play more under control.

"His passing has improved and so has his floor awareness," Ramsay said after summer league ended. "His shooting and defense are better. He has upgraded himself. He still needs to get under control better, but he's making progress."

"Last year, I was trying to play all out all the time, instead of thinking about what I was going to do," Kersey said. "I'm trying now to think ahead. I'm trying to be under control and know what I'm going to do. Everybody talks about my raw talent. I just need to harness it. I would like to get more playing time this season, but that totally depends on me. I have to show that I deserve it."

The situation in Portland was the same as the previous season, though. Kiki VanDeWeghe, Jim Paxson and Clyde Drexler were set to gobble up most of the playing time at the two wing positions.

"It's going to be hard for him to get many more minutes than he got last year," Ramsay warned. "Kiki will be playing small forward and Clyde will get some minutes at the position, too. For those two players to get enough minutes, you don't have many minutes left for Jerome."

Kersey wouldn't accept that. He figured he'd do everything he could to earn more time on the floor. He spent hours in the gym with assistant coach Rick Adelman, and he had a new training partner — rookie guard Terry Porter out of Wisconsin-Stevens Point, taken by Portland as the 24th pick in the 1985 draft.

Adelman, now 75, retired and living in Portland, calls Kersey "the hardest-working player I was ever around."

"You talk about the favorite people you've ever coached — Jerome is right up there with me," Adelman says. "From the very first day we got him, there was something different about him. Every day he would work. That's who he was. He came in a great athlete. He could run, he could jump, but he wasn't a very good shooter at all."

Adelman spent countless hours through Kersey's first few seasons doing individual drills in the offseason. Soon Porter and center Kevin Duckworth — who would be acquired via trade in late 1986 — would join them. They'd get together five days a week at places such as Mittleman Jewish Community Center or RiverPlace Athletic Club.

"We'd find a gym that was open," Adelman says. "Those guys were such a pleasure to work with. They all came from small schools. They had to prove themselves over and over.

"At first, we didn't know what we had with Jerome. I give him all the credit. He's the one who did everything. He worked his ass off to be a player in the league, and a very good one."

Paxson saw the effects of the offseason work.

"Jerome could be dribbling at 100 miles an hour and you'd think he was going to lose the ball, and he'd go through two guys and dunk it," Paxson says. "Or, he might turn it over. It wasn't always pretty early in his career. But Jerome and Rick spent a lot of time together putting in the work, and it paid off."

The Blazers' other assistant coach, Bucky Buckwalter, was the scout who had discovered Kersey. He, too, gave the player credit for his growth, along with the woman who raised him.

"It was his desire," Buckwalter says. "Jerome spent hours in the gym working on his ballhandling and shooting. He was a self-made player, really, a highly motivated young man. It's a tribute to his determination and his grandmother. She had a lot of influence on his life."

In December, a reporter asked each Blazer player for a Christmas wish.

"I'd like to have my grandmother from Clarksville here," Kersey said. The tight bond lasted through his life.

IT WASN'T all about basketball with Kersey, of course. He had always made friends easily, and it was no different during his time with the Blazers. One of those was Johnny "J.R." Harris, a Seattle resident who would become a lifelong comrade.

Harris, a Richmond, Calif., native who played collegiately at Northwest Nazarene, had played with the brother of Blazer guard Steve Colter. In 1983, Harris took a doorman's job at the Westin Hotel in Seattle. When the Blazers stayed there during the 1984-85 season, Colter introduced Harris to Kersey.

"They were in for a preseason game, and Jerome wanted to get a haircut," Harris says. "I gave a recommendation and let him take my car to go to the shop to get it cut. We hit it off. Later in the year, when the Blazers returned to Seattle, he called me up and said, 'Would you like to grab some dinner?' The relationship grew organically from there."

Harris had grown close to another basketball player of repute — University of Washington forward Detlef Schrempf, then a rookie with the Dallas Mavericks.

"One day I brought Detlef down to Portland to meet Jerome," Harris recalls. "I thought I was a pretty good player. We went to the River-Place Athletic Club and decided to play one-on-one, rotating around.

"I got humbled. Those guys wouldn't even let me get a shot off. I don't think I even scored a basket. When I walked out of that gym, I knew the difference between an NBA player and a guy like me on the basketball court."

During the preseason in 1985, teammate Jim Paxson took Clyde Drexler and Kersey to Oswego Lake Country Club to play nine holes.

"That was the longest nine holes of my life," Paxson jokes. "For both of them, it was their first round of golf.

"It was a long but a fun afternoon. I remember trying to help them choose the right club. One time, Clyde was 100 yards away and grabbed a 3-iron. It was just talking them through club selection and distance. We made it through. I don't know if I can take credit for paving the way for their love of golf or not."

Actually, it wasn't Kersey's first time hitting the links. He got his first crack while participating in the '85 Northwest Summer League. Jerome, assistant coach Rick Adelman, center Sam Bowie and trainer Ron Culp played a round in San Leandro, Calif. Kersey had never been on a golf course before.

Wrote The Oregonian's Dwight Jaynes, who witnessed the spectacle: "With a horrible-looking stance and an even worse swing, Kersey was soon booming drives. Twice in the first 15 holes he had ever played, he lined up short putts for pars. But he missed them both."

"We'll see if we ever let you shoot technical fouls," Adelman cracked afterward.

Kersey worked hard in the preseason, and had a terrific game against Seattle, scoring 24 points on 8-for-12 shooting from the field. He was 8 for 8 from the line to go with four rebounds, three assists and three steals in just 24 minutes. Still, there was little hope for increased time with Kiki VanDeWeghe, Paxson and Drexler usurping the minutes at the wing spot. For the second straight season, Kersey's primary role was mostly with Ramsay's trapping group, which someone dubbed "Ramsay's Raiders."

"Jerome is a very good trapper," the coach said. "When we trap, we have to have him out there. He has great reaction time, he rebounds and he runs the floor.

"But if Jerome is going to play, somebody ahead of him is going to get shorter minutes. That would be Clyde or Kiki. Players earn their minutes. Last year, I told Jerome he might not play at all. But he earned some minutes."

"I think I'm doing the things in practice now that I must do in games," Kersey said on the eve of the 1985-86 regular season. "I have refined my game. I am more comfortable on the floor. I'm more aware of other players, offensive and defensively."

BUT KERSEY'S one-on-one defense was still inconsistent as well as his outside shot. There were times when coach Jack Ramsay hardly used him. Other times, the second-year forward played a key role.

One of the latter came in December on a stop at Boston where, a year earlier, Larry Bird had knocked down a jump shot with Kersey in his face to beat the Blazers at the buzzer. Kersey hadn't forgotten. On the team bus to Boston Garden that night, Kersey whispered to himself, "Larry Bird, I want you."

Portland center Sam Bowie heard him. Kersey's words seemed prophetic. He had the game of his life against a Boston team that was 9-0 at home and would go on to post a 40-1 record in the Garden (50-1 including the playoffs), go 67-15 overall and claim the NBA title.

In 22 minutes off the bench, Kersey scored 22 points on 11-for-15 shooting with four rebounds and five steals in a 121-103 romp past the NBA champions. He scored 20 of his points in a 9 1/2-minute rampage bridging the third and fourth quarters and aggressively dogged Bird at the defensive end. He and Clyde Drexler hounded Bird into a 9-for-26 shooting night, then beat him downcourt for easy baskets.

"It was the best experience in basketball I've ever had," Kersey said afterward. "My quickness helped. Bird is not one of the quickest guys in the league, just one of the best.

"I felt good physically going into the game, but I didn't have any preconceived notion that something like that would happen. To play a game like that in the Boston Garden against a guy like Bird and win the game, too — it's special."

Bowie revealed to a Portland writer what he had heard on the bus.

"I didn't think anybody heard me," Kersey said with a grin. "I was just thinking about last year, when he got that shot off on me. I've had to live with that for a whole year, with the guys razzing me about it. I knew this was a chance to redeem myself."

Today, Adelman observes, "Jerome had an unbelievable game, but that's who he was. He was always ready. It was just incredible how hard he worked. He made himself into a player."

One of the players on the Celtics was second-year shooting guard Rick Carlisle.

"Jerome was dynamic," Carlisle says today. "He played with a real edge and chip on his shoulder. In that game against us, he had a couple of spectacular plays where he flew and dunked all over people. During a timeout, Robert Parish, who normally didn't say a whole lot, said, 'Somebody got to keep that young fella off the launching pad.' "

Before the Boston game, it had been a frustrating season for Kersey. His playing time was minimal, and in a loss at Washington three days earlier, he did not play. But Kiki VanDeWeghe suffered a bruised shin and suddenly Kersey was back in the picture, scoring 46 points with 10 steals in the next three games.

"We've rediscovered Jerome," Bucky Buckwalter said after the

Boston game. "When he gets minutes, he can do that, and he gives you a lot of motion on offense. He did a marvelous job on Bird. Bird just couldn't get the ball."

"I've liked the way he played the last three games," Ramsay noted. "He's quick and gets down the floor quickly. He's good at finishing fast-breaks. When he's going to the basket, he almost always scores."

Kersey admitted the season had been a letdown for him personally.

"I had that first year behind me, which everybody says is your toughest year," he said. "I expected to get more minutes this year. When I didn't, it was frustrating. When you're playing more minutes, it's fun.

"Everybody wants to play. Somebody has to sit, and when you sit, you get frustrated. Jack had explained to me a couple of times that Pax, Kiki and Clyde will be rotating, and that they need minutes. At first, I didn't understand that. After a while, I realized that they are quality players in this league and they need minutes. My job is to show what I can do within the period of time I'm on the floor."

Soon, VanDeWeghe returned to the lineup. Mychal Thompson was the starter at power forward; backup Kenny Carr missed some time resting a sore knee, opening the door for Jerome to get minutes at that position, "but Jerome has a hard time defending big people," Ramsay said. And veteran Caldwell Jones, a natural center, could play some "4," too.

Kersey got an invitation to participate in the slam-dunk contest during All-Star Weekend at Reunion Arena in Dallas in place of Drexler, who chose not to participate due to a slight leg injury. Kersey took it seriously, working with Clyde and Portland guard Steve Colter on his repertoire.

"We're working on the flash," Drexler said. "(Jerome) has to do more spins, twists, curls and pumps; the kind of things fans like to see. Not only do they want to see brute force, they want you to show them the flash."

Atlanta's Dominique Wilkins came into the contest as the favorite, but 5-7 teammate Spud Webb stole the show and claimed the $12,000 first prize. Kersey lost a sudden-death playoff with Terence Stansbury of Indiana for the last spot in the final four.

Kersey entered the second half of the regular season shooting a team-best .590 from the field.

"Confidence and shot selection," he said, explaining the improvement. "I'm not rushing myself like I did last year. I'm not putting up too many shots from 18 to 20 feet. I still don't feel comfortable shooting from that far out. I'm staying away from the things I don't do well. I'm getting to 15 feet, staying inside where I'm more productive."

Kersey was getting the majority of his points, though, around the basket and in transition. He was becoming more and more the "people's choice" at Memorial Coliseum. It made him feel good, even while sitting on the bench.

"I hear the fans," he said. "I hear them when they yell at Jack to put me in."

If Kersey didn't have his coach's full confidence, he was gaining that of his teammates.

"Jerome was energy," says Darnell Valentine, a Blazer point guard during Kersey's first two seasons in Portland. "I'll never forget his effort and determination. He improved on a monthly basis. He was always in growth mode. You knew when he showed up, he was going to be ready to play."

Valentine says he expected that Kersey would one day win the starting small forward spot.

"Kiki was such a great scorer and shooter," Valentine says. "In terms of skills, Kiki was far more advanced. With his determination, willpower and effort, though, Jerome could not be denied. He was (Dennis) Rodman-esque. He had those intangibles that create championships. It's something you can't really define, but you know it when you got it."

Valentine had deep respect for Kersey as a person, too.

"He was a sweet guy, very humble," Valentine says. "Never forgot where he was from. Not that he had to remember, but that's just who he was. When you saw Jerome Kersey, you saw his grandmother, you saw

Longwood. You saw the southern humility, that welcoming personality. He was very engaging, very soft-spoken. Just a wonderful guy."

Forward Kenny Carr would wind up playing three seasons with Kersey.

"Jerome worked himself into being a very good player, and he was a good teammate," Carr says. "He was an upbeat guy, a nice guy who communicated well with everyone. Everybody liked him. He wasn't a guy to cause trouble. Very pleasant to be around. He had a lot of friends, and I can see why because of his personality."

DURING THE SECOND HALF of his second NBA season, Kersey was keeping busy off the court. He appeared at a Special Olympics benefit in Portland, joining with Steve Colter, Terry Porter, Kiki VanDeWeghe and Mychal Thompson for a "lip sync" number. He was expanding his horizons culturally, having begun to read books for the first time. Robin Cook's "Mind Bends," he told a reporter, was a favorite. "I like fiction — adventure stuff. It helps pass the time on planes and in the hotels."

Asked about his budget as the team's trainer, Ron Culp said the Blazers went through several dozen wristbands a year and that Kersey was responsible for a good portion of them.

"He gives them out to kids after practice and games," Culp said. "I think he gives them out to his girlfriends after their dates."

Kersey, indeed, was one of the most eligible bachelors in Portland. Tall, handsome, genial and blessed with a killer smile, he was a popular addition to the nightlife in Portland.

"You got to remember, he went to Longwood," center Sam Bowie says. "That was a very small school. Even though Portland wasn't a big metropolitan area, the opportunities were immense in comparison. Jerome loved to go out and finger pop."

Finger pop?

"Yeah, like your fingers are popping when you go to a club," Bowie said. "Ah, I loved Romeo. That was my boy."

Thompson had a nickname for everyone, and sometimes two or three. He had given Kersey the "Romeo" sobriquet.

"It's a nickname that goes with Jerome," Kersey would explain. "Like 'Romey.'"

It was in part, though, due to his predilection for the opposite sex.

"Jerome loved the ladies, and the ladies loved him," then-Blazer guard Darnell Valentine says. "He was a single guy, and he liked singleness. He loved big watches. He loved to dress. He could get out the mirror. He loved who he became. He embraced who he was. He enjoyed the fruits of his labor."

"Jerome was a popular guy," Buckwalter says now. "Whenever there was a get-together, the girls would always invite Jerome. I'd hear there was a party here and there. I'd have a few talks with him. He'd say, 'I was there, Bucky, but I behaved myself. I don't do anything to take away from my body.' And I believed him. He was always around it, but he took care of himself."

AFTER A DISAPPOINTING 40-42 regular season — including a franchise-record 12-game losing streak in February — the Blazers limped into a first-round playoff matchup with Denver. The Blazers slipped past the Nuggets 108-106 in Game 2 but lost the other three contests and were eliminated. Kersey saw regular minutes off the bench in each of the games but did nothing memorable.

And suddenly the season was over.

Kersey's numbers were up considerably from his rookie season. He averaged 8.5 points and 3.7 rebounds while shooting a team-best .549 from the field. His impact was felt at the defensive end and with energy on the boards and on the fast-break. The Blazers were beginning to see they had something special in the kid from the sticks.

Soon, though, Ramsay's 10-year run as Blazers head coach was over. Milwaukee Bucks assistant coach Mike Schuler was hired to replace him. And Kersey's career path was about to ascend.

Chapter Eight

'Jerome Will Get a Lot of Minutes'

THE 1986 NBA DRAFT brought some apparent competition for Jerome Kersey at the small forward spot.

With the 14th pick in the draft, the Trail Blazers chose Walter "The Truth" Berry, a former playground legend out of New York City. The 6-8, 210-pound forward from St. John's, who had averaged 23.0 points and 11.1 rebounds as a sophomore, was honored as National Player of the Year.

The Blazers entered the draft expecting to choose a small forward, but they thought it would be either Maurice Martin of St. Joseph's or Harold Pressley from Villanova. Nothing against Kiki Vandeweghe or Kersey; they were simply going to take the best player available.

They didn't expect Berry to fall to No. 14, however. And when he did — there were concerns from teams drafting ahead of Portland about his outside shot and how well he ran the floor — the Blazers were caught in a bind. Berry, thought to be a lock to go in the lottery (one of the first seven picks), was not even one of the 10 players they interviewed before the draft.

"We just didn't think he would be available," says Bucky Buckwalter, the team's director of player personnel. And the Blazers felt they couldn't pass him up. "To not take him," Bucky says, "would have been hard."

Kersey was entering his third NBA season off a solid 1985-86 campaign in which he had shown plenty of promise. Though he'd led the Blazers in field-goal percentage, most of his shots came from the inside. In the offseason, the Blazers hired former great Geoff Petrie as Kersey's "shot doctor." After a summer of work, Kersey felt the work with Petrie had paid off.

"He helped me with my mechanics, my foot position, just squaring up with the basket," Kersey said in September. "Now I feel I can stick the jump shot from 15 to 18 feet."

Kersey's close friend from Longwood, Mitch Walker, noticed the difference.

"I worked out with him and said, 'Dude, your shot looks different,' " Walkers remembers. "It looked more refined. His elbow was in the same spot every time. He told me, 'I worked out all summer with Petrie. I was getting up 600, 700 shots a day.' That changed the whole trajectory of Jerome's rise in the organization."

Over a two-year period, Petrie worked extensively with both Kersey and young point guard Terry Porter. So did assistant coach Rick Adelman, who had conducted workouts with the two players the previous year.

"Rick and I would take Terry and Jerome in an open gym and work with them on their game and their shooting," Petrie recalls. "Jerome was one of the most motivated players and people to get better that I've been around. We played a lot of shooting games with them. They'd get really competitive.

"When we started, Jerome really couldn't shoot. He eventually became a pretty reliable midrange jump shooter."

Kersey would always be known first and foremost as a great dunker, though. In July, the Blazers stage a slam-dunk contest at Memorial Coliseum as part of a special night during the Northwest Summer League. Kersey beat out 1986 NBA Slam Dunk champion Spud Webb, Clyde Drexler and former Blazer Billy Ray Bates for the title with a score of 47, winning $3,500.

"Home-improvement money," Jerome said after his title. "I have a few things to fix up around the house. Plus, I have a vacation coming up in the Caribbean. So this is a little money for the casino."

In an era when some NBA players achieved their first dunk in seventh or eighth grade, Kersey was a late bloomer. His first dunk came as a 6-2 junior at Bluestone High.

"It was in the gym, after practice," Kersey told Dwight Jaynes of The Oregonian. "It was one of those timing dunks, a ball that bounced on the rim. But it was a flush, with my hand on top of it. I was so happy I just ran to the locker room. I didn't even try it again."

The dunk had become Kersey's trademark, an expression of his personality.

"A dunk in a game is like a great release of energy, anxiety or frustration," he said. "You know it's going to be a crowd-pleasing thing. It gets me pumped up. Once you get one, you want another one, then another one, then another one. You get addicted to dunking. At some point, just dunking isn't enough. Anyone in the NBA can dunk in the open court. Then you want to go up against somebody and dunk it over them."

Kersey was asked if he had a favorite dunk through his young career.

"I have two dunks I remember — well, maybe four or five," he said. "In a game against Utah, I was just going to lay the ball up, but Fred Roberts was coming at me from an angle. I went to lay it up and then pulled it back and dunked it backward. I didn't even know ahead of time what I was going to do.

"Then a game against Dallas, I was up a lot higher than I thought, pulled the ball down and then went up and dunked backward. It was

115

totally a surprise to me. It was situational. I was pumped for the rest of the night."

IF PORTLAND choosing Berry bothered Kersey, he didn't show it. He immediately befriended the rookie forward and helped him look for a place to live near his Mountain Park townhouse.

Kersey quickly figured he had little to worry about in terms of competition from Berry. Mitch Walker recalls a phone conversation from that summer.

"Berry is coming to the Blazers to eat into your playing time," Walker told Kersey.

"Walt came in talking all this trash," Kersey said, "but he has a long way to go."

Kersey told Walker that after a recent workout, the players retired to the weight room area.

"At that level, you had to push 225 (pounds on the bench press)," Walker said. "That was the benchmark to determine how strong you were. Jerome said Walt got under the 225 and couldn't push it even once."

"He ain't strong enough to play down on the box," said Kersey, who could bench press 225 about 15 times that season. "You got to be a grown man to command that box. If you can't push 225, we'll ride your ass out to the 3-point line."

New draft pick Berry didn't last long in Portland. He didn't care for the city, and there was plenty of competition for playing time at both forward positions with Vandeweghe and Kersey at the small forward and Kenny Carr and Caldwell Jones at power forward. Berry wound up playing 19 minutes in seven games — he did hit 6 of 8 shots from the field — before being traded to San Antonio in December for center Kevin Duckworth.

Berry had two productive seasons with the Spurs, averaging 17.6 points in 56 games in 1986-87 and 17.4 points in 1987-88. He was out of the league by 1989 at age 24, however, and spent the final 12 years of his professional career in Europe.

Duckworth, meanwhile, would become a major contributor to the Blazers over the next 6 1/2 seasons, twice making the All-Star Game and serving as the starting center on Portland's NBA Finals teams of 1990 and '92.

"I remember when I first met Jerome soon after I got to Portland," Duckworth told Hoke Currie in 1998. "In our first scrimmage together, he was on the fast-break and I saw him and tried to cut him off. That's when I took notice that you shouldn't jump at Jerome when he's about to fly to the basket, because he's going to dunk on you. It's a good thing I stopped, because he was going to dunk on my face. He jumped so high and rose up so quick.

"Jerome brought a lot of excitement to our team. The greatest fun in watching Jerome was when an opponent thought they had an easy basket or a dunk on a fast-break. Jerome would track them down and throw their stuff off the backboard. He was great at chasing somebody down the court and blocking his shot."

Like Kersey, Duckworth hailed from an off-the-beaten-path school — Eastern Illinois. Soon he learned the history of Longwood.

"We used to tease him, 'Jerome, how are you going to tell me about basketball when you went to an all-girls school? What girls did you play with?'" Duckworth told Currie. "That made him mad."

Through the years, Duckworth became one of Kersey's best friends.

"Jerome and I are like brothers," Duckworth said. "When we were teammates, we did everything together."

That included enjoying a little of the nightlife, both in Portland and on the road.

"He's definitely a ladies' man," Duckworth said. "Women love Jerome. He has that sex appeal. He's the All-American guy, a down-to-earth person. He's a sensitive guy. He plays hard-core Jerome, but he's sensitive. You know he has a soft side. He plays the tough guy, but deep down, what you say does bother him."

Duckworth wasn't convinced, however, that Kersey was a fashion plate.

"When I first joined the team, Jerome thought he could dress," the 7-footer said. "He was a terrible dresser. He'd be pissed off at me saying this. He had some white leather shoes. I used to laugh at him when he wore them. I talked about them so bad on the plane, he went home that night and threw them away. I never saw them again.

"He was talking about his mixes and matches stuff. I said, 'Jerome, you can't dress.' He'd swear up and down that he could dress, but he couldn't dress. Most of the time he can now, but sometimes he'll be cracking me up. He loves turtlenecks. Clyde and I used to laugh so much. We have better taste in clothes. That's why we can laugh."

THE BLAZERS' training camp was at Club Green Meadows in Vancouver. New coach Mike Schuler said he noticed an improvement from the last time he saw Kersey play a few months earlier.

"Jerome has had a nice camp," Schuler said. "He is much more under control of himself than during the summer."

Kersey liked having a clean slate with Schuler. "He didn't know us when he came in," Kersey said, "and he wasn't coming in pre-judging."

Kersey hoped that would result in an opportunity for additional playing time in 1986-87. Schuler's plan was to play him some minutes at power forward alongside Kiki VanDeWeghe on the Blazers' front line.

"If I play well and assert myself," Kersey said, "Mike is going to find a place for me."

Kersey's performance in a 119-117 overtime win over Philadelphia in the preseason seemed a harbinger of what was to come. He scored 29 points and grabbed eight rebounds, dunking in the closing seconds for the game-winner in the extra session.

"I'm excited for Jerome, but I'm not in awe of his performance tonight," center Sam Bowie said afterward. "I've seen him do that kind of thing before. He did nothing tonight that was special for him."

Going into the season, Schuler was duly impressed with Kersey's development.

"Jerome will get a lot of minutes somehow, somewhere, someplace," the Blazer coach said. "I like the instant offense he can generate. He probably had the best preseason of anybody. I can't say enough about him. He's the most versatile player on the team. He's such a great athlete with a great feel for himself. I wouldn't hesitate to start him, but he'll come off the bench for us at three positions."

Kersey didn't play any shooting guard — that experiment, however short-lived, would come later — but he did play some power forward. Kenny Carr was injured and Kersey got pair of starts at the 4 spot in late November. In a 118-101 romp past Indiana, he played 45 minutes and collected 22 points — on 8-for-10 shooting from the field and 6 for 6 from the foul line — to go with 10 rebounds, seven assists and four steals. Vandeweghe scored 30 points at small forward.

"My stamina has been real good," Kersey said. "I'm starting to get back to playing the way I did during the exhibition season. I find myself learning something new every game."

But when Carr returned within a week, he got his starting job back.

"I'm not going to be terribly disappointed to go back to the role I was playing before," Kersey said diplomatically. "I like to go with the flow. I don't like to get into any controversy about this or that. There is no need to ruffle any feathers. Kenny was playing well before he got hurt. Everyone wants to start, and I certainly do. But I've proved I can play minutes and be effective."

Said Schuler: "One thing is fact. When Jerome's on the floor, good things happen for us. I've been concerned about him getting minutes, making sure he gets enough playing time."

On December 5, the Blazers pulled out a 106-102 win at Sacramento on the clutch shooting of Kersey, who played power forward much of the fourth quarter. Kersey scored 13 points in the fourth quarter, including a 20-footer under defensive pressure with eight seconds left to give Portland a 103-102 lead, then a free throw with one second left to ice it.

"I had bigger guys on me tonight," Kersey said afterward. "I know I can move without the ball when that happens. And tonight my jump shot was falling."

On December 16, Kersey came off the bench to score a career-high 27 points in 36 minutes as the Blazers beat Seattle 126-118.

Cracked Schuler: "Jerome has had just a great season so far. I just wish the dumb coaches would give him more minutes."

"(Kersey) is such a great athlete," Seattle coach Bernie Bickerstaff said. "He has quickness and leaping ability, and he does a lot of things to get a team turned on. He has the skills and the dash to become a great player."

Even so, Kersey was going through periods of inconsistent play.

"He is pressing just a little bit," Schuler said at one point. "Sometimes, he goes too fast for his own good. He's trying to make something happen all the time."

"I have to let the game come to me, rather than force things," Kersey said. "Sometimes I look to make the quick pass or quick shot. At certain stages, I haven't been getting that much playing time in the first quarter. I get in there with a minute and a half to go in the quarter and feel like I have to do something real quick.

"At times, I haven't been prepared to shoot the ball. A lot of times I've been looking to get closer to the hoop when I should just shoot the jump shot. Teams are better prepared for the things I can do. People are sagging off me and making me take the jump shot."

In February, Kersey was picked for a second time to participate in the NBA Slam Dunk Contest as part of All-Star Weekend, this time in Seattle. He was chosen as a replacement for Dominique Wilkins.

"I should write Dominique and thank him, but a 48-hour notice isn't much," Kersey said. "I wouldn't be going up there if I didn't expect to win, but I think everyone expects to win."

Kersey, teammate Clyde Drexler, Michael Jordan and Terence Stansbury advanced to the semifinals from the eight-man field. Kersey survived the second round and advanced to a showdown with Jordan for the title. In the finals, the Bulls superstar scored 48-48-50–146 for his three dunks while Kersey was 46-45-49—140.

Jordan gave Kersey his due afterward.

"Jerome is an unknown player in the NBA, but I knew he had a lot of ability in dunking and creating," he said. "I wish he were playing in Chicago. He made a lot of believers out there today."

"I kind of surprised myself," said Kersey, who took home the runner-up prize of $7,500 for his next visit to a casino. "There were some things I did out there that I haven't done in a long time.

"It was a thrill to watch Michael. He's one of, if not the, most exciting player in the league. Watching him is a real treat for everyone."

AFTER THE ALL-STAR BREAK, Kersey combined his love for music with a willingness to help charitable causes at a Special Olympics fundraiser in Portland. He served as lead singer — backed by Kevin Duckworth, Kenny Carr, Steve Johnson, Sam Bowie, Terry Porter and Michael Holton — for a group of players who sang a song called the "Rad, Bad Blazers." Some time later, Kersey fronted a group that included Holton, Porter, Duckworth and Fernando Martin to record a rock video of the song to market for charity.

"Jerome could sing," says Holton, a former UCLA star who had been acquired in a trade with Chicago in the offseason. He would back up Porter at point guard for two seasons and become an admirer of Kersey.

"I used to ride with Romeo to practice or to get something to eat," center Sam Bowie says. "Some song would come on the radio and he'd be singing and I'd say, 'Romeo, I'm telling you, you got a second career. You could grab a mic and sing to an audience.' Jerome Kersey could sing."

Says guard Jim Paxson: "Jerome was never afraid of the moment, whatever it was."

But Kersey wasn't the second coming of Marvin Gaye, Johnson says.

"He really got into singing, but no," says the former Oregon State center, who played three seasons with Kersey in Portland. "There aren't too many good singers out there, period. There are guys who think they can sing, but all they are doing is karaoke. That was Jerome."

By this time, Kersey had established himself as a ladies' man.

"Jeromeo," says Johnson, offering up another adaptation of Kersey's sobriquets. "I guess you earn that nickname."

"He was a country guy with a city smooth," Holton says. "He commanded a lot of attention."

Kersey's wardrobe was expanding.

"You have to remember, most of us came from nothing," Bowie says. "When we got our hands on a few dollars, it was hard not to spend. He had more shoes or suits than he knew what to do with. Romeo loved to be a fly guy."

"He grew into that," Johnson says. "But I don't care how well you dress, (teammates) are going to talk about you. If you bought something new, you learned not to wear it right away. You waited a while to put it on so. And guys were still going to give you the business."

By this time, Kersey was also expanding his collection of automobiles.

"I remember when he bought his Ferrari," Johnson says. "That was a big deal. Somehow he shoehorned his body into that little sucker."

"He had a corny love for cars," Holton says. "I bought some rims from him off a Range Rover he had one time. He liked cars, but he was country. He was trying to figure out what was cool."

"He would buy a brand-new vehicle and spend thousands of dollars more putting on the rims and European suspension and the proper sound system," Bowie says. "He took care of his vehicles. Jerome just enjoyed life. He was a Renaissance Man."

If Kersey was a player off the court, he was one on it, too.

"Jerome was all about intensity," says Holton, now a radio analyst and studio host for Blazer Broadcasting. "He always went hard. He had that gear that he played and practiced in. It was the same every day, that passion. Even with the intensity, though, he had an easy-going personality. Usually, somebody who is intense and going hard all the time has a rough edge to their personality, but Jerome didn't.

"I remember Jerome being humble and wanting to get better.

Jerome brought so much to the table, but he always looked at it like, 'I want to do more.' He was a low-maintenance player. You didn't need to worry about Jerome. You knew you could count on him having your back, on and off the floor."

Johnson felt Kersey was a good fit for the City of Roses.

"Jerome exemplified Portland," says Johnson, who would make the NBA All-Star Game in 1987-88. "He came from a small town, went to a small school and grew up in a small city. He was a guy who did so much off of his heart. Nobody outworked him. He gave you 110 percent at all times.

"One day my first year with the Blazers we were talking about injuries. Jerome said, 'I can't imagine getting hurt.' Not too long after that in a game, he blocked someone's shot and got flipped and came down and hit the ground hard. He was stunned. Like a true teammate, once I was sure he was all right, I walked up to him and said, 'Can you imagine it now?' "

Kersey endeared himself to Holton right away.

"When I first came to Portland, Jerome was the first person who embraced me," Holton says. "I remember him telling me where the workouts were and how to get there. He was the first player I connected with. I thought, 'Man, this dude is great.' He was empathetic to what I needed in that initial transition. That stood out to me. He was a guy who cared.

'Jerome was a small-town guy, a small-school guy who played basketball. It became something he excelled at, and it enlarged his world. But it didn't get him away from the core of his upbringing and who he is."

Kersey continued to be a force off the bench. In a 135-113 rout of the Spurs in San Antonio on March 29, he scored a career-high 28 points. Two nights later, at the Meister Brau MVP Banquet at Red Lion Motor Inn/Jantzen Beach, he was named the team's top reserve by a vote of the fans.

Jerome finished the regular season with a bang. In the penultimate game on April 17, a 111-101 win over Utah, he collected 26 points and

14 rebounds. A night later, in a 144-134 home win over San Antonio, Kersey went for 28 points and nine boards.

"Going over the scouting report before the game, we felt the key to their team was Jerome Kersey," Spurs coach George Karl said afterward.

THE BLAZERS went into the playoffs as the No. 3 seed in the Western Conference off a 49-33 record, facing No. 6 seed Houston. Rockets coach Bill Fitch called Kersey "as good a rebounder off the bench as there is in the league."

Mike Schuler, voted the NBA Coach of the Year, said he was considering starting Kersey at power forward with Kenny Carr out due to a back injury. Problem was, the Rockets were starting the Twin Towers, 7-4 Ralph Sampson and 6-11 Hakeem Olajuwon. Jerome came off the bench and played only 12 minutes in the Blazers' opening 125-115 loss, grabbing seven rebounds but scoring two points on 1-for-5 shooting. Sampson (30 points) and Olajuwon (23) were effective, though Portland's Kiki VanDeWeghe (30 points) and Steve Johnson (29 with 10 rebounds) were more than their match.

Asked why he played Kersey so sparingly, Schuler said, "The only honest answer I can tell you is I was probably overly concerned about Jerome being forced to guard one of their two big guys."

The Blazers came out pressing in Game 2 and earned a 111-98 win. Schuler used Kersey, Porter, Jim Paxson, VanDeWeghe and Duckworth together for major portions of the game.

"We did it because we wanted to play certain people and not place them in situations that would be difficult for them," Schuler explained.

"(The Rockets) weren't prepared for it at all," said Kersey, who had four points and five rebounds in 18 minutes. "They were just roaming around when we went to the press. They didn't know where to be; they didn't know where to throw it."

Momentum swung back Houston's way in Game 3, Olajuwon going for 35 points in a 117-108 romp. Kersey played only 10 minutes, straining a muscle in his foot in the first half. He did not play in the second half.

The Rockets wrapped up the best-of-five series with a 113-101 victory in Game 4. Kersey had his best game of the series, collecting 14 points and six boards in 20 minutes.

Suddenly, the season was over for the Blazers. It ended in disappointment, but better times — at least in the regular season — were ahead.

Jerome waits at scorer's table for entry into game at Memorial Coliseum. *Courtesy Portland Trail Blazers*

125

Dunk you very much, says Jerome, wih teammate Kiki VanDeWeghe
looking on. *Courtesy Portland Trail Blazers*

Chapter Nine

Small Forward Controversy

THERE WAS LITTLE DOUBT Jerome Kersey was a player on the rise in the Trail Blazers organization as the 1987-88 season got underway.

Kersey had averaged 12.3 points and 6.0 rebounds while shooting .509 from the field in his third NBA season. In the eight games in which he started, he averaged 17.4 points and 10.5 rebounds. Kersey also tied with Caldwell Jones for the team high in blocked shots (77).

Jerome flew home to Longwood College for the early part of the summer to complete work on his college degree. Then he returned in mid-July for the Northwest Summer League, hosted by the Blazers.

Coach Mike Schuler made sure Kersey was used extensively at shooting guard during summer league. Schuler said it was a good chance for Kersey to work on his ballhandling, with the hope that he could merit some minutes in the backcourt in 1987-88.

"I owe a lot to the summer league (the previous year) and to

Geoff Petrie," Kersey said at the onset of summer league. "I'm looking forward to working with him again this summer. I don't think I'll have to be a great handler of the ball. I will have to get better at shooting the ball off the dribble.

"I've come a long way. I played center in college and had to move to forward. Now I'm learning to play guard."

Before training camp opened, Kersey signed a four-year, $2-million contract extension. That one-year, $92,000 rookie contract of two years ago seemed a distant memory.

"It's a good contract," he said. "I'm happy. Now I don't have to worry about anything. When I first came in, I just wanted to get the chance to play and stick. It has worked out very well."

Would he become a big spender?

"I'm still on the same allowance I got when I came into the league," he said with a smile. "That's enough for me. I like to have some money in my pocket, but I don't need a lot."

Before the season, Kersey and Terry Porter were selected as co-captains by a vote of the players.

"It was a goal of mine," Jerome said. "It's a very important position on an NBA team."

THE STARTING FIVE for the Blazers as they opened the season with a 118-104 win over Phoenix featured Steve Johnson at center, Caldwell Jones at power forward, Kiki VanDeWeghe at small forward, Clyde Drexler at shooting guard and Terry Porter at point guard.

Power forward Kenny Carr had retired at age 31 due to recurring back injuries. Center Sam Bowie, who broke his leg in the preseason, would miss the entire season.

"I'll never forget how Jerome helped me through all my injuries," Bowie says today. "There are pictures of him carrying Sam Bowie off the court when I broke my leg. He'd come to my house, to the hospital, reach for my crutches. He cried with me. He was a great human being."

Portland won its first two games of the season, then lost five in a row. Coach Mike Schuler tried Kersey in the starting lineup at power forward alongside VanDeWeghe for two games. The Blazers lost both as Kersey went a combined 12 for 30 from the field with 10 personal fouls.

On November 21, with the Blazers in the throes of the five-game losing streak, Kersey started at small forward in place of VanDeWeghe, who was suffering from a lower back strain. Kersey collected 19 points and 13 rebounds in a 120-101 win over Washington.

"Kersey is a very good athlete, which makes (the Blazers) a little quicker and a little better on the boards," Bullets coach Kevin Loughery said.

It was the start of something big. With VanDeWeghe — who was averaging 29 points per game — out of action indefinitely, Kersey was the starter at small forward. In the next game, he contributed 19 points and nine rebounds as the Blazers beat Indiana 120-110.

Next time out, he scored 15 points with a team-high 11 rebounds, playing 47 minutes in a 98-94 win over Sacramento. He got 19 points in a 97-87 triumph over the L.A. Clippers. Kersey was the star as the Blazers made it five straight with a 125-104 rout of the New Jersey Nets, scoring 21 points in the first half and finishing with 27 on 10-for-16 shooting to go with four steals.

"Kersey hurt us more than anyone in the first half," Nets coach Dave Wohl said. "We slowed down Drexler, but we didn't honor Kersey as much as we should have. He has learned to shoot the outside jumper. We gave him too much room and he made the most of his opportunities."

In that five-game rampage, Kersey was averaging 19.8 points, 8.8 rebounds, 4.4 assists and 2.0 steals in 42.2 minutes per game. Suddenly, talk around the water coolers in Portland was this: When VanDeWeghe returns, should Kersey remain the starter?

"Jerome allows us to do a lot of things defensively," Schuler said when reporters asked about the situation. "He makes us more alert and more active. We're a better pressing team. We have rebounded better with Jerome. I'm not so sure we don't run a little better, too, because Jerome is a little quicker than Kiki. But Jerome is in no way the outstanding shooter Kiki is. And when Jerome is starting, we have nobody who can come in and give us a spark off the bench."

On December 2, the Blazers blasted the L.A. Lakers 117-104 for their sixth straight win. Kersey scored a career-high 32 points and grabbed 14 rebounds. He was 14 for 22 from the field, 4 for 5 from the line and had four assists and two steals in a splendid 44-minute performance.

"My best game as a pro," Kersey told reporters. "Not my best game ever, though. I had 32 points and 26 rebounds once in college."

The streak continued. Kersey piled up 23 points and nine boards as the Blazers made it nine in a row with a 117-99 whipping of New York. Drexler was on a roll, too, having scored at least 27 points in each of the games.

Asked who should be starting when VanDeWeghe returned, Clyde was like Billy Martin in those old Lite Beer commercials. He felt very strongly both ways.

"Kiki is the best offensive player in the league," Drexler said. "Jerome has been playing very well in Kiki's absence. Getting both guys out there together is ideal. It seems like we're better with that lineup. We're so much quicker."

With Kiki still out, the string ended with a 127-117 loss to Detroit, though Kersey had 20 points on 10-for-19 shooting.

It was the first stop on a four-game road trip that would take the Blazers next to Philadelphia, where Jerome would meet up with a man he'd been missing through his life.

JOHN HARGROVE grew up in Clarksville, Va., and went to West End High, the school blacks in the area attended in the late 1950s and early '60s. Hargrove, who now lives in Willingboro, N.J., 20 miles from Philadelphia, says he graduated from high school at age 15 and enlisted in the U.S. Army at age 17.

While in the Army, Hargrove was stationed at Fort Bragg, N.C., about 135 miles from Clarksville. He says he returned often to see family. It was then that he also began to see Deloris Kersey, whom he knew as "Lois."

"I knew Lois' whole family growing up," says Hargrove, now 78. "Every time I came home, we'd get together. We saw each other for a couple of years."

At age 17, Deloris got pregnant. By that time, Hargrove was seeing another woman, someone he would wed soon after his release from the Army in 1962. They divorced in 1987 after nearly 25 years of marriage. They remarried in 2004 and have been together a total of 42 years.

"Barbara lived in Raleigh, which was closer to Fort Bragg than Clarksville," Hargrove says. "That's who I spent my time with once we began seeing each other."

On June 26, 1962, Deloris gave birth to Jerome Kersey.

"I didn't know Jerome was my son," Hargrove says today. "Nobody told me. I got married and our first son, Marquis, was born on June 4, 1963. He is almost a year younger than Jerome."

While attending school at a business institute in Philadelphia soon after he was married, Hargrove says he returned to Clarksville for a visit. He says his father told him he had been visited by Herman Kersey, Deloris' father and Jerome's grandfather.

"He was saying that Jerome was mine," Hargrove says.

By this time, Hargrove says, Deloris had gotten married and was living in Richmond. She had yielded parental rights to Jerome to her parents, Herman and May Kersey.

Did Hargrove ever ask Deloris if he was Jerome's father?

"No," Hargrove says today. "It was between her father and my father. My father came and told me. Lois was married. She had moved. I didn't think about calling. Back in those days, that's what you did. You didn't argue with your parents. Once my father told me they had decided I was his father … you didn't rebel against your parents. What they said was law and you dealt with it. They didn't have (blood) testing in those years."

(The author of this book reached out to Deloris Kersey several times via telephone seeking an interview for this book. She never responded.)

After moving to Philadelphia, Hargrove got a job as a bus driver with Greyhound. He would periodically return to Clarksville to see family or for reunions.

"Once when I came home, I saw a little kid running around, playing," he says. "The guy next door to my father's place asked me, 'Do you know who that is?' I said no. He told me it was Jerome. He was living with Herman and May."

During Jerome's childhood, Hargrove never reached out to him. He and Barbara would have three sons — Marquis, Martin and Marvin. In the 1991 book entitled "Blazers Profiles," written by this author, Kersey said, "I'll never forget the time he came to Clarksville when I was a kid. He came one block from where I was staying — and he knew I was there — but he didn't come by. From that point on, I just felt it didn't matter anymore."

Hargrove says he would hear little about Jerome through his childhood years.

"Once my father died in 1969, I didn't make it back to Clarksville for quite a while," he says.

Many years passed.

"Then one day, one of my friends who worked in Philly as a bus driver called me," Hargrove says. "He said, 'I picked up this kid who was heading toward Norfolk and he said, 'My father is a Greyhound bus driver, too.' I asked who it was and he said, 'John Hargrove.'

"It was Jerome. I think he was 17. That's when I started realizing that we needed to do something."

It was years, though, before Hargrove would.

Hargrove says he was unaware that Jerome was making a name for himself at Longwood. He says he didn't follow Kersey's first couple of seasons with the Blazers. Then one night, he was at home, drinking a beer as he was watching on TV a game between Portland and Philadelphia.

"The announcer said, 'starting at forward for the Trail Blazers, Jerome Kersey,' " Hargrove says. "That name jumped out at me. Before that, I had no idea what he was doing."

Once he confirmed that it was the same Jerome Kersey, Hargrove began to contemplate attempting to meet Jerome, who was 25 years old. By this time, Hargrove was divorced from Barbara and dating another woman.

"I mentioned to her that Jerome was my son," he says. "Somehow, she got in touch with (Blazer forward) Maurice Lucas."

Hargrove says he bought tickets for himself and his friend for the Blazers' game against the 76ers at the Spectrum on Dec. 9, 1987.

"We were in the stands before the game and Maurice came over and nodded to my friend," Hargrove says. "I didn't know, and Jerome didn't know, what was happening."

After the game, Hargrove recalls, "somebody came over and said, 'Don't leave.' They told us to wait around."

Eventually, Jerome came out of the locker room and was introduced to his birth father.

"It wasn't uncomfortable for me," Hargrove says. "It was sort of a relief."

In 1998, Jerome would address briefly with Hoke Currie his recollections of the meeting.

"It was never discussed what happened between my (birth) mom and my (birth) father," Kersey said. "I met (Hargrove) at a 76ers game in Philadelphia. His girlfriend wrote me a letter and said he was going to be at the game. She said he had come to some other games, but didn't come up and say anything to me. After 25 years, I guess I made him a little nervous."

Told more than 22 years later of Jerome's account, Hargrove says this:

"I'd never gone to one of Jerome's games in person before that night. I don't think she wrote to Jerome because he wasn't expecting to see me at the game. I wasn't expecting to be able to meet with him, either. Maurice was the person she went through to get us together."

That seems to be supported by the recollections of several friends and teammates of Kersey who were there that night in 1987.

"It was very uncomfortable for Jerome," recalls Mitch Walker, who lived in New York and was at the game to watch his close friend play. "I remember that as being extremely stressful. We were walking out of the locker room, and his dad was there. It was very uncomfortable. Initially, he didn't want to be bothered. Jerome was always a respectful person in general. There were a lot of emotions."

Kersey didn't act like a person who had been alerted that his father was at the game, according to a couple of his Blazer teammates.

"After the game, Jerome was in tears at his locker stall," says one, who asks to remain unidentified. When told his father was there waiting to meet with him, "he didn't want to leave the locker room. He was shaken up. We had to coax him to walk out of the room. It was one of those lifetime things."

"Jerome was confused," center Kevin Duckworth said in 1998. "He was like, 'Why come now?' "

Hargrove says during their postgame meeting, Jerome took him over to meet Charles Barkley, with whom he was going out to dinner that night.

"He told Charles, 'This is my father,' " Hargrove says.

Hargrove says in ensuing years, "we developed a relationship." If the Blazers were playing games in the Philadelphia/New York/Washington, D.C. area, he would often attend games and/or meet Jerome for dinner the night before, or for lunch on game days.

"We spent time together within the confines of his schedule," Hargrove says.

In 1991, a little more than three years after they met, Kersey told the author this for an article in The Oregonian: "I see him now when we go back east. We talk. But it's like he's a cousin I'd never met. It's hard to consider him a father. Any time you go through something like that, there's kind of — for lack of a better word — a hatred. It's like, 'Where were you? How come you never came to see me?' "

In the book "Blazers Profiles," Kersey said this: "That first time (in Philadelphia), it was like meeting a stranger. When we're on the East

Coast, he comes to games and we talk, but I guess I'm apprehensive."

The relationship changed some and Jerome mellowed about the situation through the years. Hargrove says he did what he could to assure Jerome that all he wanted was to get to know his birth son.

"Whenever I went to the games, I paid for my tickets," Hargrove says. "Maybe one time Jerome got me tickets. Because I hadn't been there for him growing up, I would never accept them.

"I never asked him for money, either. He was taking care of a lot of his relatives. He never had to pay a check with me. When we'd go out to eat, I would pay. He didn't owe me anything. I owed him because I didn't give him a chance to grow up with a father."

In later years, Jerome got to know Hargrove's wife. He also got to know his stepbrothers. The youngest, Marvin Hargrove, was also a professional athlete. A receiver and return specialist out of Richmond, he played a season with the Philadelphia Eagles.

"Barbara and him got along great," Hargrove says. "He called her 'Little Mama.' The other boys got along with him fabulously. All three of them just loved him."

There was some irony to the fact that Jerome ended up attending Bluestone High, which opened in 1963. It was at the time when Civil Rights legislation was passed, requiring states to integrate all schools.

"After I got out of the service, I came home to spend some time with my father," Hargrove says. "They were looking for people to serve on a committee to help with the integration process."

Hargrove says he volunteered and joined a four-person committee that traveled to Virginia State University in Petersburg to meet with Dr. Martin Luther King.

"We were in the room discussing the freedom of choice with Dr. King," Hargrove says. "In Virginia, they didn't integrate schools at the time. If the parents didn't advocate for a kid to join (an integrated) school, they left it alone. It cut down the amount of children who were going to come in."

Hargrove says the committee influenced four black families to send their kids from Clarksville to Bluestone the first year.

"They made the black high school I went to — West End — into a junior high," he says. "By the time Jerome came up, all the (high school) kids were going to Bluestone. It made me feel good that I had a hand in Jerome going to a place where he got a better education."

Hargrove says he and Jerome never discussed why he wasn't involved in Jerome's life as a child.

"He knew what happened," Hargrove says. "I don't think he ever brought it up."

John and Barbara flew to Portland for Jerome's wedding in 2013. Jerome's best man, Ron Sloy, got 20 friends of Jerome together for a scramble at Columbia Edgewater Country Club before the rehearsal and invited John to play.

"We're at breakfast before golf," Sloy recalls. "Jerome walks in talking on his cell phone and spots his dad. He backs up and walks straight out the door. He was so nervous."

Sloy placed his own father, John and Jerome in a foursome.

Says Sloy: "Before the round, Jerome tells me, 'I need to get a Jack and Coke. I'm so nervous to play with John.' About the fifth hole, the cart girl drives up and asks if we want refreshments. 'I'll have a Jack and Coke with a lime,' John says. He didn't know that's what Jerome had ordered an hour earlier."

John was wearing a pair of weathered golf shoes.

"At the turn, Jerome says to me, 'What would you think if I bought him a pair of golf shoes in the pro shop and gave them to him at the 10th tee?' He does and says, 'Dad, these are for you.' You should have seen John's eyes well up."

Hargrove says he has regrets over the way he handled things during Jerome's childhood.

"I didn't see him grow up," he says. "I feel bad about that. I had nothing to do with him becoming the great man he became. I wish it could have been different."

In the end, there was a relationship. It just wasn't father/son.

"Jerome said he respected him as a person, but did not know him as a father," says Jerome's close friend, Kevin Brandon. "Herman Kersey was his father."

THE BLAZERS kept rolling. On December 15, Portland ripped Seattle 128-109 as Kersey led the team in scoring (24) and rebounds (12). Kiki VanDeWeghe returned to play just his second game in a month, scoring 16 points in just 17 minutes off the bench.

Three nights later, the Blazers disposed of Phoenix 129-114. Kersey hit 10 of 15 shots and scored 20 points while VanDeWeghe tallied 23 points in a 22-minute reserve role.

"You're concerned about Jerome Kersey, and then here comes Kiki VanDeWeghe into the game," Suns coach John Wetzel said afterward. "They can beat you in so many ways."

On December 21, the Blazers were clicking on all cylinders in a 148-126 drubbing of San Antonio. Clyde Drexler bombed in 40 points, Kersey nearly got his first career triple-double with 21 points, 10 assists and nine rebounds and Terry Porter added 18 points, 16 assists, eight rebounds and three steals.

"I think me and Clyde are the best backcourt in the league," Porter said afterward.

Kersey had 21 points in 26 minutes as Portland buried Golden State 136-91 on December 31 for its fifth straight victory and 14th in 17 games. The Blazers were now 11-1 at home, 16-8 overall and the hottest team in the NBA, despite the absence of injured veterans Sam Bowie and Jim Paxson and with VanDeWeghe still dealing with back issues.

Kersey stayed red-hot. On New Year's Day, he went for a career-high 36 points, making 15 of 22 shots from the field, in a 127-125 win over Philadelphia.

By January 8, Kersey — who was averaging 13.3 points before VanDeWeghe was sidelined — had increased his seasonal scoring average to 19.1 and was leading the Blazers in rebounding. Even so, when Schuler called for an optional practice on the day after a win over

Sacramento, Kersey was the only starter present, scrimmaging with the reserves.

"I'm used to doing something every day," he explained. "It's hard for me to sit around and do nothing. I wanted to come out and get in a good run. My work ethic is what got me this far. I know it's always going to be there."

Said Schuler: "The day that changes is the day he'll stop getting better. I think he still has a lot of improvement left."

VanDeWeghe finally felt good enough to return to action on a regular basis, but Schuler said he intended to keep Kersey in the starting lineup with the Blazers playing well.

Drexler and Kersey were both asked back to the slam-dunk contest as part of All-Star Weekend, this time in Chicago. Kersey failed to survive the first round; Drexler finished third behind Michael Jordan and Dominique Wilkins in what is considered one of the epic battles in the history of the event.

Drexler told reporters he felt Jordan won the competition on his own merits, not with the help of hometown judges in Chicago. Jordan later guffawed at that, revealing that he, Drexler and Kersey were on an ensuing flight together to Portland (Jordan was on his way to Eugene, where a doctor was scheduled to examine an injured foot) and spent the entire time playing poker.

"I took $350 from them — I think $250 from Clyde and $100 from Jerome," Jordan said. "I killed 'em. But right before we landed, I was a nice guy and gave it all back to them. Drexler remembers. He must, or else he wouldn't have said I deserved to win the dunk contest."

AFTER THE ALL-STAR BREAK, Kersey scored 34 points and grabbed a career-high 20 rebounds in a 120-105 walloping of Denver on Feb. 12. The fourth-year forward was earning mention as a candidate for the NBA's Most Improved Player Award along with teammate Kevin Duckworth, who was starting now in place of the injured Steve Johnson.

On Feb. 27, the Blazers stormed back from a 16-point fourth-quarter deficit to win 123-120 at Atlanta. After Clyde Drexler swished a 19-foot fallaway jumper with three seconds left to tie it at 120, Kersey — who finished with 25 points, seven rebounds and five steals — stole the inbound pass and banked in a 29-foot 3-pointer at the final horn. It was just enough to offset the sensational performance by the Hawks' Dominique Wilkins, who scored 47 points.

Kersey, who was 1 for 23 from 3-point range the previous season, would go 3 for 15 from beyond the arc in 1987-88.

"I dribbled once and thought about shooting," he said afterward. "Then I dribbled again and let it go. I'm not a great 3-point shooter, especially off the glass."

Though referee Bennett Salvatore ruled the shot good, Atlanta coach Mike Fratello argued long and loudly that it was after the horn. There were no video replays in those days.

"An outright disgrace to basketball," Fratello told the media. "I hope the refs are fined for their lack of knowledge of the game."

That night on "SportsCenter," ESPN's Tom Mees, reviewing tape of the game, said without a doubt the shot came late.

On March 9, Portland won its sixth of the last seven games on the road, edging Dallas 112-110. Kersey was sensational with 33 points and 15 rebounds in 45 minutes.

The next week, Basketball Digest picked Jerome to its all-underrated first team along with teammates Johnson and Terry Porter, Sacramento's Otis Thorpe and Detroit's Joe Dumars.

THE BLAZERS kept winning. On April 14, they beat Utah 128-123 behind 42 points by Clyde Drexler and 25 points and 19 assists by Porter. Kiki VanDeWeghe, who scored 10 points while playing only 16 minutes off the bench, was beginning to wonder about his role with the team and relationship with coach Mike Schuler.

"I don't know how to say this," he told a reporter, "but I really don't figure into Mike's plans."

In the next game, a 147-113 blowout of Golden State, Kiki scored 36 points in 20 reserve minutes. Drexler got in a dig at Schuler afterward.

"When Kiki came in and won the game for us tonight, it shows you the mistake Mike made," said Drexler, ever a loyal friend. "We're talking about Kiki VanDeWeghe, a premier player in this league."

By this time, there was formation of two sides by the players — the pro-Schuler group (Kersey, Porter and Kevin Duckworth) and the anti-Schuler group (Drexler and VanDeWeghe). Kiki was clearly disenchanted with the coach and how he was being used.

"Mike was a coach who liked to practice," Kersey said in his 1998 interview with Hoke Currie. "We spent a lot of time in the gym working on things. Some players took exception to that. We had a little split during that time. There was Clyde and Kiki, and there was me, Duck and Terry.

"Clyde and Mike didn't get along. Kiki and Mike didn't get along. There was no secret about that. It definitely divided the team. Kiki and Clyde had personality clashes with Mike. Me, Kevin, Terry — we just wanted to play. We didn't care about the politics. We were up and coming. Who cares about the innuendo stuff? Mike was the kind of coach who, if he had a question for you, he wanted an answer. I didn't mind a coach who wants you to practice hard, because it only makes you better for games. He evaluated you for what you put into it. What more can you ask for?

"There was no personal animosity (between me and Clyde); it was all directed toward the coach. Kiki was in and out with his back and, quite frankly, I started playing well (in 1987-88). I was more consistently available to play. You had some split among the fans, too. Kiki VanDeWeghe was a household name. I wasn't. How can a guy from Longwood be starting ahead of Kiki VanDeWeghe?"

At least one player agrees that Drexler's relationship with VanDeWeghe didn't affect his relationship with Kersey.

"I never felt that way," former Blazer guard Michael Holton says today. "The way Kiki and Clyde were close wasn't awkward for anybody else. It was like they were the 'Odd Couple.' It didn't bother Jerome."

More than 30 years later, Drexler offers his opinion on the subject.

"Kiki was an All-Star," the Hall of Famer says. "When you're a good player, you don't care what other good players do — you feel like you're going to get your minutes. Kiki got hurt, and he and the coach didn't see eye to eye. We were starting to play more slowdown. Jerome got his break, and then Kiki wanted to get traded. The Blazers started thinking seriously about moving him because he wasn't healthy. He wasn't the same Kiki anymore.

"If Kiki had stayed healthy, I don't think anybody would have played ahead of him, at least then. Jerome got his break when Kiki got the back problem. That was Jerome's opportunity, and he made the most of it. He should have been an All-Star that (1987-88) season."

Drexler says both players handled the situation well.

"No one was happier for Jerome than Kiki," he says. "Even though they played the same position, there was no adversarial relationship. They were good friends.

"With Jerome, we didn't lose much. Offensively, he wasn't Kiki, but defensively we picked it up a couple of notches. Jerome worked his butt off and was a great teammate. He always wanted to win; we had that in common. No one wanted to win as much as I did. When we lost, he was visibly upset. I loved that about him. Show me a guy who's a good loser, I'll show you a loser."

Drexler averaged 27.0 points, 6.6 rebounds and 5.8 assists in 1987-88 under Schuler, then career highs in points (27.2) and rebounds (7.9) with 5.9 assists under Schuler and Rick Adelman the following season.

"I had my best offensive years under Mike," Drexler says now, his assessment perhaps softened over the course of time. "For most of the time, he let us run. I thought he was a good coach. The second year, after he got Coach of the Year, he came in with a lot of mandates. But he was still a nice guy."

In 1986-87, VanDeWeghe finished fifth in the NBA in scoring

average at 26.9, behind only Michael Jordan, Wilkins, Alex English and Larry Bird. In 1987-88, he was able to play only 37 games, posting a 20.2-point average.

"My relationship with Jerome was always great, but it turned a little bit because I was not able to play my fourth year (in Portland)," VanDeWeghe says. "I wasn't quite the same player. I couldn't run or jump anymore. My game changed; I became less of a driver and more of an outside shooter. I was never a super defender, but I couldn't react anymore. I hurt my back my last year in Denver (1983-84) and was never the same after that.

"Jerome started to play more. I was out for an extended period of time and then came back. Our roles were reversed. He was a great player and fit perfectly. I came off the bench, could only play limited minutes and couldn't play every game. After first hurting my back, I played another nine years, though. I was super lucky."

There's no question Kersey looked up to VanDeWeghe, who would be dealt to the Knicks the following season.

"I'd like to think I was a bit of a mentor for him, but he'd have been great no matter where he was," Kiki says modestly. "He wanted to be good. He worked on his shot, but he could contribute to a team whether he was shooting well or not. His defensive and rebounding energy and consistent hustle every single second was impressive. But he never changed his attitude. He always kept asking questions. I was grateful for that. I was frustrated with my own situation from a physical standpoint, but it gave me a different purpose.

"Jerome continued being that same person — still curious, still wanting to get better. He was having great success and a fantastic career, and his attitude never changed. Even when I was traded to New York, it was still the same Jerome. He became even better and a big part of a great team."

Most teammates and those in the organization agreed with Schuler's decision to continue to start Kersey.

"Jerome was ready to go," says Adelman, then a Blazer assistant coach. "Once he was given that starting job, he added another phase to our team. The way he played was so physical, so aggressive."

"There were a lot of discussions within the coaching staff that season," says Geoff Petrie, then serving as a shooting coach but soon to be the club's vice president/operations. "It was a choice between a young, up-and-coming player and a terrific established player. Based on practices and the type of team we were evolving into, it looked clear we'd be better with him at starting small forward. It made us a better team. No disrespect to Kiki, who was a fabulous scorer, but Jerome had the athleticism and a will to play. With Clyde and Jerome leading the way, we could run teams right out of the gym on some nights."

Assistant coach Bucky Buckwalter — the one who scouted and in effect found Kersey — liked the way Drexler and Kersey interacted on the court, too.

"By Jerome's fourth year, he and Clyde were reading each other," Buckwalter says. "They were very fast up and down the floor on the break. Between the two of them, they made some spectacular passes to each other. I can think of many times when Clyde would give a lob to Jerome and he would dunk it off the pass or kick it off the board back to Clyde."

Adds Adelman, who would take over as head coach midway through the 1988-89 season: "A lot of things we did were because of Clyde and Jerome. They did form a connection. On our turnout play, they knew exactly what they were going to do. Clyde would post, with Jerome on the outside, and they would read each other."

Today, Schuler— 80, retired and living in Phoenix — says the decision to play Kersey became a simple matter of who was the better player at a time when VanDeWeghe's health was becoming an issue.

"Kiki went down twice that season," Schuler says. "Both times Jerome went into the starting lineup to replace him, we won (nine) straight games. Jerome was a great athlete, a great teammate and a very good player. You could always depend on him to give you his best effort every night. He was very coachable. A terrific guy. One of my all-time favorite players."

Everyone respected VanDeWeghe, but Kersey's time had come.

"His defense, rebounding and intangibles outweighed Kiki's scoring ability," center Steve Johnson says today.

Center Sam Bowie sat out the entire season with a broken leg. Guard Jim Paxson, who had lost his starting job to Drexler, struggled with a bad back, then was traded to Boston at midseason. Both saw what was happening with the team at small forward.

"Kiki and I were in similar situations," Paxson says today. "Both of us had injuries that opened the door for younger players. Clyde took over for me. Jerome was younger than Kiki. He just kept getting better. When he got his opportunity, he was ready. He was one of those guys who was always ready. If he played 10 minutes or 40 minutes, he'd give you everything he had.

"I considered Jerome one of my favorite teammates in Portland. We always got along. Did we hang out a ton off the floor? No. But I always admired him. From where he came from and what he did, he was such a great success story."

Said Bowie: "Kiki had his back issues, and Jerome was not afraid of the moment. He grabbed the opportunity and ran with it. Kiki was giving us 25 a game, but Jerome was not intimidated or afraid. I loved playing with Kiki. You talk about a guy who could put the ball in the basket, but Jerome brought another dimension. He'd score 18 points, but he'd get you the equivalent of 30 points. He played both ends of the floor. He never balked, never pouted, never complained. He was a pro's pro."

ON APRIL 17, the Blazers beat Sacramento 112-102 for their 50th win of the regular season. It was just the second time a Portland team had won that many, joining the 1977-78 club that won 58.

"No question, 50 is a big deal," Kersey said. "We've had a lot of injuries to overcome."

Portland finished the regular season 53-29 to earn the No. 4 seed in the West and home-court advantage. Problem was, the Blazers would be facing Utah in the first round. It wasn't a good matchup. The

Jazz, led by Karl Malone and John Stockton, had beaten them in four of their five regular-season meetings.

Kersey was outstanding as Portland won the opener of the best-of-five series 108-96. He scored 16 of his 26 points in the first quarter, hitting 8 of 10 shots from the field. He would finish 13 for 18 and would also contribute five rebounds, three assists, two steals and two blocks in just 30 minutes.

Malone then bullied his way to 37 points and 16 rebounds in Utah's 114-105 Game 2 victory at Memorial Coliseum to square the series at 1-1. After the game, "the Mailman" guaranteed the teams would not be returning to Portland for a Game 5.

"He's going to be eating his own words," Kersey responded.

Malone didn't have to. The Jazz won twice in Salt Lake City to wrap up the series and end Portland's season.

The Blazers were building with a young nucleus. There would soon be a new coach to steer them home.

Jerome rips a rebound. *Courtesy Portland Trail Blazers*

Chapter Ten

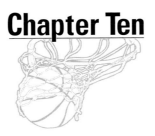

Finally a Starter

WITH HIS STOCK on the rise, Jerome Kersey entered his fifth NBA season brimming with confidence. During the 1987-88 season, he had averaged what would end up as a career high in points (19.2) to go with 8.3 rebounds, 3.1 assists and 1.6 steals while shooting .499 from the field. Teammate Kevin Duckworth claimed the NBA's Most Improved Player Award. Utah point guard John Stockton finished second; Kersey was fifth in the voting.

Kersey had grown comfortable in Portland and purchased a house in suburban West Linn.

"Portland is a small big city, if you know what I mean," he would tell Hoke Currie in 1998. "It's different than if you step into New York or D.C. — not to put those cities down, because there are nice people in those cities. Portland is like country with city buildings, and everybody is much more friendly.

"There's some racism in Portland. Not like in the South — North

Carolina or Alabama. Being in Portland was the first time I experienced inter-racial dating. (People there) seem to be very accepting. It's the first time I've resided in a place where other cultures are represented. The attitudes of people are not that different, but being on the Trail Blazers, you're being eyeballed all the time.

"The fans in Portland appreciate their players. Every time you go back (with another team) you hear rousing applause — a standing ovation sometimes. It makes you feel good. I still live in the area, and I see people who say, 'I wish you guys were back on the team again!' We had some solid, hard-hat guys who went to work every night, and the fans appreciated that. They appreciated us more than the organization did."

THE TRAIL BLAZERS had won 49 and 53 regular-season games in the first two seasons under Mike Schuler, who was honored as the NBA's Coach of the Year in 1987-88. Inside Sports Magazine was picking Portland to play the Atlanta Hawks in the NBA Finals.

The Blazers were under new ownership. Microsoft co-founder Paul Allen, who lived in Mercer Island, Wash., and for several years had held season tickets for the Seattle SuperSonics, purchased the club from Larry Weinberg for $70 million.

Allen and Kersey hit it off immediately. For the next five seasons, Kersey was one of Allen's favorite players.

In his first month as owner, Allen placed calls to most of the players to introduce himself. He found a special connection with Kersey. One day, Jerome drove to Allen's Bellevue estate for a personal meeting and was taken with the owner's Ferrari Testarossa.

"Jerome asked Paul if he could drive it," friend Eddie Bynum recalls. "Paul threw him the keys."

Geoff Petrie, who became the Blazers' vice president/operations, has a memory of that.

"Jerome burned up the engine and had to call for roadside assistance," Petrie says.

Bynum tells a slightly different story.

"The car broke down on the way back to Portland from Seattle," he says. "The wheel bearing went out."

Bynum worked at Beaverton Nissan at the time. He met Kersey when Kersey visited the dealership one day.

"I sold him a Nissan 300 ZX," Bynum says. "Through the years, he bought more cars from me and I met Kevin Duckworth and a lot of his teammates. I wound up selling cars to more than 20 NBA players."

Kersey and Bynum became running mates.

"We were two peas in a pod in the '80s and '90s," Bynum says. "Everybody knew Jerome and Eddie. We had a real cool friendship. We just kicked it."

Kersey was a generous sort by nature.

"I'd be working in the afternoon and Jerome would call and say, 'Whatcha doing tonight? I have tickets for you,' " Bynum says. "For a gift one time, 'Gee' gave me a really nice painting. I still have it up at my house. I was like, 'That's so expensive; you can't give that to me.' "

"What do you mean?" Kersey responded. "The most important thing you can give a person is time, and look at the time we spend together. I'd like to give you more than that."

"That's a lesson Jerome taught me," Bynum says. "Time is something you can never get back. You can only get it once."

There was one tradition they shared in which Kersey was often on the receiving end.

"When we'd go out to eat, we'd play liar's poker to determine who paid," Bynum says. "Whoever lost paid for dinner."

A WEEK BEFORE training camp came a report that Kiki Van-DeWeghe had told the Blazers he'd like to be traded. He didn't think it was wise the way former Blazers Darnell Valentine and Jim Paxson had been dealt at midseason, "when the whole league knows the coach wants to trade you."

Kiki's high salary — $1 million for the 1988-89 season and a total of $3.2 million over the next three — plus his chronic back issues scared off most potential suitors. He had gone through two stints on the injured list the previous season. The Knicks were showing the most interest, offering a first-round draft choice.

Coach Mike Schuler tried to assuage him, saying as camp began that Kiki would be given every opportunity to win the starting small forward job.

"I'd be an incompetent coach if I went into this with a closed mind," the coach said. "I suppose if we had to play tonight, Jerome would be our starter. But if someone plays better than someone else …"

Today, VanDeWeghe offers his version of the scenario.

"I didn't directly ask for a trade," he says, "but I was in a fair amount of pain constantly and I wasn't truthful about it. The coach and I weren't on the same page. Though I loved Portland and my team-mates, that combination made me feel that maybe I needed a change of scenery. It became not a great environment for me."

The Blazers and Knicks were close to completing the deal, but Paul Allen put the quash to it.

"I'm the owner and I make the final call," he told one writer. "I want (Vandeweghe) on the team. He can help us win a championship."

It was a moot point. Kiki began the season on the injured list due to the back injury. Kersey wasted no time establishing that he was deserving of a starting spot. He scored 23 points to lead Portland to a 120-105 victory over Phoenix in the season opener at Memorial Coli-seum. He had 26 points and six rebounds as the Blazers moved to 2-0 by blasting Sacramento 121-103.

Soon Kersey was big again, with 25 points and eight rebounds, though the Blazers lost their third in a row, a 143-132 shootout with Denver. The next game, a 125-103 romp past the L.A. Clippers, Kersey had a moment that exemplified why teammates took to calling him "Jerome Crazy."

In the third quarter, he stole a pass, raced downcourt and was clipped by Benoit Benjamin as he went up for a dunk.

The collision flipped Kersey off-balance and he landed on his head and right shoulder. He wound up with a cut over his right eye that needed five stitches, a sprained left wrist and a sprained right shoulder.

An enraged Schuler ran onto the court and yelled at Benjamin, who had to be restrained from going after the coach. "It was a very hard, nasty play," Schuler said. "He grabbed Jerome's head and threw him down — a clothesline effect." Benjamin was given a flagrant foul and ejected.

Five days later, playing with a shoulder so sore he didn't think he'd be able to play, Kersey went 38 minutes and scored 29 points with 10 rebounds to lead Portland past New Jersey 117-106.

Two days after that, Kersey had his first major skirmish with Xavier McDaniel — and there were several over the years — in the Blazers' 125-104 romp past the Sonics at Seattle Center Coliseum.

Late in the first half, they were jostling for position. Kersey fouled McDaniel from behind, and McDaniel whacked him in the chest with an elbow. Kersey wound up wrapping his hands around McDaniel's neck — something the "X-Man" had done to the Lakers' Wes Matthews the previous season. "I think I beat him to the neck tonight," Kersey quipped. "I'm not afraid of him."

The players were separated, but McDaniel wasn't through. He had to be restrained by several teammates and two referees as he was leaving the floor. Portland's Steve Johnson and Seattle's Michael Cage also had an altercation in a game featuring eight technical fouls, one punching foul and two ejections — McDaniel and Johnson.

"We outplayed them after those two scuffles," said Kersey, who finished with 27 points and nine boards. "Those two incidents set the tone for the night. They try to intimidate us when we come up here and we weren't going to take it."

On November 27, Kersey scored 21 points and made what Golden State coach Don Nelson called the biggest shot of the game — a 25-foot 3-pointer under duress as the clock expired to end the third quarter of the Blazers' 109-94 win over the Warriors. "Making that shot with somebody all over him was a tremendous physical feat," Nelson said.

"We had momentum and would have finished up (the quarter) just six behind, but that made it nine."

Two nights later, Kersey did what he could in the Blazers' 119-114 loss at Milwaukee, scoring 30 points with eight rebounds. He banged home a 3 with 21 seconds left to draw Portland to within 117-114.

THINGS WEREN'T GOING SMOOTHLY, though, for the Blazers, who after a 114-106 defeat at Philadelphia were 1-6 on the road (though they were 6-1 at home). There was some dissension in the ranks. Some people in the Blazers' front office were calling Schuler "His Royal Tightness." Suddenly, the reigning NBA Coach of the Year didn't seem bulletproof.

On December 11, Kersey totaled 25 points and 13 rebounds in 47 minutes of a 128-123 overtime win over San Antonio at Memorial Coliseum. Clyde Drexler was even better, contributing 41 points, nine assists, five rebounds and five steals in 50 minutes.

Kersey missed three games with a sprained ankle. In his first game back, he suffered a broken nose during an attempted shot block by the Warriors' Manute Bol and was out for another contest.

By late December, Kiki VanDeWeghe was practicing and said he was ready to return to the active roster. Bucky Buckwalter, serving in the capacity of GM and working the trade market, told him he needed a few more days of rest and practice. Kiki then told a reporter he was not the one who brought up the idea of trading him.

"I know three or four deals they tried to make before I ever asked them to trade me," VanDeWeghe said. "I did not ask them to trade me until a good friend of mine who works for the league told me they were trying to ship me all over the league."

The next day, Kiki told the media, "I want to make this clear. None of this is Bucky's fault. He has been trying to do the right thing. The people making the decisions (Paul Allen and his right-hand man, Bert Kolde) are hiding behind Bucky."

VanDeWeghe made his season debut on January 1 in a 111-95

blowout of hapless Miami, scoring eight points in 22 minutes off the bench. Four days later, Kersey got into the act, telling the media either he or Kiki needed to be traded.

"Kiki isn't going to be as effective as he can be if he doesn't get enough minutes," Kersey said. "Myself, I think the same thing. No matter what anyone says, it's something that has to be done. We both need (playing) time."

Kersey said he wanted to continue to start. "I've worked hard for a starting role," he said. "I intend to keep it. If (VanDeWeghe) is playing better than me, then he should start. If I'm playing better, then I should start."

Kersey acknowledged feeling the pressure with VanDeWeghe back in action.

"I know that every time I miss a jump shot, people are going to think that Kiki would have made it," he said.

There was a logjam at small forward, with Richard Anderson and Adrian Branch also vying for minutes. It meant for some unhappy campers, which made it even harder on the taciturn Schuler.

"Any time you have a controversy like this, it hurts the team," Kiki told the media. "These kind of things are not a positive influence. It's pretty messed up."

After a January 14 win over San Antonio, the Blazers were 14-1 at home but only 6-13 on the road. They then lost five straight, including four in a row at home. A team meeting was held to "clear the air," the day before a 127-109 setback to Milwaukee 127-109 for their fourth straight loss at MC.

With rumors flying about Schuler's job security, Paul Allen said, "My personal preference is to stick with the guys we have — the staff and the players."

On February 1, Kersey was ejected in the second quarter of a 108-107 win over Clippers, the Blazers' 16th in a row over L.A.'s junior team. After Kersey and the Clippers' Ken Norman engaged in a shoving match, Norman took a swing and Kersey decked Norman with a solid right hand to the jaw. Vandeweghe, meanwhile, scored 24 of his 28 points in the second half.

Three days later, Kersey would get the only triple-double of his career — 14 points, 10 rebounds, 10 assists — in only 33 minutes of a 137-100 rout of San Antonio. Three days after that, he scored a season-high 33 points to lead the Blazers past Dallas 134-125. Kiki added 11 in the fourth quarter as the Blazers rallied from 12 points down after three periods.

Kersey and Clyde Drexler again represented Portland in the slam-dunk contest during All-Star Weekend in Houston — Clyde's fifth appearance in six years, Jerome's fourth in a row. Drexler lost to Kenny "Sky" Walker in the finals. Kersey, who did not make it out of the first round, said it would be his last unless he was also playing in the All-Star Game.

"I'm not an exhibitionist dunker," he said. "I'm a game dunker. All those kicks and spins — that's not me."

ON FEBRUARY 16, Kersey scored 22 points in the Blazers' 110-101 loss to the Lakers at MC. It would be his final game under Mike Schuler. Two days later, the coach was fired and replaced by assistant Rick Adelman on an interim basis for the rest of the season.

Adelman inherited a difficult situation. The Blazers stood in eighth place in the Western Conference with a 25-22 record. Drexler was out of action for three games with a broken nose.

"I don't envy Rick," Kersey told reporters.

Adelman had Vandeweghe for three games. On February 23, Kiki was traded to the Knicks for a first-round draft pick. Adelman's hiring didn't affect Kersey's standing — he had a good relationship with both Schuler and Adelman — but it eased the tension in the locker room with Clyde Drexler, who had no use for Schuler.

On February 26, the Blazers snapped a six-game losing streak and Adelman got his first win, a 124-102 pounding of the Heat at Miami. Rick went to a three-quarters-court press featuring Kersey and

Drexler; Jerome had five steals to go with 14 points while Clyde had a triple-double with 26 points, 11 rebounds and 10 assists.

Kersey continued on a roll, contributing 31 points and seven boards in a 139-134 win over Phoenix. Terry Porter, also coming into his own, bombed in 34 points and 12 assists. Kersey scored 23 points and tied his career high with 20 rebounds as the Blazers made it four in a row with a 129-121 victory over Philadelphia.

Two weeks later, Kersey exited in the third quarter with a broken nose after scoring 19 points in just 25 minutes of a 139-110 rout of Golden State. He didn't miss any games.

On March 28, the Blazers visited Madison Square Garden and faced Vandeweghe for the first time. Kiki got a measure of revenge by scoring 24 points in 26 minutes of New York's 128-124 win. Knicks coach Rick Pitino raved about his defense, though Kersey — matched up against VanDeWeghe much of the time — finished with 26 points, 12 rebounds and seven assists.

By April 1, the Blazers were in a battle just to make the playoffs. Kersey had 21 points and 13 rebounds as they beat Charlotte 125-121 in overtime to get to 33-38 for the season. Three days later, Portland shocked Detroit — the team with the NBA's best record — 118-100, scoring 71 points in the second half. Afterward, Adelman's best player was lobbying for him publicly.

"Rick did a super job preparing us," said Drexler, who had 25 points, 13 rebounds and 10 assists. "That was the best coaching job from anybody all season on any team in the whole league."

Kersey chipped in 14 points, six rebounds and four blocks. Before the game, he showed his vocal chops, combining with Andy Stokes of local R&B band "Cool'R" to sing the national anthem.

"Jerome contacted me and said, 'Do you want to do it together? It would be cool,' " says Stokes, who has been singing professionally now for four decades. "We rehearsed and I was surprised at his voice. I'd never heard him sing. He had a little something. It came out great. We were all over ESPN that night."

Kersey and Stokes shared a bond. Both were from Virginia — Jerome from Clarksville, Stokes from Danville, about 50 miles down the road. They'd met earlier in the year when Cool'R was playing at Salty's Restaurant in the Sellwood area of Southeast Portland and Jerome walked in the door with Kiki Vandeweghe.

"We talked, and from then on, we began to hang out," Stokes says today. "I lived in Mountain Park and he was living across the street. We were homeboys. We both came out of little towns and made it to the big stage.

"For us to get out of (rural Virginia) was a big deal. We grew up hard. We'd talk about knowing nothing about Oregon before we came. I thought there were cowboys and Indians out here. We're both blessed, man. We both came from all-black neighborhoods and grade schools. To come to an area that was like a melting pot was a real cool thing for us. It was a breath of fresh air. Only people from the South would understand it."

Stokes considered Kersey a close friend.

"I would have taken a bullet for him," Stokes says. "He was like a brother. He'd give you the shirt off his back. A beautiful soul. We'd talk stuff back and forth. When I was going through tough times, he'd always tell me to keep my head up, keep pushing. He would tell everybody he taught me how to sing. I'd tell him, 'Yeah, but you're afraid to come out on the basketball court with me.' "

At Kersey's public memorial service, Stokes sang the Spinners' "I'll Be Around."

"That was Jerome," Stokes says "If you needed him, he'd be there. Heart of gold. There wasn't a negative bone in his body. Just positive all the time."

AT THE BLAZERS' annual MVP banquet at MC, Kersey shared the Most Inspirational Player Award with Sam Bowie as voted by the fans.

On April 20, Kersey scored 30 points, but it wasn't enough for the Blazers, who lost 124-118 to Seattle, still needing one win to clinch the eighth and final playoff spot. They got it three nights later, beating Sacramento 126-120 in overtime to finish the regular season 39-43. Clyde Drexler led the way with 40 points, 10 assists and eight rebounds while Kersey collected 25 points and 15 boards.

That set up a best-of-five first-round series with the Lakers, the two-time defending NBA champions led by the likes of Magic Johnson, Kareem Abdul-Jabbar and James Worthy. The Lakers had swept five games from the Blazers in the regular season.

"All the guys on the team think we can win," Kersey said bravely before the series. "We played the Lakers tough this year at times and we know we can do it again. We have to keep our concentration level up and work hard at the defensive end."

The Lakers took the first three games to end Portland's season. Drexler was superb in the series (27.7 points, 8.3 assists, 6.7 rebounds) and Kersey (20.3 points, 8.0 rebounds) and Terry Porter (22.0 points, 8.3 assists) were up to the task, but they had too little help against an opponent that powerful.

The outlook for the Blazers would get much brighter very quickly.

Portland players stand for the national anthem at the Coliseum during the 1990 NBA playoffs. *Courtesy Portland Trail Blazers*

Chapter Eleven

Tripping' to the NBA Finals

WITH CLYDE DREXLER, Terry Porter, Jerome Kersey and Kevin Duckworth the returning nucleus, the Trail Blazers figured they were a power forward away from fielding a team that could challenge for supremacy in the Western Conference in 1989-90.

During the summer they got the final piece to the puzzle in a trade that sent oft-injured center Sam Bowie and a first-round draft pick to New Jersey for veteran Buck Williams.

Williams was an undersized but extremely effective two-way player who, at 29, was hitting his peak years at the same time as his new teammates in Portland. An excellent rebounder and defender, he was a fitting bookend at forward with Kersey, who carried the same lunch-bucket attitude. And both could run and were capable of finishing fast-breaks with dunks and driving layups in the Blazers' vaunted transition game.

Portland also added 6-10 forward Cliff Robinson from Connecticut, who somehow fell into the second round of the draft. The Blazers chose him with the 36th overall pick, and it would prove to be one of the best selections in the franchise's long history.

The coach would return, too. Rick Adelman, who had taken over at midseason for the fired Mike Schuler on an interim basis, was given a one-year contract. The message from owner Paul Allen: Make good immediately or hit the road, kid.

Geoff Petrie, on an ascension up the management ladder, had become vice president/business operations on his way to vice president/operations, meaning he would soon be taking over for Bucky Buckwalter in running the basketball side of the franchise.

In August, the Blazers decided to stage a happening, hosting their first "Slam 'n Jam" event at outdoor Civic Stadium, the home of baseball's Triple-A Portland Beavers and soccer's Portland Timbers. Before a crowd of 20,000, local bands Quarterflash, Nu Shooz and Body & Soul and comedian Jay Leno performed along with the Phoenix Gorilla.

There was an unusual dunk contest, too, featuring Drexler, Kersey and Billy Ray Bates. The competitors dunked on a basket that was incrementally raised via a hydraulic lift. Clyde dunked on his first attempt at 11 feet, six inches, and Jerome made it on his second. When the basket was raised an inch to 11-7, Clyde made it — for an unofficial world vertical record — while Jerome didn't. Drexler earned $6,500 and Kersey $4,500 as an apprehensive Adelman looked on, relieved neither was injured in the act.

Kersey began a season without Kiki VanDeWeghe for competition for the first time in his six years with the Blazers.

"I feel a little more relaxed," he confessed as he cooled down after a training camp session at Willamette University in Salem. "The dissension we had last year — not knowing if the pressure from the fans and media would influence the coach to play certain players — wasn't an easy thing. I'm much more relaxed since I know the position is mine. I can work on some of the things to get prepared for the season rather than worrying about if I'm going to have the position or not."

Kersey started all 76 games he played during the 1988-89 season, averaging 17.5 points and 5.6 rebounds while shooting a respectable .469 from the field. But he pressed when taking an outside shot.

"Last year, if I missed two or three (shots) in a row, I'd start worrying about everyone thinking, 'Jerome can't shoot. VanDeWeghe should start,' " Kersey said. "I'll probably never be the shooter Kiki is, but I'm not a bad shot, and I'm going to work toward improving."

Adelman said he wasn't going to worry about Kersey's shooting as long as he continued to provide so many other things.

"Jerome did not shoot as well last year as he has in the past," Adelman said. "It had a lot to do with him and Clyde feeling they had to do so many things because there was no other answer. He seems to be more at ease this year, just trying to play his game and not worrying that a lot of weight is on his shoulders.

"Jerome is a guy who makes things happen. No one ever questions his effort, his intensity, his enthusiasm.

"He is not a pure shooter, but he is a better shooter than he showed last year. But hey, Dennis Rodman is one of the worst shooters in the league and he's a heck of a player. When you make a judgment, you have to ask, 'Is he an effective player or not?' Jerome Kersey is a very effective small forward."

Kersey felt comfortable playing for the guy with whom he had worked so closely in his first few seasons with the Blazers.

"Rick is a players' coach," Kersey said. "He has played the game and has the instinctive feelings only a player can have. He has kept things simple and lets people play their games. You want to go out there and work hard for a coach like that."

Before the season, the NBA signed a four-year, $600 million TV contract with NBC, of which players were to reap 53 percent.

"It will give everybody more incentive to play a little better … 53 percent of that kind of money is a lot," Kersey said. "It makes you want to add another 10 percent to the 100 percent effort you're already giving."

OPENING NIGHT was special as the Blazers put away Sacramento 114-96 at Memorial Coliseum. The team was celebrating its 20th year as a franchise. Bill Walton's No. 32 jersey was retired and most of the players from the original 1970-71 team, along with coach Rolland Todd, were honored during a pregame ceremony.

Kersey had 22 points and nine rebounds and Williams debuted with 18 points on 8-for-10 shooting to go with 12 rebounds as the Blazers pounded the Kings on 54-31 on the boards. Over the next three seasons, Portland would rank as one of the best rebounding teams in basketball.

Kersey was in classic form two weeks later as Portland bounced Seattle 119-109. He collected 16 points, 18 rebounds and six steals despite sitting out the entire fourth quarter with the Blazers comfortably on top. He dominated rival Xavier McDaniel, who had a quiet night with 12 points and five rebounds.

On November 21, as the Blazers took care of Michael Jordan and the Chicago Bulls 121-110 at the Coliseum to improve to 9-3, radio broadcaster Bill Schonely came up with a catch phrase for the ages.

"Jerome took a pass from Terry (Porter) and sent it down with a two-hand dunk," says Schonely, now 92 years young and still serving as an ambassador and broadcaster emeritus with the Blazers. "It just came out of my mouth: 'Mercy, mercy, Jerome Kersey!' And it stuck."

Schonely is considered by many the most popular figure in the Blazers' 51-year history. "The Schonz" served as play-by-play voice — mostly on radio — through the franchise's first 28 years. In 2012, he was honored with the Curt Gowdy Media Award at the Naismith Memorial Basketball Hall of Fame annual banquet.

"Jerome was one of the nicest young men to come down the line in all my years with the Blazers," Schonely says today. "I've been friends with many players through the years, but my friendship with Jerome was special. The two of us hit it off right off the bat. He was a great friend and compatriot. The crowds never bothered him. He was good to everybody."

Rookie Cliff Robinson was playing well off the bench, and some wondered if he might win the starting small forward job. Robinson, not short on self-confidence, made it clear that was his goal. Adelman quieted any notion that was going to happen.

"The chemistry and balance of a team is a delicate thing," the coach said. "Our starters have been playing together, they've earned their spots and they've all been through this before. I've been around long enough to know you don't mess with that unless we go through tough times as a team, or if a player is really struggling. Besides, Cliff gives us a spark off the bench. I can put him in for any of three guys and I don't worry for one minute about it."

On December 7, the Blazers improved their record to an NBA-best 15-4 with a 96-86 win over Charlotte. Nine days later, rookie forward Ramon Ramos was critically injured when his automobile slid off Interstate 5 south of Portland and overturned. He was not wearing a seat belt. What was scheduled as a practice turned into a team meeting replete with anxiety and some tears.

"It puts your life as a basketball player in perspective," said Kersey, serving with Porter as the team's co-captains. "You live such a fabulous life and you are always in the limelight. It tends to make you overlook what life really is. This makes you forget about basketball and think about Ramon and his family. All you can do is pray for him. I feel help-less and emotional about this."

Ramos eventually came out of a coma and spent years in rehabili-tation and recovery, but was never the same. He never played a minute in the NBA.

ONE OF THE AMENITIES provided by owner Paul Allen was concierge air travel. In January, the Blazers began to lease a private jet through Louisiana-Pacific for road trips. Radio play-by-play man Bill Schonely dubbed it "Blazer One." Portland became the third team, joining the Detroit Pistons and L.A. Lakers, to either own its plane or lease one.

The aircraft, once used by New York hotel magnate Leona Helmsley and built to carry 84 passengers, was reconfigured to seat 21. It was equipped with captain's chairs, a buffet table and wet bar. Flight attendants passed out food and drink. Instead of getting up early for commercial flights the day after games, the team generally flew out of a town and on to the next city immediately after a game.

"It makes a big difference," Adelman said. "We always worried about the players not eating well after games. Now we know they'll get a good meal. No one falls asleep until after midnight anyway, and now we're usually in the next city by then and the players can go to bed at their usual time and sleep in the next morning."

It also eliminated the possibility that a player might stay out late and get himself into trouble after a game. The Blazers were generally off to another city 90 minutes after the final buzzer.

The Blazers flew out of suburban Hillsboro Airport rather than Portland International Airport. Players avoided lines at security and at check-in and didn't have to deal with crowds anymore.

"If I were a free agent, I'd definitely take this into consideration," Kersey said. "If it means traveling like this for the rest of your career, it could make a big difference for you."

The Blazers were doing a lot of winning. After going 12-1 in a 13-game stretch from late December to the end of January, they held a Western Conference-best 31-11 record just past the midway point of the regular season. In a 115-100 romp past Charlotte, Kersey totaled 26 points and 13 rebounds, knocking down 12 of 18 shots from the field. He hit his first four shots — three from the perimeter — and kept banging them home against the Hornets' Kelly Tripucka.

"Kelly's not known as one of the greatest defenders in the league," Kersey said afterward. "I just kept working hard and moving without the ball, and the guys did a great job of finding me."

Kersey contributed 19 points, 10 rebounds and six steals as the Blazers outclassed Milwaukee — which had won 13 of its last 16 games — 119-90.

"They played a magnificent game," Bucks coach Del Harris said. "If Portland is not the most athletic team in the league, it's right up there in the top echelon."

Kersey was one of the leaders as the Blazers totaled 46 fast-break points. "It looked like the way the Lakers used to run on us," he said.

On January 31, Portland fell 135-130 to Golden State, but Kersey collected 18 points, 10 rebounds and five assists, sinking 7 of 12 shots from the field. Five of his baskets came from the perimeter. Over the last 27 games, he was shooting .503 from the field while consistently knocking down jumpers from 15 to 20 feet.

"I still don't think people respect my outside shot," he said. "So my job is to be in a spot where Clyde (Drexler) or Terry (Porter) can get the ball to me off their drive. People close in on them and — boom! — I'm drilling it."

Perhaps understanding that consistent perimeter shooting would never be a Kersey strength, coach Rick Adelman emphasized his other gifts.

"I don't know if there's a small forward in the league who rebounds like he does," he said. "He makes more effort plays than just about anybody in the league. He just never gives up on a play. He doesn't need to get 20 points to be effective because he causes the other team so many problems."

In a 131-100 rout of Dallas on February 3, Kersey had 23 points and nine rebounds and made 7 of 8 attempts from the 16-to-20-foot range. A night later, in a 123-121 win over Phoenix, he enjoyed one of the best games of his career, equaling season highs in points (28) and rebounds (18).

On February 6, the Blazers faced their biggest test of the season so far, an MC date with the vaunted Lakers. Portland (35-13) trailed the Lakers — who had won eight straight Pacific Division championships, earned five NBA titles over the previous decade and lost to Detroit in the Finals the previous year — by a half-game.

"We're looking forward to the challenge," the Lakers' Magic

Johnson said on the eve of the game. "We look at it the same as going against Detroit and New York — big game. It's going to be a dogfight."

That it was. The Lakers prevailed 121-119 in overtime. The Blazers, who rallied from a 14-point halftime deficit, nearly won despite making only 2 of 11 attempts from 3-point range and 25 of 40 from the foul line. Drexler scored 32 points and Kersey, playing 46 minutes, contributed 17 points and 14 rebounds.

"There was so much hype," Adelman said. "I told somebody before the game, 'This is the first chance I've had to coach the seventh game of the world championship series.' We're still one of the best teams. This doesn't change at all what we've accomplished so far. Even if we'd won, I don't know if it would have proved we're right there with the Lakers."

A week later, Mount McDaniel blew up in Seattle Coliseum as the Blazers nipped the SuperSonics 110-106. Growing nemesis Xavier McDaniel, who scored 35 points, was the instigator of a third-quarter altercation that nearly resulted in a brawl.

Late in the period, Drexler drove to the basket and appeared to be fouled, with no call. On the next trip down, Drexler tried to dunk. McDaniel clotheslined him as he went up. Players from both sides rushed in, words were exchanged, and Kersey took a swing at the Sonics' Olden Polynice. After the break, McDaniel and Kersey got into a verbal exchange that didn't end until referee Jake O'Donnell called a technical on Kersey. When Kersey protested, referee Jim Capers heard him curse out of earshot of O'Donnell. Capers raced over to tell O'Donnell, who then gave Kersey a second technical, which meant automatic ejection.

"If I get a T, then we both should," Kersey said afterward. "I can't see me getting two and McDaniel none."

"I'm not afraid of him," McDaniel said, issuing a challenge to Kersey he would echo in the future: "I'll take him out in the alley and we'll see who comes out alive."

The next week, the Blazers got revenge on the Lakers, winning a hotly contested road game 132-128 in double overtime to pull back within a half-game of their division rivals. Portland had lost nine straight and 19 of its last 20 visits to the Forum.

Two days after that, the Blazers used a 32-4 edge in fast-break points to vanquish Boston 120-101.

"It's not very often that a team can take the ball against the Boston Celtics on a made field goal and score at the other end so quickly," Boston coach Jimmy Rodgers said.

Kersey won his individual matchup with Larry Bird, who collected 21 points, eight rebounds and six assists but made only 1 of 10 shots in the second half. Kersey had 24 points and 13 rebounds, taking Bird to the well often. He ran the court superbly, hit the open shot and played strong defense on Bird.

"I didn't do it myself," Kersey said. "Bird rubs off picks so well to get open, but in the second half, Buck (Williams) and Duck really helped out."

Beginning with a March 3 win over Seattle, Portland went on a 10-game winning streak, going 4-0 on a trip through New York, Boston, New Jersey and Washington — accomplished in a five-day span. It was the Blazers' first four-game sweep of an eastern trip since 1978.

"We can beat anybody in this league, any night, anywhere," Adelman said.

The Blazers kept on rolling. After their streak ended with a 108-107 loss at San Antonio, they destroyed Denver 140-126 for their 20th road win of the season. Coach Doug Moe said the Nuggets played "like a bunch of dogs. Actually, that's too kind. That would be an insult to any canine."

Kersey had perhaps his best game of the season with 26 points, 12 rebounds, two steals and two blocks. Adelman said he was "tremendous in the transition game."

Even on bad nights, the Blazers were often able to pull games out. They beat the Clippers 106-99 at home in a game in which they shot .418 from the field, committed 20 turnovers — 10 in the second quarter and 16 in the first half — and got outrebounded 49-47 by one of the poorest rebounding teams in the league.

"It was like a trip to the dentist," said Kersey, the brightest light for the Blazers with 28 points and 10 rebounds. "Or maybe like the dentist coming to you."

THE BLAZERS were in the postseason for the 11th time in 12 years but had won only two playoff series during that time. This team expected more of itself, and so did everyone else. Portland finished the regular season at 59-23, best in franchise history and tied with Detroit for second-best in the NBA behind only the Lakers (63-19).

The Blazers, No. 3 seed in the Western Conference, opened the playoffs against No. 6 seed Dallas, led by the outstanding guard tandem of Derek Harper and Rolando Blackman and forwards Sam Perkins and Roy Tarpley. The 7-foot Tarpley averaged 16.8 points and 13.1 rebounds but had missed nearly half of the regular season on NBA suspension after being arrested for driving while intoxicated and resisting arrest.

Portland won the first two games of the best-of-five series at home, then completed the sweep with a 106-92 win at Dallas. In Game 3, Kersey gave a tremendous performance with a career playoff-high 29 points plus nine rebounds while holding Perkins to 13 points and eight boards. The Blazers paid a heavy price, however, losing power forward Buck Williams (corneal abrasion) and center Kevin Duckworth (broken right hand) to injuries.

Williams would return to action for the Western Conference semifinal series with San Antonio but with goggles, something he would wear for most of the rest of his career.

The Spurs were led by a Hall of Fame coach (Larry Brown) and a Hall of Fame center (David Robinson). Forwards Terry Cummings and Sean Elliott and guards Rod Strickland and Willie Anderson also posed a formidable threat.

Without Duckworth, the Blazers were left with veteran backup Wayne Cooper and rookie Cliff Robinson to guard David Robinson. Prior to the series, "the Admiral" — somewhat out of character — told a reporter, "I don't think (Cliff) can guard me. I don't think he can guard me as well as Cooper, and I don't think Cooper can guard me."

That provided bulletin-board material for the Blazers, who swarmed the Spurs' befuddled Robinson and held him to nine points and nine rebounds in 40 minutes in Portland's 107-94 win in the opener. Cliff, Cooper, Williams and Mark Bryant took turns guarding the Spurs' center and got help from teammates.

Kersey came up big with 25 points and 16 rebounds. With the game still tight early in the fourth quarter, he went on a rampage from the perimeter, sinking four straight jumpers in a four-minute span to help Portland boost its lead to 97-82.

"I felt good," said Kersey, who was 8 for 11 on midrange jump shots. "I was catching and shooting instead of hesitating. I took one shot that didn't feel like it was going to get there, and still, it was all net."

Portland also won Game 2 at Memorial Coliseum; San Antonio evened the count with two wins at HemisFair Arena.

Game 5 was a classic, the Blazers prevailing 138-132 in double overtime in a 3-hour, 11-minute marathon.

Portland led 91-69 midway through t he third quarter, but the Spurs stormed back, and the Blazers, playing without Duckworth and Cooper — who had suffered a back injury in Game 3 — couldn't hold the lead.

"That's the most exciting game I've ever played in," said Kersey, who totaled 23 points and 10 rebounds in 54 minutes and made a pair free throws with 11.1 seconds left in the second extra session to give the Blazers a 137-132 lead and put the game on ice.

Despite a team-high 22 points by Kersey, the Spurs manhandled the visiting Blazers 112-97 in Game 6 to set up a deciding contest in Portland. It didn't help that Drexler was ejected in the third quarter after an altercation with Anderson.

The day between Games 6 and 7, Anderson told the media that the Blazers would "fold" if the Spurs could get off to a good start in the finale. He also said this of the player with whom he was matched up at shooting guard. "Clyde is one of the dirtiest players I've ever played against. He's always punching me in the stomach and he cries all the time. He cries and cries and cries."

Game 7 was another classic. The Spurs led 97-90 with 2:32 left in regulation. The Blazers scored seven straight points to force overtime, the last two on a Kersey breakaway dunk with 1:17 remaining.

The score was tied at 103-103 when Strickland threw an over-the-head pass from the baseline that Kersey picked off. He passed down-court to a streaking Drexler, who was chased by Robinson. Robinson was called for a breakaway foul — and disqualified with his sixth personal — giving Clyde two free throws and the Blazers the ball with 26.2 seconds left.

Drexler made both, and another pair with 16.4 seconds left to push Portland ahead 107-103. After the Spurs narrowed the gap to 107-105, Clyde was fouled again with 7.3 seconds left. He made the first attempt; the second curled out, the Spurs rebounded and called timeout trailing 108-105 with 5.6 ticks left. Terry Porter stole the inbound pass to seal the Blazers' 13th straight home-court win over the Spurs.

Porter, who had scored a career playoff-high 38 points in Portland's double-overtime win in Game 5, bombed in 36 in this one along with nine assists. Drexler, fighting a head cold, scored 12 of his 22 points in the final four minutes of regulation and the overtime, and finished with 13 rebounds and eight assists. Kersey contributed 21 points, 15 rebounds and six steals.

Duckworth — expected to miss the entire series with the broken hand — played, too, making an entrance that would remind some of Willis Reed's Game 7 return for New York in the 1970 NBA Finals. It wasn't determined until the day before that Duck would be able to go, and it was a closely guarded secret. When fans saw him exit the locker room and jog onto the court for pregame warmups, they greeted him with an ovation anyone in the arena that day will never forget. The 7-footer would later call it "the greatest moment of my life."

Cooper, moving gingerly because of his back injury, played 13 minutes, too. They combined to hit only 4 of 17 shots but provided an emotional lift and did a nice defensive job on Robinson, who made only 2 of 12 shots through the first three quarters.

"That's the most emotional series I've been in as either a player or coach," Adelman said afterward.

"The greatest series I've been involved with in my 20 years in the league," Spurs owner Red McCombs said.

It was on to the Western Conference finals for the Blazers and a matchup with the Phoenix Suns, led by high-scoring forward Tom Chambers and explosive guard Kevin Johnson.

Portland won the first two games at MC, though the second one was a bit on the miraculous side. The Blazers were down by 18 points at intermission and by as many as 21 in the third quarter. Porter's jump shot with 12 seconds left capped an emotional 108-107 win as the Blazers ran their home playoff record to 8-0.

"I can't think of another win I've experienced as satisfying as this one," Adelman said.

At least half of the sellout crowd of 12,884 stayed on hand for 15 minutes, clapping in unison like a rock concert throng waiting for an encore. When Porter and Drexler emerged from the locker room, they were greeted by an uproar.

The Blazers suffered one-sided losses in Phoenix the next two games. Kersey was the Blazers' leading scorer in both games. He tallied 29 in Game 4, hitting 14 of 20 shots from the floor and making nine shots from the perimeter.

Portland returned home to win Game 5 120-114 with Kersey again coming up big with 21 points and 11 rebounds.

The Blazers finally broke through in Game 6, claiming a 112-109 victory at Veterans Memorial Coliseum in Phoenix. Kersey provided the biggest play of the game. With Phoenix ahead 109-108 inside the final minute, Jeff Hornacek drove the lane for a running one-hander, and Kersey — who would finish with 15 points and 10 boards — came from nowhere to block it. Seconds later, Drexler got him the ball at the other end and he converted the layup to push Portland ahead 110-109 with 27.2 ticks left.

"Everybody has always said, 'You guys can't win,'" Kersey said in a jubilant visitors locker room. "I've heard it so much for so long. Everybody on this team is sick and tired of it. We've known all year we have a good team. We can get it done. Maybe now we've finally got some respect. We've earned respect."

It was a terrific series for Kersey, who averaged 21.5 points and 8.5 rebounds while shooting .505 in the six games. Now he was about to taste what NBA Finals action was all about.

THE OPPONENT was defending NBA champion Detroit, a veteran crew with a tremendous backcourt tandem in Isiah Thomas and Joe Dumars and a physical cast on the front line led by Bill Laimbeer, James Edwards, John Salley and Dennis Rodman. The Pistons were the best defensive team in the league and had just taken care of Michael Jordan and the Chicago Bulls in seven games in the Eastern Conference finals.

During the regular season, the Blazers had crushed the Pistons 102-82 at home and lost a close one at Detroit 111-106. Even so, some wondered if the Blazers would be intimidated by the physicality of the "Bad Boys."

"We are one of the most physical teams in the league," Kersey said before the series. "I don't think they want to play a physical game with us. They're a team that can definitely be beat."

The Blazers let a big opportunity slip away in the opener. They led much of the way, but Detroit finished the game with a 25-9 spurt to erase a 10-point deficit and win 105-99.

"We should have really exploded on them, but we allowed them to hang around," said Kersey, who had 18 points and eight rebounds.

Like everyone on the Portland side, he complained about the officiating. "We got a championship-team whistle down the stretch," Kersey said. "They were holding and pushing and nothing was called for whatever reason. The Pistons or not, championship series or not, fouls are fouls. You know you're not going to get the baby calls, but the refs can't just quit calling the game."

But, Kersey said, "We'll be back. We should have won this game tonight. We know we can beat that team. There's no doubt in our minds."

The Blazers did just that, with Clyde Drexler scoring 33 points, including two free throws with 2.1 seconds left in overtime for a 106-105 win to even the series at 1-1.

With Games 3 through 5 in Portland, the battle cry in the Blazers' locker room was, "We're not coming back to Detroit." The thought was, win three straight and wrap up the series at home. The Blazers were right; they weren't going back to Motown. The Pistons were — with another NBA title.

Detroit won Game 3 by a 121-106 count, breaking a string of 20 straight losses by the Pistons at the MC despite a team-high 27 points by Kersey. "If you're going to end a 16-year losing streak," Detroit coach Chuck Daly said, "this is as good a time to do it as any."

Kersey was sensational in Game 4, going for a career playoff-high 33 points — on 11 of 17 from the field and 11 of 14 from the line — to go with eight rebounds. But the Pistons, erasing a 16-point second-half deficit, pulled out a 112-109 victory, with Thomas scoring 30 of his 32 points in the second half.

Portland was in prime position to win Game 5 and send the series back to Detroit, but again the Pistons responded. They scored the final seven points, then won 92-90 on Vinnie Johnson's last-second, death-defying 18-footer over Kersey's outstretched hands.

"Maybe it was just meant for them to win," a dejected Kersey said.

Buck Williams summed up the Blazers' feelings this way: "We felt the thrill of victory twice, maybe three times in this series, and (the Pistons) came back and stole our dreams. But they deserved to win the title. They were the better team this year."

Later, Kersey reflected on the 1989-90 season as "a great learning experience. As a team, we learned how important it is to hang in there.

As a player, I learned that no matter what happens, you gotta keep working at it. There's always a brighter side. Times when we were defeated on and off the court, we were able to come back and learn from the experience."

The Finals experience and the loss to the Pistons, Kersey said, made the Blazers hungrier to win a championship in 1990-91.

"You've had a taste of it now, and you know what it feels like," he said. "When you get that you'll do anything to get back. And we have the confidence now. We have that feeling that nobody out there can beat us."

Two days after the Finals, an estimated 7,000 people jammed Pioneer Courthouse Square in downtown Portland for a tribute to the team. A steady drizzle fell during the 35-minute ceremony, but as Jerome told the throng, "You fans make it sunshine every day in Portland for the Blazers. The greatest fans in the NBA are right here in Portland. You guys make it happen."

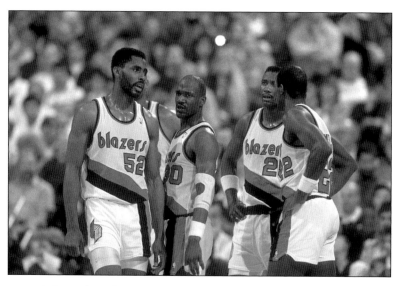

From left, Buck Williams, Terry Porter, Jerome and Clyde Drexler talk it over during the 1990-91 season. *Courtesy Portland Trail Blazers*

Chapter Twelve

Coulda Been, Shoulda Been Champs

AFTER SPENDING five years as the radio analyst and serving as shooting coach and vice president/business operations, Geoff Petrie became senior vice president/operations for the 1990-91 season, putting him in charge of the basketball side of the Trail Blazers organization.

That set the wheels in motion for a number of moves in the summer of 1990.

Rick Adelman got a three-year contract extension after coaching Portland to the NBA Finals.

Though he was beginning only the second year of a four-year, $2-million contract, Jerome Kersey's deal had already become below market value. The Trail Blazers brought him up to speed with a four-year, $11-million extension that carried through the 1994-95 season.

"Jerome was part of the heart and soul of the team," Petrie says today. "I really cared about the guy. I was so glad to see him grow and become such a terrific player and a great fit for the team. None of those contract negotiations are easy, but that was one I really wanted to get done."

Petrie also gave one-year contract extensions to teammates Buck Williams ($4 million for the 1993-94 season) and Clyde Drexler (a record $8 million for the 1995-96 campaign) to bring their overall deals closer to market value.

And Portland added an important piece in veteran guard Danny Ainge, acquired in a trade with Sacramento. Ainge, a Eugene, Ore., native who had helped the Boston Celtics win NBA championships in 1984 and '86, would come off the bench and provide backcourt help for Drexler and Terry Porter.

Kersey put a weight room in his West Linn home and added about 10 pounds to push him to 235.

"I feel stronger, and I'm in good enough shape to carry the weight," Kersey said as the Blazers hit training camp at Willamette University.

At 28, Kersey was coming into his own as both a basketball player and as one of the most eligible young bachelors in Portland.

"His friends called him 'Romeo,' or 'Jeromeo,' " says J.R. Harris, one of Kersey's close friends and running mates. "He was a single guy with a great smile, and his face was on a (Nike) mural on a building in downtown Portland for several years. He was very visible. That made a difference for him socially."

By this time, Kersey was dressing in style.

"That got an upgrade when we started getting his suits custom-made," Harris says.

Kersey liked to have things his way in a relationship.

"If he was dating you, when he called, he expected you to be available," Harris says. "He couldn't handle the woman who said she would get back to him later. He'd say, 'I can't believe she was too busy to talk to me.' He struggled with that kind of woman. He wanted the freedom to come and visit. If someone would say, 'you can't come over now,' that was tough for him."

During the late '80s, when both Kersey and Harris were single, they would occasionally venture into the Portland night life. Jerome could sometimes be an impediment to J.R.'s pursuit of female company.

"One time we were in Champions bar at the Marriott," Harris recalls. "I was talking to a girl. Her girlfriend came over to join her. Jerome came over — and all the attention's on him now, right? I told him, 'From now on, whenever I'm with you, I'm going to be on the other side of the club. Just don't come over here. Let me come over to you.' "

If they were out and were joined by a female, it wasn't a level playing field.

"This was Jerome's big-time move," Harris says. "We might be having dinner or appetizers. The conversation was going real well. Then when the bill came, it could be $300 or $400. He'd be showing off — 'Come on, give me the bill.' It was like, 'I'm going to get the girl; you move to the back of the line.' So one night I said, 'You're going to get the bill, anyway. I'm going to get the girl this time.' "

In an interview that season, Kersey spoke about life as a celebrity in the public eye.

"I like to be silly sometimes and not have people look at you real funny," he said. "The people who really know me know that side of me. I'm a big kid at heart. I like a lot of music and going to clubs, but I don't dance. I'm a people-watcher. I like to relax, kick back, have a few cold Heinekens. People say, 'They let you guys drink?' We're responsible adults. We know what we have to do.

"Some people act like we're gods, that we shouldn't do anything wrong. That's not the way it is. I have to live my life by my own rules and standards. I have to say that to myself sometimes. I can't let somebody else run my life. If I make a mistake, it's my own mistake."

He tried to emulate one of his sports idols, Julius "Dr. J" Erving.

"For me as a kid, it was about Dr. J.," Kersey said. "I wanted to be as good as him. The adulation I had for him … I'd like to leave that for some kid. Pro athletes set examples, and I think I set a good example on the court. If a kid watches me and says, 'Hey, I like the way Jerome Kersey plays, I want to be like him,' that would be a good way to look back at my career."

Kersey's interest in cars was growing. As the season began, he owned a 1986 Mercedes 500 SL, a 1989 Porsche 911 and a 1989 BMW 750.

"Cars are kind of an extension of your personality," he said. "They get your blood boiling."

"He knew his cars," Harris says. "I used to joke that you could put a blindfold on Jerome and drive by him and he could tell you what the car was. He knew them that well."

The last time Harris bought a car — a BMW 650i — he had Kersey test-drive it for him.

"He said, 'It's nice,' " Harris says. "I didn't ask any other questions. I bought the car."

It's not surprising, given the way he played basketball, that Kersey liked to drive fast.

"He was from Virginia," Harris says. "That's auto racing country. Once after he bought a new car, we drove down (Oregon Route 43) toward Lake Oswego. He said, 'Let me show you what this car can do. A fin comes up to break the wind at a certain speed.' He hit about 90. I said, 'You need to pull over and let me out, or I need to put a helmet on. We're going to flip this thing over.' "

WITH A VETERAN starting unit and a strong bench led by Cliff Robinson and Danny Ainge, the Blazers felt they had the ingredients to claim the NBA title they had missed out on in 1989-90. They won their regular-season opener — but just barely, nipping Houston 90-89 at Memorial Coliseum. Kersey collected 23 points and 14 rebounds in 41 minutes as Portland rallied from 16 points down midway through the third quarter.

The Blazers eked out another win, this one 95-93 in overtime at Sacramento despite Clyde Drexler going 1 for 16 from the field. Kersey clinched it with a driving layup and a pair of free throws in the final 7.3 seconds of overtime.

The Blazers went overtime again to beat the vaunted Lakers 125-

123 at the Forum and go to 3-0. Kersey suffered a cervical strain late in the first quarter when he flipped over teammate Cliff Robinson trying to block a Magic Johnson layup and fell on his neck. Jerome went to the locker room and did not return. But he was back in action for the next game.

"I can't play any other way," he said afterward. "You can't worry about injuries. You just have to play the game."

The Blazers kept winning — and winning. On November 18, they shot a superb .623 from the field in a 125-112 beat-down of Michael Jordan and the Chicago Bulls at the Coliseum to run their record to 9-0. Easy victories over Golden State and San Antonio jacked the mark to 11-0.

"I feel like we can't be beaten right now, really," Kersey said afterward, which proved to be the proverbial kiss of death. Next time out, Phoenix ended the streak with a 123-109 victory, snapping its 20-game skid at MC. Clyde Drexler's second-quarter ejection didn't help matters.

"When you win 11 in a row, you have to feel invincible," Phoenix forward Eddie Johnson said afterward. "The way they were playing, you have to have a lot of confidence. No way Portland was going to go 82-0. Somebody was going to get lucky and beat them."

Added teammate Jeff Hornacek: "They still have the best record in the NBA. As far as that goes, they're still the best team."

The wins kept coming. After a 122-96 lacing of Indiana on December 11, Portland was 19-1, equaling the second-best start in NBA history. Only the 1969-70 New York Knicks (23-1) had gotten off better. Pacers star Reggie Miller was calling the Blazers "even better than the Laker teams of the early '80s." Seven-year Indiana veteran Chuck Person said, 'They're the best team I've seen since I've been in the NBA."

The Blazers stumbled in their next outing, falling 100-88 at Sacramento in a game in which they led 35-19 after one quarter. They got back on the winning track and improved to 22-2 with a 122-94 romp over Golden State in which Portland jumped to 35-9 advantage after one period. It was the fewest points an opponent had scored in a quarter in franchise history. "We tried to control the tempo a little and execute in the half-court offense," Warriors coach Don Nelson said. "It didn't work."

On December 29, Portland defeated Cleveland 120-114 to go to 27-3 for the season. But Kersey pulled a calf muscle in his left leg, an injury that would sideline him for a total of nine games and end his consecutive game streak at 150. Robinson moved into the starting line-up for Kersey, who was averaging 14.3 points, was second in the team in rebounds (7.3) and leading in blocked shots and dunks. The Blazers lost their next two outings and four of the next seven.

"I think they'd have gone undefeated in those games with him," Golden State guard Tim Hardaway said. "He's so valuable to their team. He plays so hard. I think he's an All-Star player."

"You take away Jerome, you take away a major part of our team," Drexler said at the time. "His defense, his scoring, his unselfish play, his hustle … and he makes a lot of things happen with his athleticism. Cliff has done a great job, but you just can't replace that."

"The thing we miss more than anything is his energy," coach Rick Adelman said. "He'll come up with a big rebound or a great block. He'll run down a ball, or he'll rotate at the right time to stop a basket. He might make three or four hustle plays, and in close games, they mean everything."

The idle time didn't sit well with Kersey.

"It gets a little agonizing," he said of sitting out for an extended period. "You just want to be out there with the guys."

Kersey suited and went through warm-ups but was not expected to play as the Blazers visited Minnesota at the end of a road trip on January 14. Then Buck Williams exited with a groin injury 2:31 into the game. Jerome said nothing when Williams departed. He just took off his warm-ups and reported into the game. Wrote The Oregonian's Dwight Jaynes: "Kersey ended up giving his team 34 hard minutes, 22 points, four rebounds and two terrific put-back baskets after knifing in for offensive rebounds in the final quarter."

On January 18, the Blazers observed Bernard King Day by blasting the Washington Bullets 123-99. Kersey did a splendid defensive job on King, the NBA's leading scorer at 31.1 points per game, holding him to 15 points on 6-for-15 shooting.

"You want to make him put it on the floor," said Kersey, who had 16 points and eight rebounds. "You don't want to give him any real easy shots. If he drives, you want to push him to help. We played great team defense, got him frustrated and took him out of his game."

After the game, King talked about his toughest matchups, mentioning James Worthy, Scottie Pippen and Dennis Rodman but singling out Kersey.

"He brings a lot of different things at you," said King, who finished third in the NBA during the 1990-91 campaign with a 28.4-point scoring average. "He's a finesse player, but also a power player. He can hit the jump shot consistently. He can put the ball on the floor, but he also has the aggressive attitude of a big forward. He's very physical. He's tough for me."

Four days later, Kersey met up at the Coliseum with an old adversary — Xavier McDaniel. The X-Man had been traded from Seattle to Phoenix the month before after 5 1/2 seasons with the Sonics.

"This probably makes Jerome's job a little easier, me not being in Seattle," he said before the Blazers-Suns meeting. "The only thing is, we're still in the same division. And if (the Blazers) thought I was a bitch in Seattle, I'm going to be a real pain in the butt now."

A couple of weeks earlier, a Seattle writer had asked the Blazer players for their impression of the Sonics without McDaniel. Their seemingly innocuous quotes made their way to McDaniel and Phoenix coach Cotton Fitzsimmons, the latter only too anxious to stoke the fire inside his volatile small forward.

"What I read out of Portland was all of the Blazers think the trade helps Seattle's club and will hurt mine," Fitzsimmons said. "I was glad to hear that. I'm sure 'X' enjoyed the article. I'm delighted to have him.

We're a much better team than we were a year ago. If Seattle is happy about him being with us, if Portland's happy about him being with us, I'm happy."

"Just as long as I have those guys thinking more about me than what they have to do … if I remember right, the Blazers did a lot of bickering among themselves a couple of years ago," McDaniel said before the game. "All the problems with Clyde and Jerome going at each other … if there were a situation where they started to play the young kid, (Cliff) Robinson, more than Jerome, you'd hear some bickering. That's the way it is in this league."

The Blazers (35-7) emerged with a 123-116 victory over the Suns, and sure enough, there was extracurricular activity. Play was physical, and Kersey and McDaniel were ejected after a third-quarter altercation.

The Blazers were in front 82-70 when tempers flared. Kersey and McDaniel were battling for position under the Portland basket when McDaniel intentionally threw a forearm, hitting Kersey in the back. Players from both sides moved in to break up the altercation, Adelman grabbing McDaniel. After nearly 10 minutes discussing the situation, the referees called a personal foul on Kersey and — much to the Blazers' dismay — ejected both players.

"I have nothing to say — see the film," Kersey fumed afterward.

Said the X-Man: "I had just told the referees Jerome was getting a little too aggressive. He knocked me off balance, he was holding on to me and I just knocked him away. I barely touched him … if they want to end it, they should put us in an alley."

ON JANUARY 23, the Blazers sent disgruntled guard Drazen Petrovic to New Jersey in a trade that brought veteran swing man Walter Davis to Portland. The 6-6, 195-pound six-time All-Star, at 36 in his 15th NBA season, was averaging 18.7 points for Denver when the deal was struck. Blazer management felt "The Greyhound" could be a valuable addition off the bench through what they hoped would be a long playoff run. That didn't prove to be the case. Davis averaged only 6.1 points the rest of the regular season and wasn't a factor in the postseason. By the start of the 1991-92 season, Davis was back in a Nuggets uniform.

Kersey failed to make the NBA All-Star Game again, but he finished fifth in voting for forwards in the West for the second time in his career — the closest he would come to being a starter. Kersey was behind Utah's Karl Malone, Golden State's Chris Mullin, the Lakers' James Worthy and Phoenix's Tom Chambers — the four forwards to make the West squad that year. Jerome's candidacy wasn't helped by the fact that teammatesDrexler, Porter and Duckworth made the team.

Over the All-Star break, The Oregonian (actually, the author) rated Kersey as the ninth-best small forward in the league, behind Charles Barkley of Philadelphia, Worthy, Dominique Wilkins of Atlanta, Bernard King of Washington, Scottie Pippen of Chicago, Mullin, Dennis Rodman of Detroit and McDaniel. All but McDaniel — who was averaging 21.8 points and 6.9 rebounds at the time — would make the Naismith Hall of Fame.

"Small forward is probably the toughest position in our league because of the wide variety of skills necessary at that position," Portland coach Rick Adelman said. "There are so many great ones, and they're so different. It's a heck of a position to play. Every night, you face somebody who is going to be a problem. At some positions, it's not that way.

"Jerome is perfect for our team. We don't run many plays for him, but he really doesn't demand anything of our offense. He gets his shots off of offensive boards and running the floor on the fast-break. We need a player like that. On our team, the forwards do most of the dirty work."

The strained calf continued to bother Kersey through February. On February 19, Davis was ticketed to get a rare start in a game against Dallas. Maybe because he was worried about losing his starting job, Kersey warmed up and decided he could go. He started and contributed 10 points, four steals, three blocks, three assists and two rebounds in 33 minutes in a 107-100 victory.

The Blazers were rolling again. On February 22, they manhandled Phoenix 127-106 at the Coliseum for the fifth of what would become a seven-game win streak. Portland committed three turnovers, a record for efficiency since the NBA began keeping turnover records in 1970. Kersey had 20 points and 11 boards — eight at the offensive end — plus three steals, three assists and three blocked shots.

"Jerome was incredible tonight," Adelman said. "He was everywhere. He had so much energy — it's hard to keep him down."

Kersey also did a nice defensive job on old rival McDaniel, who finished with 10 points and 10 rebounds in 27 minutes and was laden with foul trouble in the second half. The X-Man said everybody was just waiting for him to stir up some trouble.

"The officials were looking at (Kersey and McDaniel) with binoculars," McDaniel complained. "The fans were watching us, the media. Even (supervisor of officials) Rod Thorn was watching on the satellite. I heard one whistle and it was a foul on me. I said, 'Hey, I ain't done nothing yet.' " He added: "(The Blazers) were looking for Jerome early, trying to get him off and get his confidence up."

Kersey was still not fully over the calf injury, but said, "It feels good not to be tentative going after the ball." On McDaniel: "He got a couple of fouls and never really got into the game, but I don't think the game was called any differently. I got pumped up for him. He's a great player. When he gets going, he's capable of getting his numbers."

The following night, Kersey and Terry Porter, along with teammate Danny Young, served as honorary chairmen for the "Kids Auction," a benefit for Boys and Girls Clubs of Portland at the Portland Hilton. The auction netted $201,000.

The affiliation with the Boys and Girls Clubs for Kersey and Porter began shortly after Terry joined the Blazers in 1985. As a youngster, Porter had practically taken up residence at the nearest Boys & Girls Club in Milwaukee. Jerome had often visited a recreation center during his childhood in Virginia.

"They recognized where they came from," says Traci Rose, a

former vice president/corporate communications and community relations for the Blazers who managed community service affairs for the players. "They both visited the Columbia Boys and Girls Club a few times. They would go out on their own, just show up and play basketball and spend time with the kids. At one point, they bought a group of game tickets for the kids."

The previous season, Kersey, Porter and Young had backed the cast of Portland hip-hop group "U-Krew" to lay tracks for the song "Rip City Rhapsody." Proceeds from an ensuing cassette single and video were earmarked for the Portland Boys and Girls Clubs.

That led to the establishment of the "Portland/Phoenix Exchange Club" (see Porter's preface in this book).

"It was an initiative program in which the kids had to show improvement in several areas: club attendance, school attendance, grades, community involvement and so on," Rose says. "Jerome and Terry funded the whole thing. Their time spent with the Boys and Girls Clubs of the Portland Metropolitan Area was the reason the Blazers got involved."

"It's a chance to put a smile on some kids' faces, to broaden their horizons," Kersey said. "It tickles you sometimes. Some of the kids try to act like they're not in awe, but they're in awe."

In 1996, the Blazers built a new facility on MLK Boulevard in Northeast Portland that today is called "the Blazers Boys and Girls Club."

"When we were master planning for the Rose Quarter and developing plans to give back to the community, it was a no-brainer that we would want to invest in that club," Rose says. "Terry and Jerome are the reasons there is a Blazers Boys and Girls Club."

SAN ANTONIO started the Blazers on a four-game skid with a 95-88 victory in a game in which Kersey was ejected after drawing two technicals from referee Jake O'Donnell, the second for kicking the ball after O'Donnell had called him for a charging foul. Kersey said he didn't do it on purpose: "I didn't kick it. I was running toward it and it hit my foot. He just wanted to (eject me)."

Afterward, Rick Adelman, who also got a T, said he couldn't comment on O'Donnell's work. "You're talking about Zeus. I can't say anything about the officials or I'll get a fine." But, said Adelman, "every time we have him, something happens."

On March 4, Portland ended the losing streak with a 116-107 victory at Boston in the final stop on a four-game road trip. Larry Bird collected 28 points and 13 rebounds, but Kersey made him work at the defensive end, scoring 23 points on 9-for-12 shooting.

"I don't know if the rest of the guys felt pressure, but I did," Kersey said. "I didn't want to come home 0-4 from a trip."

On March 12, Kersey sank 8 of 13 shots from the field and totaled 21 points, nine rebounds and five assists as the Blazers beat Cleveland 104-96 at home for only their second win in seven games. A week later, Golden State handed Portland (47-18) its eighth loss in 11 games with a 136-126 thumping. Suddenly, the Blazers — who had been perched atop the Pacific Division since opening night and had held an eight-game lead on January 8 — were trailing the Lakers (48-18) by a half-game.

"We're back in the position of chasing the Lakers again," said Kersey, who scored a team-high 35 points, one shy of his career high, while making 14 of 21 shots from the field. "It's anybody's division (championship) now."

It would be the last game the Blazers would lose for more than a month. They ran off 16 straight wins before losing the final regular-season game at Phoenix.

In the second game of the streak, a 117-102 rout of Charlotte, Kersey was 11 for 13 from the field and scored 22 points with five rebounds, four assists and three steals in 31 minutes. He was back to his old tricks, picking up opportunity baskets, finishing fast-breaks, following missed shots with dunks and chasing down loose balls.

"I've gotten myself back into shape, practicing hard every day," he

186

said. "I went through a period where I wasn't able to do that. I'd play in games but would have to miss practices because of soreness in the leg. That threw me off my game. I think I'm back. There's still a little soreness, but I don't think that will go away until … well, hopefully the championship series. I'm not thinking about it anymore, and I can run the court and be aggressive all the time."

The Blazers were sometimes down but never out during the streak. On March 27, they rallied from 24 points down to beat Seattle 112-107 in Tacoma, Wash. Only once had a Blazers team ever come from so far behind to win. Two nights later, they erased a 21-point deficit to overtake the Lakers 109-105 in overtime.

They swept every game of a six-game, nine-day trip, including a 104-93 win at Minnesota. Kersey led the way with a game-high 25 points, including 13 in the third quarter. He had five second-half-dunks, including four in the third while finishing fast-breaks. He was 10 for 17 from the field and had eight rebounds and four assists.

"It was 'Jerome Kersey Dunk Night,' "teammate Kevin Duckworth said. "Every time I looked up, he was out on the break. That's his game."

The Blazers routed Orlando 115-98 mostly without Drexler, who was ejected late in the first quarter after drawing a pair of technicals. Terry Porter (29 points, 12 assists), Buck Williams (14 points, 21 rebounds) and Kersey (26 points, 11 rebounds) helped the Blazers rally from a 12-point third-quarter deficit.

In a 103-93 win at Houston, Kersey had the play of the game — a spectacular block of a Sleepy Floyd breakaway layup late in the game. The next possession, Kersey took the ball to the hole and was fouled with one second left on the shot clock. He swished a pair at the line with 47.7 ticks left for a 99-93 lead.

Portland finished the long trip and a "Texas Three-Step" sweep (Houston, Dallas, San Antonio) with a 105-100 triumph over the Spurs. Kersey sank a 20-foot jumper and two free throws on successive possessions down the stretch to key the victory. He had scored only two points on 1-for-7 shooting when he took a pass with three seconds left on the shot clock and drained a shot from deep in the corner for a 97-93 lead with 1:22 to play.

"That killed us," Spurs coach Larry Brown said afterward.

Added Adelman: "An enormous shot. I wasn't surprised. The way Jerome plays, I knew he'd respond. We have so many guys like that. No matter what kind of game they're having, they're going to come through when it counts."

The Blazers wrapped up their first Pacific Division crown since 1977-78 with a 118-113 win over Lakers at MC on April 13.

"This is the way to win the division — beating the Lakers in a dramatic way," Kersey said. "All the pressure was there. We could have lost this game and probably still won the division — but we didn't want to do that."

The Blazers entered the playoffs with an NBA-best record of 63-19.

A division title and the league's best record "are two of the goals we set for ourselves at the start of the year," Adelman said. "This team deserves a lot of credit for getting that done. Now we have one more thing to try to accomplish — the big one."

PORTLAND OPENED the playoffs with a 110-102 home victory over Seattle in a best-of-five first-round series. Clyde Drexler scored 39 points — one shy of Mychal Thompson's franchise playoff high — to go with nine assists, seven rebounds and three steals.

Kersey scored 18 of his 31 points in the first half and finished with seven rebounds and five assists, hitting 11 of 19 from the field and 9 of 10 at the line. He was knocking down jumpers and punctuating fast-breaks with flying dunks.

"Jerome was relentless," Adelman said. "He kept working the whole game."

The Blazers won Game 2, then fell in Games 3 and 4 to put themselves in position to become the first top-seeded team ever to lose to a No. 8 seed. That wasn't to happen. Portland jumped to a 20-point halftime lead and cruised to a 119-107 victory to win Game 5 and set up a Western Conference semifinal series matchup with Karl Malone, John Stockton and the Utah Jazz.

Portland breezed to a 117-97 win in the opener, with Drexler going for 20 points, a career playoff-high 15 rebounds and eight assists. Kersey added 17 points and 13 rebounds.

The Blazers blew all of a 23-point fourth-quarter lead only to prevail 118-116 in Game 2.

"Whew," exclaimed Kersey after scoring a career playoff-high 34 points, sinking 11 of 16 shots from the field and 12 of 15 from the foul line. "That was one sent down from heaven."

Malone busted the nets for a career playoff-high 40 points and set an NBA playoff record by making 19 of 20 free throws in the second half.

The Blazers lost Game 3, then stole Game 4 in Salt Lake City 104-101 behind 30 points and 11 rebounds from center Kevin Duckworth. Portland wrapped up the series back home in the Coliseum, using a 16-0 run to start the second half and pull out a 103-96 win.

"Everybody was determined that we weren't going to go back (to Salt Lake City) again," said Kersey, who chipped in 15 points and six boards. "We all wanted to take care of business at home."

There was not much celebrating in the winning locker room.

"Last year, every series win was a tremendous thrill," Kersey said. "But this is a team that thinks we should be in the Finals again and then win it. We're not letting this get to our heads. We're glad to beat Utah because that's a very good team — better than a lot of people give them credit for. But the big emotional thing — hopefully that will come later."

The Western Conference finals was a heavily anticipated matchup between the team with the best record in the league and the Lakers of Magic Johnson and James Worthy. Portland had won three of the five regular-season meetings between the clubs. The last five times the Blazers had opened a series at home, they'd gone 10-0 in the first two games.

"Contrary to what some people say on NBC, we match up well with them," Kersey said before the series began. "I think they're more scared of us than we are of them. I don't think we're scared of them at all, really."

The Lakers, though, did what it took to claim the opener 111-106, rallying from a 14-point deficit late in the third quarter. The Lakers outscored the Blazers 31-14 in the final period. Portland — which shot 57 percent from the field through three quarters — was 4 for 14 in the fourth and made one field goal over the final 5:20.

"We gave them a chance to win the game, and they took it," Adelman said.

Worthy scored a team-high 28 points, including 15 in the first quarter. Magic had 15 points and 21 of the Lakers' 29 assists. Drexler (28 points, 12 rebounds, eight assists) and Kersey (21 points, nine rebounds) had big games for Portland, but it wasn't enough.

The Blazers came back to win 109-98 in Game 2, Porter leading the way with 26 points on 12-for-15 shooting to go with eight assists. Kersey contributed 18 points and nine boards.

The Lakers rolled in Games 3 and 4 at the Forum, winning 106-92 and 116-95. Kersey scored 25 points in the latter affair but had too little help, and the Blazers were on the brink of elimination.

Adelman switched defensive assignments for Game 5, taking Kersey off Worthy and putting him on Vlade Divac. That allowed Buck Williams to guard Worthy and Kevin Duckworth to defend Sam Perkins. It worked well in a 95-84 victory. Portland won the rebound battle 52-33, grabbing 26 off the offensive glass.

"Reminded me of college when I played center," said Kersey, who led the way with 20 points and nine rebounds.

The teams returned to L.A., where the Lakers escaped with a 91-90 win to clinch the series. Porter missed a 17-footer from the baseline with four seconds left that could have won it. The biggest miss, though, came with the Blazers trailing by one point inside the final minute. Cliff Robinson let a pass from Kersey slip off his fingertips on a four-on-one breakaway; had he caught it, it would have been a sure dunk.

Suddenly, Portland's season was over. The Lakers would go on to lose to Chicago in five games in the NBA Finals. The Blazers felt they should have been there.

"This is really hard to take, because we worked so hard," Adelman said after the final game of the Lakers series. "We accomplished a lot, but we're in this for the long run. We'll be back."

THAT SUMMER, there was one intriguing trade possibility that never reached fruition. Charles Barkley wanted to be a Blazer. The "Round Mound of Rebound" had lobbied for a trade while still with the Philadelphia 76ers.

"I thought they had the best home-court advantage in the NBA," Barkley says today. "They were loaded. It was a nightmare playing against them. That is probably the most talented team I ever played against, top to bottom. They were two-deep at every position."

Barkley called Geoff Petrie, by then Portland's vice president/operations.

"I told Geoff, 'I really need to sit down with you face to face and talk,'" Barkley says. "I flew to Portland in the middle of the summer on my own dime. Didn't tell anybody in the world. We sat down and talked for a couple of hours."

"You're one of the few teams that can give up enough players to get me," Barkley told Petrie. "The only weakness is you can't score in the halfcourt when the game is on the line in the playoffs. That's my specialty. I don't care who you give up. I'll still have enough (talent) here to win a title."

"We'd love to have you, but I'm not sure what it would take," Petrie responded.

"Do whatever it takes," Barkley said.

A few days later, Barkley said he heard back from Petrie. He likely would have had to give up something like Kersey, Buck Williams and a pair of first-round picks to acquire Barkley.

"We're going to stick with what we've got," Petrie said.

"I said, 'No hard feelings,' " Barkley says. "And the rest is history."

Barkley was 27 then, beginning the prime of his Hall of Fame career. After the 1991-92 season, he would be traded to Phoenix, with whom he won the NBA's Most Valuable Player Award in leading the Suns to the NBA Finals in 1992-93.

Through their shared association with Nike, and the fact that Barkley made frequent trips to Portland to visit Nike's headquarters and to play annually in a celebrity golf tournament, he and Kersey grew close.

"Over the years, Jerome became one of my best friends," Barkley says. "I would come to Portland every summer and we'd spend a lot of time together. Whenever our teams faced each other, we'd get together. He was one of the best people you're ever going to meet."

Barkley says Kersey was his kind of player.

"Gritty," he says. "Tough. For a kid like him to make it out of Longwood, it was really something. I might be going out on a limb, but I don't think there's been another NBA player from Longwood.

"You never had to worry about him trying to get attention. I never heard him complain about his contract or playing time. He just went out and did his job. That's one thing I admired and respected about him. He was probably the most important part of that Portland team. What I mean by that is, he didn't have an ego. When you're playing with a really good team, you have to have that.

"I knew I was in trouble after my first year in Phoenix. The first year, I got the guys together and said, 'We're going to the Finals and we're going to play the Bulls. I'm telling you right now, that's our goal.' It was great the first year. We exploded onto the scene. After that, it wasn't the same. There were guys thinking, 'This guy's making more money than me. This guy's getting more playing time.' We were never the same."

Chapter Thirteen

Another Big Swing and Miss

"GREAT EXPECTATIONS" was the theme for the Trail Blazers as they headed into the 1991-92 season. Geoff Petrie was bringing back the entire rotation, minus only reserve guard Danny Young, who was waived to make room for rookie Robert Pack. Sport Magazine forecast Portland as the NBA champion.

"We have the potential to win it all," teammate Clyde Drexler said. "It's really up to us."

Jerome Kersey was ready for action. He had taken a month off after the loss to the Lakers in the Western Conference finals, spending time with friends and relatives in Virginia. He did some weight lifting, "but not as much as I've done in the past," he said. "I was drained after the playoffs. I didn't want to even see a basketball for a while. It's the first summer I've felt like that. It was probably a combination of the last two years — going so far, but not capturing the ring."

After the third day of training camp, coach Rick Adelman called

Kersey "the most impressive player" in camp.

"He's in great shape, he's shooting the ball well and he's running the floor hard," Adelman said. "Jerome is playing the way Jerome can play."

"Jerome has been even more active in camp than he was last year," teammate Buck Williams noted. "If we get that kind of effort out of him, we're going to be that much better this year."

At 29, beginning his eighth NBA season, Jerome was approaching a decline in terms of athleticism. But with continued work through the years, his perimeter shooting had grown more consistent to help make up for it. His scoring average dipped in 1990-91 to 14.8 from 16.0 the previous season, but he played fewer minutes (32.3 to 34.7) on one of the deepest teams in the NBA.

"You never feel established when you're playing the 3-spot until you start knocking down your jumper from the outside," Kersey said. "I think I did that last year for the first time. I've taken advice that good shooters like Walter (Davis) and Terry (Porter) have given me. The important thing is to face up, take my time and take my shot when it's there. If I don't rush it, I do pretty well."

Kersey came to camp carrying about 245 pounds on his 6-7 frame.

"I feel like I'm real quick at that weight, but I'll probably end up at 235 when the season starts," he said.

"He's really our power forward right now, as big as he is," Adelman said.

The Blazers' power forward, Williams, was undersized at 6-8 and 225.

"Jerome is a physical player," Williams said. "I enjoy playing with him because I don't have to do all the banging. It takes some of the pressure off me in that department."

Kersey was the only one of the Portland starters to have never made an All-Star team.

"Jerome is one of the top small forwards in the conference," Adelman argued. "He doesn't score a lot of points and he's not a go-to guy on our team because we have a lot of other players, but we know how important he is for us. We're not the same team without him. He does all the little things.

"He's the most underrated player we have — maybe in the whole league. But all you have to do is go around the league and ask people if they'd like to have him. Not too many teams wouldn't want a Jerome Kersey."

Kersey said he was focusing on the team's ultimate goal.

"I know we can win it all," he said. "We have all the tools. We have so much talent it's incredible. No one can stop us but ourselves. I just want our team to do well. If that happens, the accolades will follow."

BEFORE THE SEASON, Kersey was featured in a segment on TNT's "Basketball's Funniest Pranks." The show's producer contacted John Lashway, Portland's director of media services, and asked him to suggest a player who would enjoy helping stage a prank. He chose funny guy Alaa Abdelnaby, who enlisted Danny Ainge for support.

The scenario: Alaa and Danny were supposed to be going in on the purchase of a prize racehorse. Each had chipped in $50,000 and was looking for a third partner. Alaa tabbed Kersey because he had mentioned he was interested in buying a stable of horses one day.

"I knew he'd be a total sucker for it," Abdelnaby said.

The three met in the Coliseum parking lot to view the horse, which was said to be unbeaten in three races and a young up-and-comer. Truth was, the horse was a nag with one eye and a swayback and looked about 15 years old.

Alaa: "We're talking about an ugly horse."

Alaa and Danny were unbending in their support of the venture.

"I told him the one eye might be an advantage, because he could concentrate on the rail," Ainge said.

Kersey admitted the pair "had me going for a while." He said he had reservations about the horse, "but I was trying to be nice. I was thinking, 'Are they sure they want to invest $50,000 apiece in this?' "

When Abdelnaby left to discuss terms with the trainer — an actor for the show — Ainge changed his story, pointing out the horse's shortcomings to Kersey and saying he was going to ask for his money back. Then the trainer returned and said he had money from Alaa and Danny and needed Kersey's check.

Kersey told him he needed more time to think about the purchase, but the trainer said he already had Jerome's signature on the contract. When Alaa sheepishly told Kersey he'd forged his teammate's signature, Kersey exploded.

"I said, 'You did what?' Kersey said. 'I was really mad.'"

"He'd have hit me in the mouth if the other people hadn't been around," Abdelnaby said, laughing.

A steamed Kersey was stalking off when Alaa led him back to the camera and let him in on the prank. Kersey took it well, in part because he was relieved it was just a gag.

"It was pretty funny," he said.

THE BLAZERS were up and down in the early season, rolling to a 117-106 win over Cleveland in the opener at home — Kersey contributed 16 points, five rebounds and five assists — but losing the next three. They won the next four, beginning with a 121-96 pasting of Cleveland in which Kersey collected 19 points, 11 rebounds — seven at the offensive end — and four steals despite playing on one bum ankle and injuring the other.

Over the next month, Kersey played in every game but was unable to practice and wasn't at full strength. He had 20 points, five rebounds and five steals in a 122-111 loss to Denver. He went for 28 points and 10 rebounds in a 132-112 pounding of the Clippers. Kersey had another nice game against Chicago at the Coliseum, collecting 21 points and 10 boards. But he missed an open 17-foot jump shot with 10 seconds in regulation and the score tied at 99-99. The Bulls went on to win 116-114 in double overtime behind 40 points from Michael Jordan.

"Jerome has played really well," coach Rick Adelman said. "He knows only one way to play, and that's hard. In the last three games, he's been all over the boards and has been keeping things alive, diving on the floor and hustling after loose balls. The way he plays adds energy to our team. It carries over to the rest of the guys."

With the sore ankles, Kersey said, "You definitely don't feel like you're on as solid a base as you should be. Sometimes you don't feel like you can take a hard cut — you think about that. I've just been trying to get to the boards and do things that won't put pressure on my ankles."

The Blazers knocked off Washington 91-87 on December 1, but there was a scary moment. Late in the game, Kersey was flying in for a dunk when he slammed into the Bullets' Pervis Ellison and fell onto his right side. Kersey was taken to Meridian Park Hospital for X-rays on his right forearm, which showed no breaks but revealed a deep bruise in the ulnar bone. He missed no games, which didn't surprise trainer Mike Shimensky.

"There was a game against the Lakers in the Forum," says Shimensky, Portland's trainer from 1987-94. "Jerome was on a breakaway and went up for the shot and got undercut. He did a flip, landed on his upper back and head. I ran out on the floor. The Lakers' doctor, Stephen Lombardo, was talking to him and asking him questions. So was I. Dr. Lombardo wanted to take him to the locker room. Jerome said, 'I'm fine.'

"After a few moments, he got up and walked to the bench. He sat out for a couple of minutes and got back into the game. I took some grief from some people for not putting him on a gurney and taking him to the hospital, but we relied on the medical people, and Dr. Lombardo signed off on sending him back in."

Shimensky cites another occasion that cemented his belief in Kersey's steely composition.

"We were scrimmaging during a practice at Mittleman Jewish Community Center," Shimensky says. "Jerome took a nasty spill, and Kiki Vandeweghe picked up the ball and took off the other way on a breakaway. Jerome jumped up, chased Kiki down and swatted (a layup attempt) out of bounds. For him to shake that off. … only Jerome could do that. He was so tough."

Shimensky spent 26 years as an NBA trainer with the Blazers, Seattle SuperSonics, Utah Jazz and Los Angeles Clippers.

"I worked with Clyde Drexler, Terry Porter and Buck Williams," says Shimensky, now retired and living in Vancouver, Wash. "John Stockton and Karl Malone. Gary Payton and Ray Allen. I'd put Jerome right in there with all of those guys. You talk about a professional, he was one. They came to play. You couldn't ask for better people to work with. (Former Jazz coach) Jerry Sloan used to say he liked those guys who came to work with their hard hat and their lunch pail. That was Jerome."

Shimensky connected with Kersey on a personal level, too.

"I went to a sushi place to have dinner with my wife one night," he says. "Jerome was at the sushi bar. He came over, bought us a drink and visited for a while. He suggested some things for us to try. He couldn't have been more personable.

"Another day, one of my kids had a birthday and we celebrated at Chuck E. Cheese. Jerome found out. We were in the place, and all of a sudden, in pops Jerome with this huge present for my kid. He stays there and talks to everybody. You never expect a player like that to show up, especially with a gift, and spend time and talk to people. You don't find people like that very often."

ON DECEMBER 13, Kersey accompanied Santa Claus to Doernbecher Children's Hospital as part of the Make-a-Wish Foundation's annual Christmas visit. Jerome wore an elf's costume. "Just seeing the look on (the children's) faces is enough for me," he said. "I'm excited to be here."

That night, the Blazers lost 113-103 to Detroit to fall to 13-9. The previous season, they hadn't suffered their ninth loss until February 15. But everything came together after that. The Blazers would go 44-16 — 25-3 at home — the rest of the season and never lose more than two in a row.

Kersey's ankles finally healed. In a 123-118 loss to Golden State, he collected 24 points, 10 rebounds and five assists. In a 98-88 win over the Lakers, he hustled his way to a 16-point, 16-rebound game.

In a 132-128 loss in overtime to Phoenix, Kersey took an elbow from Tom Chambers over the right eye in the fourth quarter that required 10 stitches to close. That didn't slow him down. In the next game, a 113-109 win at Seattle, Kersey got loose for a half-dozen slams. He finished with 19 points and nine boards.

The next night, the Blazers ran their home win streak to 10 and won their 15th of 19 games overall by beating Atlanta 125-117. Kersey had 20 points, 10 rebounds, four assists and three steals in 43 minutes.

On January 28, Portland took over first place in the Pacific Division with a 124-116 overtime win at Golden State. Drexler was magnificent, putting up 39 points, 13 rebounds, nine assists and four steals, while Kersey added 23 points and 14 rebounds.

Portland won 10 of its next 14 outings leading into a March 1 showdown with Chicago at United Center. The result was an embarrassing 111-91 defeat, after which Michael Jordan — who had compiled 31 points, nine rebounds, seven assists and three steals — brought up the subject of the Blazers' collective basketball IQ.

"They run the open court so well, we try to get them in a half-court game and make them utilize their minds as much as possible," Jordan said. "They have more athletic ability than we do. But to win, you have to play together as a team, and you have to play smart."

A good portion of the Blazers' 23 turnovers, Jordan said, was due to "no thought process. When you're playing against good teams, you can't let that happen."

Added Scottie Pippen, who collected 20 points, 10 assists and eight rebounds: "You have to force them to have to make decisions. They're a very athletic team, but against a good, smart team like us, you have to be a smart team, too."

It was a sore spot with the Blazers, who had cringed when Magic Johnson said they weren't a smart team in the 1991 playoffs. They took offense when Phoenix coach Cotton Fitzsimmons said earlier in the 1991-92 season that they were long on natural ability, implying that they were short on gray matter. The subject would dog them the rest of the season.

On March 15 at Boston Garden, Larry Bird bombed in 49 points — including a leaning 3-pointer with two seconds left that sent the game into overtime — to go with 14 rebounds and 12 assists in Boston's 152-148 double-overtime win, ending Portland's seven-game win streak. Clyde Drexler had 41 points and 11 assists and Kersey contributed 23 points, 14 rebounds and five assists.

In early April, the Blazers won back-to-back games against Golden State to boost their division lead over the Warriors to four games with six to play. Kersey collected 23 points and eight rebounds in the first game and scored on a one-handed heave from 55 feet to end the third quarter and give Portland a seven-point lead in the latter contest.

Portland finished the regular season with the best record in the Western Conference (57-25), guaranteeing home-court advantage through the conference finals. Kersey averaged only 12.6 points on a team with a multitude of scorers but was also the No. 2 rebounder on the best rebounding team in the league. He averaged 8.3 boards a game, more than any small forward except Charles Barkley, Dennis Rodman and Larry Johnson. Adelman said he made more hustle plays than any 3-man in the game.

"Jerome may not score as much as some guys, but he'll hurt you in a lot of other ways," the coach said. "Jerome will be there when it counts the most."

"I'm a different type of small forward," Kersey said. "There aren't as many plays run for me as there are for a lot of the guys I guard. I get my points out of movement and in transition. If I keep hustling and going to the boards, I'll get my points. I don't make nearly as many shots just standing and shooting as I do when I set a down-screen and move or come off a screen. I can take some people in an isolation and get a good shot off, but I haven't had to do that too much with this team."

Kersey looked forward to the postseason. He averaged 20 points in the previous four playoff seasons, well above his 16.9 regular-season average during that time.

AS THE PLAYOFFS DAWNED, Portland radio station "Z100" released a new single, "Bust a Bucket," performed by local artist Dan Reed and his band. Kersey and teammates Terry Porter, Buck Williams, Kevin Duckworth and Lamont Strothers helped with background singing, and Kersey provided a lead vocal cameo. Proceeds, of course, went to Portland Boys and Girls Clubs.

Just as the postseason was about to begin, Kersey got into a conversation with a woman in a local grocery store. She mentioned that her child — who loved the Blazers — was ill and in the hospital. She didn't ask for anything, but Kersey was moved. The next day after practice, he called Traci Rose — the club's director of community relations — when she was in her office and said he needed a favor.

"I need a shirt and a hat for this kid," Kersey told Rose. "Can you run it down to the parking lot?"

"He was going to the hospital to see the little boy," Rose would recall later. "I put a little package together and brought it down. Jerome was there, but so were Clyde, Buck, Terry and Duck. The entire starting five were in their cars, headed for the hospital. Jerome had arranged the whole thing."

Rose worked 27 years for the Blazers (1986-2013), finishing as vice president/corporate communications and community relations. For many years, she managed community service for the players.

"In all my time there, there were a couple of players who were far above the rest — Terry and Jerome," Rose says today. "They were two peas in a pod. We'll never know the full extent of all Jerome did. When we made those two trips to the Finals, I would get calls, probably one a week, saying, 'Just want to thank you guys. Jerome Kersey was here at the hospital,' or, 'Jerome was here,' or 'Jerome was there.' And we would never know about it beforehand. He was out there on his own.

"Jerome's sincerity was 150 percent. He was never into any publicity. If I needed help with an appearance or whatever it was, he was one I knew I could call. I knew he would do what I needed him to do. He was totally dependable."

THINGS WERE much different than the playoff scene a year earlier. The Blazers were matched up in the first round with the No.

8-seeded Lakers. But they were not the team that had knocked Portland out in the West finals the year before. Magic Johnson was gone from the game after testing positive for HIV and James Worthy was out after undergoing knee surgery in March.

Portland won the first two games of the best-of-five series handily at home. The Lakers managed a 121-119 Game-3 win at the Forum despite a playoff career-high 42 points by Clyde Drexler, after which Game 4 was moved to Las Vegas due to civic turmoil in Los Angeles following the Rodney King jury verdict. The Blazers closed it out in "Sin City" with a 102-76 rout.

"We felt badly that we had extended the series this long by losing with a not real good effort in L.A.," said Kersey, who contributed seven points, eight rebounds, five assists and two steals in only 25 minutes of the finale. "We didn't want it to go any further. We felt pressure to get this done because we have a good team waiting for us."

Phoenix — the opponent in the Western Conference semifinals — posed a more difficult challenge. The Suns, led by guards Kevin Johnson and Jeff Hornacek and forwards Tom Chambers and Dan Majerle, had won three of the five regular-season meetings between the clubs and had swept San Antonio in the first round.

Portland won a spine-tingling opener 113-111 at the MC by making 19 of 24 free throws in the fourth quarter, including 10 of 10 by Porter, who finished with a game-high 31 points. The Blazers pulled out another close one 126-119 in Game 2, with Kersey contributing 25 points on 10-for-17 shooting and nine rebounds in 33 minutes. "The Run-Down Man" chased Chambers to block a breakaway layup from behind, then converted a key three-point play down the stretch.

"Damn, my arm is sore," Kersey joked afterward. "It's been a long time since I've shot that many times."

"He was an offensive machine tonight," teammate Danny Ainge told reporters. "He got mad at you guys telling him his offense had disintegrated."

"Jerome was tremendous," Adelman said. "Once he gets going and into a positive flow, he can make plays like that."

Phoenix won Game 3 by a 124-117 count at Veterans Memorial Coliseum, then fell 153-151 in double overtime in Game 4, which will long go down as one of the most memorable contests in franchise history.

Adelman said it ranked with Portland's Game 7 win over San Antonio in 1990 as the two most exciting games in which he had participated through his 17 years as an NBA player or coach. Ainge, who had won a pair of NBA titles with Boston in the 1980s, could recall only two comparable games while with Boston — a game in the 1988 Finals in which Larry Bird stole Isiah Thomas' inbound pass and swiped an NBA title in the process, and one in 1984, when Gerald Henderson's steal and solo layup sealed a win in the finals against the Lakers.

The Blazers scored 74 points in the first half and shot .581 in Game 4, but still needed 58 exhausting minutes to put away the Suns, who committed only six turnovers — fewest ever for a Blazer playoff opponent.

Portland had many heroes. Porter's statistical line was sensational — 31 points on 10 for 16 from the field, 14 assists, six rebounds and one turnover in 51 minutes. Drexler provided 31 points, 11 assists and eight rebounds. Kersey shot well, knocking down five outside jumpers, while scoring 21 points and snagging a team-high 10 rebounds. He also made the defensive play of the night, tying up Majerle as he tried to hit a game-winning shot at the end of regulation.

The Blazers iced the series at home with a 118-106 victory in Game 5. Kersey put together 16 points, 12 rebounds, eight assists, five steals and two blocks in 42 furious minutes.

"I've said all along, they're the best team in the West," Phoenix coach Cotton Fitzsimmons said afterward. "The way they are playing, they could be the team to beat for the whole thing."

That set up a Western Conference matchup with old rival Utah, featuring Karl "The Mailman" Malone and John Stockton — basically the same team the Blazers had ousted in five games in the West semis a year earlier.

Portland had it going in a 113-88 rout at home in the opener, hitting 24 of its first 30 shots and taking a 65-37 lead into the half.

"I don't know that we can play any better than that," Adelman said.

Kersey's first five shots — all from the 16-to-18-foot range — were all on the money. He was 6 for 6 from the field in the first quarter.

"It felt good to get out of the blocks like that," said Kersey, who finished with 20 points, four rebounds and three assists in just 29 minutes.

Asked about adjustments he might make for Game 2, Utah coach Jerry Sloan quipped, "We're going to get David Robinson, Hakeem Olajuwon and four or five other guys and see if we can play with this team."

The Jazz were overmatched again in Game 2, falling as Portland won 119-102 behind 77 combined points from Porter (41) and Drexler (36).

Utah got back into the series while winning a pair of physical, emotional games at the Delta Center. The Blazers were whistled for five technicals in Game 4 in a game in which the Jazz to shoot 55 free throws. "They lost their composure," Utah guard Jeff Malone said afterward.

Kersey led the way in a 127-121 overtime victory in Game 5, Portland's 12th straight win over the Jazz at home. He was constantly in motion, collecting a team-high 29 points on 13-for-20 shooting, with 10 rebounds and five assists.

"Jerome will do anything to score, anything to get a rebound, anything to get a loose ball," teammate Kevin Duckworth said. "He's the kind of guy who just can't be replaced."

Kersey played another all-around game as the Blazers wrapped up the series with a 105-97 win in Salt Lake City, contributing 18 points, five rebounds, four blocks and three assists. He averaged 19.5 points while shooting .551 from the field in the series.

"A lot of people said we wouldn't get back to the NBA Finals this year," said Kersey, ice packs covering both knees and an ankle in the visitors locker room afterward. "Now we have one more thing left to do."

THE NBA FINALS matchup was what many fans had hoped for — the Chicago Bulls against the Trail Blazers, featuring Michael Jordan and Clyde Drexler, the players who would rank 1-2 in Most Valuable Player voting that season. The defending champion Bulls had won both regular-season meetings with the Blazers and had disposed of Cleveland in six games in the Eastern Conference finals.

"I always thought it would be (the Bulls)," coach Rick Adelman said. "They've been the best team all year."

"It's a great challenge to play the defending champs," Kersey said on the eve of the series. "What better team to beat than them? I had the same feeling against Detroit (in 1990), and we didn't beat them. I hope we can do it this time."

Chicago coach Phil Jackson announced that Scottie Pippen would likely cover Drexler and Jordan would probably guard Kersey, who was shooting .523 from the field while averaging 16.8 points in the playoffs.

"I would invite that," Kersey said. "I would love that. They're going to be rotating their defense away from me because they're concerned about defending Clyde and Terry. I'm going to be active and doing the things I've been doing through the playoffs."

Jackson entered the series poor-mouthing his team by saying, "Physically, (the Blazers) overmatch us at every single position. Maybe Michael and Drexler are the two guys who can compete physically. Other than that, they really have physical dominance."

"It's amazing to me how he says that when they're the world champions," Adelman responded, shaking his head. "The team that executes defensively the best is probably going to win."

"The first game will set the tone for the whole series," Kersey predicted. "How we come out and establish our style of play is important. If we play the way we've been playing, it's going to be a very tough game for (the Bulls). If we stay on top of them and keep our defensive pressure up, things are going to look good for us."

Things did not go well for the Blazers in the opener at the United Center. Jordan went wild, knocking down six 3-point shots in the first half en route to a 122-89 blowout victory. He finished with 31 points, nine rebounds, seven assists and three steals. Kersey had the worst statistical playoff game of his career, going 0 for 8 from the field while managing two points and four rebounds in 20 minutes.

Portland evened the count with a 115-104 overtime victory in Game 2, rallying from a 92-82 deficit with 4 1/2 minutes to play in regulation. Drexler and Kersey both fouled out in overtime, but reserve Danny Ainge scored nine points in the extra session, tying an NBA record.

"The basket got a little smaller (for the Bulls)," Ainge said, "and we were able to get back into it."

Back in Portland, the Blazers could muster little offense in a 94-84 Game-3 loss, matching a franchise low for points in a playoff game. They came back to win Game 4, winning 93-88 after falling behind 10-0 and 18-5 at the start. Kersey has his best game of the series with 21 points, making 8 of 12 shots while contributing five assists, four rebounds and two steals.

Jordan wasn't going to let the Bulls lose Game 5 at the Coliseum. He scored 46 points and the Bulls shot .548 from the field in a 119-106 triumph.

The Bulls returned to Chicago hoping to close out the series in Game 6, but the Blazers ruled the action through three quarters, leading by 17 points until the final seconds of the third quarter and taking a 79-64 advantage into the final period. Back home in Portland, fans watching on TV were whooping it up and looking forward to a Game 7.

It was not to be. With Jordan and most of the Chicago starters taking a blow on the bench, Scottie Pippen and reserves Bobby Hansen, Scott Williams, B.J. Armstrong and Stacey King put together an 18-4 run to get the Bulls to within 83-82 with 5:57 remaining. Five straight calls by the officials seemed to go against the Blazers, who wound up on the short end of a stunning 97-93 decision.

"It's hard to play against more than five people," groused Kersey, who led the Blazers with 24 points and nine rebounds. "It seemed like (the referees) wanted Chicago to win."

Buck Williams was more magnanimous: "The Bulls came out and showed the world they're the best team tonight."

ANOTHER NBA FINALS appearance had ended in disappointment in Rip City. In the weeks following, talk turned to whether it was time to break up the Blazers.

"It would be ridiculous to break us up," Kersey said. "We're right there. We have a lot of guys in our prime. As long as you have the capability to win it, one of these years you'll crack through."

Portland's veterans had great chemistry amongst them that had made them the Western Conference's top team for three years. Kersey was in the middle of it all.

"Jerome was extremely tight with Terry (Porter) and Duck (Kevin Duckworth)," Clyde Drexler says today. "He and Duck were like two brothers on the planes and buses. Sometimes you had to separate them. They were so funny.

"But our whole team was close. It was truly a family atmosphere. It was the best of times. We were always trying to be better than the best team. That's a tough pursuit, to be the last team standing. We put in the effort and work. We didn't get the ultimate reward, but we were always around there. And Jerome was a beloved member of our team.

"A lot of guys on other teams would say, 'When we played you, we knew it was going to be a long night.' When you have guys like Jerome and Buck, you know that was true. We played hard every night. That's how our team was characterized. (Opponents) knew you'd better put in some work to beat our guys."

Jerome dunking on the Lakers' Elden Campbell. *Courtesy Portland Trail Blazers*

Jerome dunks on Philadelphia's Charles Barkley in 1986. The two became good friends during their years together in the NBA. *Courtesy Portland Trail Blazers*

Jerome launches fallaway jumper over future Hall-of-Famers James Worthy and Kareem Abdul-Jabbar of the Los Angeles Lakers in 1987. *Courtesy Portland Trail Blazers*

Jerome and Terry Porter fawn over new-born Taylor Harris in 1988. At left is the baby's mother, Susan Harris, ex-wife of Jerome's close friend J.R. Harris. *Courtesy J.R. Harris*

Jerome elevates to slam one down against Sacramento in 1988. In background are the Kings' Reggie Theus and Blazers' superstar Clyde Drexler. *Courtesy Portland Trail Blazers*

Jerome fires up a jump shot from the baseline in 1989. Kersey wasn't a pure shooter, but worked hard to improve and got better during his NBA career. *Courtesy Portland Trail Blazers*

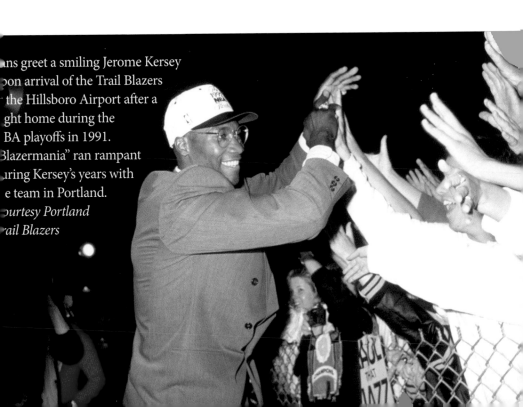

ans greet a smiling Jerome Kersey
on arrival of the Trail Blazers
the Hillsboro Airport after a
ght home during the
BA playoffs in 1991.
Blazermania" ran rampant
uring Kersey's years with
e team in Portland.
ourtesy Portland
ail Blazers

The starting five — from left, Buck Williams, Kevin Duckworth, Jerome Kersey, Clyde Drexler and Terry Porter — during the 1992 NBA Finals against Michael Jordan and the Chicago Bulls. *Courtesy Portland Trail Blazers*

Bird's-eye view of Jerome jockeying for position under the basket with Dennis Rodman, then with the San Antonio Spurs, in 1994. *Courtesy Portland Trail Blazers*

Jerome battles A.C. Green (left) and Charles Barkley of the Phoenix Suns for rebound positioning during the 1995 playoffs. *Courtesy Portland Trail Blazers*

Jerome smokes victory cigar as he and San Antonio teammate Gerard King celebrate after the Spurs wrap up the 1999 NBA championship. *Courtesy Mitch Walker*

Jerome with golfing partners (from left) Terry Porter, Mike Tudor, Ron Sloy. Kersey started out as a 25-handicapper but improved his game enough through the years to get it down to single digits. *Courtesy Ron Sloy*

Jerome and Kevin Duckworth serve food to homeless during the Trail Blazers' annual "Harvest Dinner" before Thanksgiving at the Rose Garden in 2007.
Courtesy Portland Trail Blazers

Teri and Jerome Kersey.
Courtesy Teri Kersey Valentine

Jerome reads to schoolchildren as part of the Trail Blazers' SMART (Start Making a Reader today) program. Jerome served in various public outreach roles for the Blazers after his playing career. *Courtesy Portland Trail Blazers*

Jerome relaxes with former Blazer Brian Grant around the fire pit in 2014. *Courtesy Teri Kersey Valentine*

Kiara Kersey, at age 3, with her papa Jerome in 1997.
Courtesy Anjela Stellato

Jerome touches the left hand of his granddaughter, Harley Rae Kersey, shortly after her birth in 2014.
Courtesy Teri Kersey Valentine

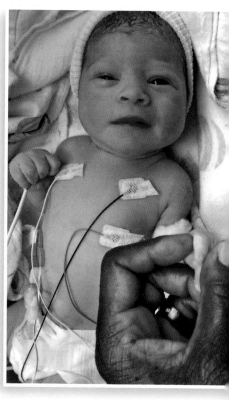

Kiara Kersey with her daughter, Harley, at age six in 2021. *Courtesy Kiara Kersey*

Chapter Fourteen

Downward Turn

Three seasons in a row, the Trail Blazers had arrived at the steps of the NBA throne — or close to them — without experiencing the grand, glorious look down as champions.

The first near miss, an unexpected berth in the 1990 finals, gave much hope for a title to follow. The Western Conference finals loss to the Lakers the next year was a shock to the team that had posted the best regular-season record in the NBA, but it firmed the Blazers' resolve to get the job completed in 1992. Now they had been stopped short of their goal again, victims of Michael Jordan, the Chicago Bulls and, perhaps, fate.

The Blazers had averaged nearly 60 regular-season wins and taken home two conference titles over three seasons, but they couldn't get over the hump. Against the Bulls, Clyde Drexler had averaged 24.8 points but shot only .407 from the field. Terry Porter — so good in the clutch so many times over three playoff runs — was simply another player, averaging 16.1 points and 4.7 assists. Jerome Kersey was the only Blazer who stepped up his game in the Finals. He averaged 16.2 points while shooting .510 from the field. Over the final three series in the 1992 postseason, Kersey led the Blazers in rebounding 10 times.

The Blazers picked up the one-year option on the contract of Rick Adelman but did not grant him an extension, leaving the coach with lame-duck status entering the 1992-93 campaign. Could it really be that owner Paul Allen was dissatisfied with a coach who had gotten his team to the Finals in two of his first three full seasons?

Still, Portland appeared to be in the thick of things in the hunt for the NBA championship. All of the rotation players returned except Danny Ainge, who signed a free-agent contract with Phoenix, and reserve center Wayne Cooper, who retired. The Blazers added talented point guard Rod Strickland and free-agent swing man Mario Elie, who could play shooting guard and small forward.

Everyone was still in what seemed to be the prime of his career except Buck Williams, who would turn 33 in March. Drexler and Kersey were 30, Porter and Elie were 29, Kevin Duckworth was 28 and Strickland and Cliff Robinson were 26.

Kersey, Williams, Duckworth, Drexler and Porter were heading into their fourth year as a starting unit. With balloon payments for Drexler and Williams set for future seasons, Kersey — beginning a four-year contract extension that called for him to make $11 million — would be the highest-paid Blazer for the 1992-93 campaign at about $2.5 million.

"We think he will be a productive player over the next four years," Geoff Petrie, Portland's vice president/operations. "Every player goes through an evolutionary process over the course of his career. Jerome has become a smarter player, and he has become so comfortable playing with our other starters. We want to maintain that group. Besides, Jerome is such a competitor. He's a guy you want to go to war with."

Over the summer, Kersey underwent surgery to remove bone spurs from his right ankle but was back and able to take part in the first intrasquad scrimmage.

"I was surprised Jerome was able to practice," Adelman said. "That's a good sign."

"Last year before every game, it was like, 'How does it feel? Can you play on it?' " Kersey said. "And after every game it was, 'How's it holding up?' It had been building up for two years, and I wanted to take care of it."

Kersey was facing more competition from the 6-10 Robinson, who in his fourth season was growing into one of the most versatile big men in the game. The previous season, Robinson had come off the bench to average 12.4 points — fourth on the team behind Drexler, Porter and Kersey — and serve as an effective reserve at all three front-line positions.

From the time he arrived in Portland as a second-round draft pick out of Connecticut in 1989, Robinson felt he was good enough to be a starter. Small forward was his most natural position.

"Jerome made Cliff a better player," assistant coach John Wetzel says today. "Cliff was a little upset when he went in the second round. Based on his talent, he should have gone in the first round. Cliff was a bit of an ego guy and thought he was going to take the starting job (at small forward). Jerome said right from the start, 'Uh uh, you're not going to take my minutes. This is my job.'

"Jerome made Cliff work his ass off every day in practice. Jerome never laid down in practice. He was always playing hard. If Cliff didn't play hard, Jerome would have embarrassed him. There was a lot of high intensity between the two of them. They were both competitive."

Williams says today that it was that way from the time Robinson came in as a rookie.

"Cliff was pressing him from Day One," Williams says. "Jerome felt he always had to prove he deserved to be the starter. Jerome held Cliff off for as long as he could.

"In practice, Jerome's thing was, 'I'm the starter. If you get to the point where I am, maybe you will be a starter.' Cliff always thought he was the better 3-man, but Jerome had so much grit and determination, Cliff couldn't take it over for quite a while. But at some point, he was

6-10, with a huge wingspan and good 3-point range — hey, Cliff could do it all. And that was difficult for Jerome because he felt he would always start for the team.

"It was an interesting practice session when those two would go at it. It would get very physical, but they remained good teammates. They understood the business. Jerome pushed Cliff, and Cliff pushed him, too. He made Cliff earn what he got, and he became a better player playing against Jerome in practice."

Kersey held on to the starting spot through most of the 1992-93 season, and Robinson played well enough off the bench to claim the NBA's Sixth Man of the Year Award.

Drexler was coming off a fabulous season in which he was second in voting behind Michael Jordan for the NBA's Most Valuable Player Award and was a member of the Dream Team that won the Olympic gold medal in Barcelona. Clyde had arthroscopic knee surgery after he returned to Portland in September and missed most of the preseason but was ready to go when the Blazers took the court for their regular-season opener on November 8, 1992.

The acquisition of Strickland, though, meant Drexler wouldn't have to play as many minutes as he did in 1991-92. The idea was to give him more rest and let Porter pair up with Strickland in the backcourt.

"Our core group has been together really only three years," Adelman said before the season. "We've progressed more than any team other than the Bulls over that span. Our future is now."

THE BLAZERS rolled to an 8-0 start to the 1992-93 campaign, including victories over Phoenix, Cleveland, New York and San Antonio, all bound for the playoffs. In a 130-116 win over Golden State, Terry Porter set an NBA record with seven 3-point baskets and scored a franchise-record 25 points in the fourth quarter.

"We've got so much balance on this team," coach Rick Adelman marveled. "It's a different guy coming through every time. It doesn't matter who scores."

Phoenix, led by offseason acquisitions Charles Barkley and Danny Ainge, stopped the streak with a 121-117 home win. Kersey had his best offensive production of the young season with 23 points.

But there were warning signs. Kersey had developed patellar tendinitis in his left knee.

"I expected to come into this year healthier than I am — no aches or pains," he said. "I am getting a little frustrated. You're seeing me take more jump shots because I just don't have the explosiveness right now to drive."

On December 4, Kersey went on the injured list. He would remain there until January 2 and missed 15 of 16 games through the process of recovery. By the time he recovered, Kersey's value was evident. Since the start of the 1990-91 season, Portland was 123-38 with him in the starting lineup, 10-12 when he was missing.

On December 30, Clyde Drexler joined him on the injured list with tendinitis in his right knee. He wound wind up sitting out 33 games through the remainder of the regular season.

Kersey returned on January 3 for a 103-101 overtime loss to Houston, totaling 13 points, seven rebounds and five steals in 37 minutes before fouling out in the extra session. Hakeem Olajuwon stole the show with 40 points, nine rebounds and 10 blocks.

The Blazers opened a three-game Texas trip by drilling Dallas 109-95, as Kersey scored a team-high 17 points with nine rebounds. He also sent a driving layup by Doug Smith back toward midcourt.

"That play was so typical of Jerome," Adelman said. "They were coming in there for an easy basket and he sends it the other way. It's good that he's not having any problems and is playing very well for being out so long."

Soon Drexler returned and the Blazers put together a six-game win streak to improve to 28-11 and overhaul Seattle (27-12) for the Pacific Division lead.

But near the end of that streak came an incident that would put a tarnish on the reputations of four players and cause considerable embarrassment to the Blazers organization.

ON TRIPS to play games against Utah, the Blazers would always stay at the Marriott Hotel in downtown Salt Lake City. It was adjacent to a shopping mall, where there was usually a bustling amount of activity.

On January 23, 1993, the night before Portland was to play the Jazz at the Delta Center, that was the case. Some of that activity spilled into the halls of the Marriott. The next night, the Blazers knocked off the Jazz 124-113 behind 28 points and eight rebounds from Clyde Drexler. Two days later, a police report was released that delivered allegations of sexual misconduct by Blazer rookies Dave Johnson, Reggie Smith and Tracy Murray … and veteran Jerome Kersey.

According to the report, one 16-year-old girl said she had sex with Johnson, Smith and Kersey. Another 16-year-old said she felt forced by the other player, Murray, to have sex with her. The two girls said they spent the night in the players' rooms.

The investigation ensued for more than two weeks. On February 11, the Salt Lake County attorney announced that the four players would not be charged with criminal conduct. In a press conference, David Yocum said he had decided against filing felony charges because didn't think he could prove "beyond reasonable doubt" that the girls were enticed or coerced. He said he told the girls he believed he could win if the players were charged with a misdemeanor — contributing to the delinquency of a minor. If convicted, the players would have been subject to six months in jail and a $1,000 fine.

The girls were unwilling to go through what would have been a highly publicized jury trial for a potential misdemeanor conviction.

"I'm firmly convinced there were sexual relations between the players and the girls," Yocum said. If the evidence had been strong enough, he added, he might have pressed first-degree felony charges. That would have been rape, which carries a possible five years to life sentence in the state prison.

The age of consent at the time in Utah was 16. One of the girls told the players she was 17 and another said she was 19. One of the girls said she had sex with Kersey at about 1 a.m. in Johnson's room after first having sex with Johnson. Both of the girls said they had been in Kersey's room earlier in the evening.

A third girl, aged 15, said she was with the other two but chose not to have sex with the players. Yocom said if she had, the player would have been charged with a third-degree felony for unlawful sexual intercourse.

Kersey and Smith issued apologies for their involvement, but Kersey denied that sex was involved: "I met the girls, but that was it." His attorney, Kevin Kurumada, said the girls may have briefly been in Kersey's room but that Jerome "was not involved in any way, shape or form with these individuals."

The players were fined by the Blazers —Murray and Johnson $20,000 apiece, Kersey and Smith $15,000 apiece. Murray and Johnson were also suspended for three games for "breaches of policies and team rules."

"Based on our review of the information available to us, we had to make judgments we felt were appropriate," Geoff Petrie, the Blazers' vice president/operations, said at a press conference. "In the case of Jerome and Reggie, we did not feel their involvement merited a suspension."

Petrie said club management was relieved no charges would be filed but was concerned about what he called "gross errors in judgment" by the players.

Asked by media about it, Kersey said he'd used "very poor judgment." He declined to elaborate, saying, "I've given my lawyer my version. We're heard the other version 100 times. Just because we don't say anything doesn't mean what the girls say is right."

Kurumada said Kersey "saw some girls in the hall, and they asked directions, and he went into his room with teammates. At one point, when he was inside his room with other teammates, the girls knocked on the door and came in and wanted to talk. He called security. They came up and the girls were asked to leave. He was never socializing with these people. They were there for about five minutes."

Five years later, Kersey would speak with Hoke Currie about the incident. He denied having sex with the girls.

"It was the day before a game," Kersey said then. "These girls were running through the hall. I actually called security because they were knocking on doors. It was kind of baffling. After we got back to Portland, I got a call from Horace Balmer (the NBA's director of security) and he was talking about this and that. And I'm like, 'No!'"

Kersey said he was at a nightclub that night.

"There were two people I met at the club who came back to my room that night, so I couldn't have been where (the girls) say I was," he said. "The two people who were in my room, they said they were with me. During the investigation, they found a lot of other stuff the girls were saying wasn't true."

Kersey told Currie he had trouble coming to grips with the situation.

"For a while, it was like an inner turmoil thing for me," he said. "I just tried to deal with it without telling people like my grandma or close friends. I was like, this can't be happening. It makes you feel violated, that people can say just anything. People automatically go with it because the press says it, or they hear it somewhere. Once the allegation is made, the damage has been done."

A while later, Kersey was asked about it during an appearance on Roy Firestone's nationally syndicated TV talk show.

Said Kersey: "I told Roy, 'One thing you get out of that is you don't think your name is valuable, but you find out how valuable it can be. People are so shallow, when they listen to the media, even if they don't know the truth at the end, they just hear the beginning.'"

After beating Golden State in the next game, the Blazers fell flat while losing to Northwest rival Seattle 108-86, beginning a four-game losing streak.

"It drained a lot of emotional energy that month," Petrie said at the time. "There's no question it cost us some games."

Kersey admitted it was a difficult time for him.

"I didn't sleep for three days," he said. "I was trying to play as you hear all the people's comments. The people who knew me stood behind me. You find out who your real friends are. It was part of the whole falling out with the team. Rick had to take a look at it. You learn from it, though. It helped me grow up. It made me a lot more wary of people."

Currie asked Kersey if his lifestyle — as a young man who liked to party — had caught up with him.

"I was a single guy for all those years," he said. "I had girlfriends along the way. But who cares if Joe Blow dates girls? As a pro athlete, you're so visible. Everybody cares about what you do. If they see you talking to a girl, then automatically you're sleeping with her.

"If you spent 11 years in one place and were in the limelight, I'm quite sure there would be a lot of girls you dated, slept with or whatever. I wasn't married. I wasn't in any serious relationship. I did what any normal adult is going to do, pretty much. Maybe I got a few more curtain calls than other people, but it's like people don't know.

"You're under a microscope. I'm not a saint, but I just try to live my life the way I want to without hurting people. Living in Portland is like being in a goldfish bowl. You have everybody pulling at you."

Kersey was in a serious relationship, of course, for part of that time. At one point, he was engaged to be married to Anjela Stellato.

ON FEBRUARY 26, with the Blazers having lost seven of 10 games, Rick Adelman made changes in his starting lineup, inserting Cliff Robinson at small forward and Mark Bryant at center while moving Kersey and Kevin Duckworth to the bench.

"The status quo isn't working," Adelman said.

In the first game after the changes, Duckworth collected 17 points and nine rebounds in 37 minutes as Portland beat New Jersey 102-91. Robinson had a nice game, too, with 20 points in 42 minutes. Kersey contributed five points on 1-for-6 shooting and five rebounds in 22 minutes.

Two nights later, Portland ended a four-game trip with a 122-110 loss at Boston. Clyde Drexler strained a hamstring and would be out of action for almost a month. Robinson started at center and fouled out in 18 minutes. Mario Elie started at small forward and scored 16 points. Kersey came off the bench and made 1 of 6 shots from the field, scoring four points with two rebounds in 25 minutes.

The Blazers would play .500 ball over the next month. Tracy Murray started several games at small forward with Robinson at power forward. On March 15, Kersey came off the bench to lead the Blazers to a come-from-behind 110-94 win over the Nets, going for seven points, 13 rebounds, three assists, three blocked shots and a bag full of hustle plays in 27 minutes.

"Jerome was incredible," Adelman said. "He just picked everything up, and then Cliff came in and we got really active defensively. That opened up our offense and turned it around for us."

"I'm still searching for exactly what I can do, but I've tried to play hard and hustle," Kersey said. "I think the way I played this game is what they want bench players to do."

Four days later, Kersey had his best game of the season as Portland rallied from four points down inside the final minute of regulation as the Blazers ended Houston's 15-game win streak with a 106-98 victory in overtime. Kersey had 22 points, six rebounds and three assists in 41 minutes off the bench.

A week later, Kersey returned to the starting lineup, collecting 13 points and 11 rebounds in 32 minutes to help the Blazers past Sacramento 113-111. Next game, Kersey had 18 points and a season-high 15 boards in a 122-110 win over the Clippers.

The Blazers would close the season by winning 14 of 20 games. Adelman said he had reinserted Kersey in the starting lineup for defensive intensity: "He has been much more active. He has performed consistently."

"Just when I thought I was back on the bench for good," Kersey said, "here I am in the starting lineup."

Kersey's outside shot had come back "maybe more than ever," he said. "I've been looking to shoot when I'm open. I've been more active moving without the ball; that's the big thing about getting open shots. I would not say I'm 100 percent healthy yet. I've still got a little tendinitis (in the knee), and it's probably not going to go away unless I take a month off."

Drexler, meanwhile, was even more hobbled. After missing 22 games with a sore right knee and a strained left hamstring, he reinjured the hamstring on April 2 against Philadelphia and would miss most of the rest of the regular season. Kersey also missed some time with sore ribs and pleurisy. He came back to spark the Blazers to a critical 105-101 win over San Antonio, collecting 17 points and 16 rebounds in 30 minutes.

The Blazers finished 51-31 and had home-court advantage as the No. 4 seed in the West against the fifth-seeded Spurs.

"They've proved what kind of a team they are, getting to the Finals twice," Spurs coach Larry Brown said. "The only thing they have to do is win it all. If Clyde is healthy and gets his legs back, he might just get them there this time."

Drexler wasn't healthy, though. He sat out the opener of the best-of-five series and the Blazers gave one away, losing 87-86 while missing 14 of 36 free throws. Portland held a 13-point lead with eight minutes to go. The Spurs scored the final eight points, including a pair of free throws by Sean Elliott with 5.3 seconds remaining.

Coming off the bench, Cliff Robinson was 1 for 15 from the field and missed two free throws with 10.9 seconds left that would have given Portland an 88-85 lead. Kersey, starting at small forward, went for a game-high 24 points on 9-for-13 shooting with nine rebounds.

"I'm feeling better than I have all season," he said. "I can do virtually everything on the court I have in the past. I can let it all hang out."

Drexler returned for Game 2 and didn't skip a beat, contributing 21 points, five assists, five rebounds and three steals in a 105-96 win. Jerome didn't start, coming off the bench for 10 points and five rebounds in 18 minutes. "I definitely wanted to play more than 18 minutes," he said, biting his tongue. "I'm just glad we won. That's the main thing."

It was a time of turmoil for Adelman, who missed a practice between Games 2 and 3 to attend the burial of his father in Los Angeles. This happened not long after his wife's sister was killed in a car accident, leaving her two young children for the Adelmans to raise.

Portland lost Games 3 and 4 and was eliminated from the playoffs. In Game 3, the Blazers led by nine points in the fourth quarter but failed to score in the last three minutes, falling 107-101 as the Spurs scored the final nine points. In Game 4, the Blazers rallied from a 15-point halftime deficit only to lose 100-97 in overtime. Kersey had 15 points and 14 rebounds in 23 minutes off the bench.

Jerome was easily the most productive Blazer in the series. He wound up averaging 14.3 points and 8.5 rebounds in 24.5 minutes, shooting a team-best .524 for Portland, which shot .407. Robinson had a miserable series, shooting .262 while averaging 10.3 points and 4.3 rebounds in 32.8 minutes a game.

It was the first time in four years Portland had failed to advance past the first round.

"Because of injuries, we never had continuity, and it hurt us," Drexler said. "It's frustrating because this team never reached its potential."

CHANGE WAS IN THE OFFING as the 1993-94 season began. Off the court, Kersey had recently purchased a black Ferrari Testarossa with black leather interior. "It's my so-called 'pick-me-up,' " he said.

Portland traded center Kevin Duckworth to Washington for small forward Harvey Grant. Mused Kersey: "Harvey's not going to play center, is he? That's crazy. Who's going to guard David Robinson or Hakeem Olajuwon for 48 minutes?"

The answer came a couple of weeks later when Portland signed center Chris Dudley to a free-agent contract. Grant was going to vie for the starting job at small forward with Kersey, Cliff Robinson and Tracy Murray.

Kersey had an excellent preseason and claimed a spot in the starting lineup alongside Chris Dudley and Buck Williams on the front line, with Drexler and Kersey in the backcourt. Robinson, Grant, Murray,

Rod Strickland and Mark Bryant were the mainstays of a deep bench.

"Everybody is talking about Phoenix and Seattle in the West, and it's probably justified," coach Rick Adelman said. "But I don't see why we should be discounted. It's not like it's been five years since we've been there. I don't see any reason why we can't compete with anybody in the league. We're no older than a lot of good teams in this league. Our guys have a lot of basketball left in them."

Good fortune was not on the Blazers' side, though. In the season opener in L.A., the Clippers beat them 97-95 on a Mark Aguirre 3-pointer at the buzzer. Kersey was 3 for 15 from the field and the Blazers shot 36 percent.

After two games, Kersey went to the bench in favor of Grant. In the next game, a 109-102 win over the Lakers, Dudley fractured an ankle and missed most of the rest of the season. Kersey, 6 for 33 shooting in the first three games, turned an ankle in the game. Grant had a big game, making 11 of 20 shots — most from the outside — while scoring 22 points.

Grant was the starter now. Playing as a reserve, things were up and down for Kersey. He had a string where he scored at least 10 points in five of six games but then averaged 4.3 points in only 16 minutes a game on a four-game trip.

"If you don't have any idea how much you're going to play, you can go nuts," he said. "I'm trying to go with the flow and stay positive about the whole thing, but it's tough sometimes. I'm disappointed. I played 11 minutes the other night (in Miami), and it's probably been five years since I played only 11 minutes in a game."

Actually, it had been seven or eight years.

Kersey had his moments. He scored 18 points on 8-for-10 shooting to go with six rebounds and four assists in 22 minutes off the bench in a 117-99 pounding of the Lakers on December 10.

"I think I can still do great things for this team," he said. "It's a matter of being ready when I'm called upon."

But Kersey was frustrated. On December 18, he tossed a towel high in the air as he walked to the bench after being replaced by Robinson midway through the fourth quarter of a 105-95 win over Minnesota, landing not far from the feet of Adelman. The coach walked to where Jerome sat on the bench and made it clear he didn't appreciate the public spectacle.

"Everyone wants to play," Adelman said. "I don't have a problem with that, as long as it's not there for everyone to see. Things like that should be taken care of in the locker room. That's the only thing I told him. I've made it very clear, I'm going to play the guys I want to play, and people have to accept it."

Kersey, who had played as much as 20 minutes only once in the previous 11 games, had four points and no rebounds in 15 minutes against the Timberwolves.

"It's nothing personal," Kersey said afterward. "Having been a larger contributor over the years, it's just hard. I'm trying to fit into my role as best I can. I just think I can give this team more than I'm being allowed to give."

Said Adelman: "Jerome is going to be fine. I've known him for too long. He's going to come out and work his tail off and get us some energy going. That's just part of him."

Years later, Kersey would say, "I just had to vent. I didn't care at that point. I wasn't playing well. I felt I was getting jerked around. At that point, I was like, 'Trade me, whatever. Just let me go.'"

With Grant injured, Kersey got a rare start on December 29 in a 114-98 win over the Clippers at MC and had a big game — 10 points, 12 rebounds, five blocks and four steals in 32 frenetic minutes.

But mostly, he was a reserve now. Terry Porter was, too, supplanted by Strickland at point guard in January.

On March 4, after playing four minutes and sitting out the entire second half of the Blazers' 115-96 win over Chicago, Kersey told a reporter he'd had enough.

"I want out of here, and you can quote me on that," he said. "I can't take any more of this, and you can quote me on that, too. They've got to do something."

After a 122-99 victory over Utah on March 9, Portland was 38-22 and in position to make a deep run in the playoffs. Grant was starting at small forward and Murray — who would lead the NBA in 3-point percentage — was getting his minutes, too.

"I know Jerome wants to play more, and I want him to feel that way," Adelman said. "I know however much he plays, he'll give us everything he has. I just get real tired when you're on a roll and have won eight of nine and the only issue that comes up is somebody not getting enough minutes."

Then things turned. In a 110-102 loss at San Antonio — Portland's fourth in a row — Kersey got a DNP-CD (did not play/coach's decision) for the first time since his rookie season.

"It's a weird feeling," said Kersey, who had played an average of 10.4 minutes in the previous 14 games. "Some guys tell you that time will come when you don't play at all, but I didn't expect it. I don't think my game has gone down at all. Tracy is playing well, but I think I can do things that can help us win. That's the frustrating thing. I'm not mad at anybody. I just want to play. I'd rather stay here than play anywhere else. I want to earn my money and be a contributor to this team."

On March 22, Kersey scored 15 points and made two free throws with 30 seconds left to help the Blazers, who had lost five of the previous six games and trailed by 16 points in the third quarter, past Sacramento 96-94.

"Jerome was terrific," Adelman said. "He was the one who set the tone and brought us back."

It was up and down for Kersey, who started in a 111-109 loss to Milwaukee, then didn't play in the first half and had two points in five minutes of a 111-100 win over Philadelphia.

He kept his humor up. In a 105-100 win over the Lakers on April 15, Kersey stripped Vlade Divac of the ball, raced downcourt on a fast-break and tripped over his own feet to turn the ball over.

"I was about to make a vintage dunk, but the laws of gravity caught up with me, coupled with the inanimate object of a shoelace," he said after scoring 12 points on 6-for-9 shooting with nine rebounds in 26 minutes of the victory. "If this was football, it would have been a first down. I controlled it and we went more than 10 yards."

Said Drexler: "That performance was vintage Jerome. He was everywhere in this game — rebounding, defending and making tough shots."

In a 119-110 home loss to Houston on April 17, Kersey was spectacular, leading the Blazers with 24 points and 11 rebounds. The fans cheered every second and cried for more.

"That makes me feel great," said Kersey, who had shot 50 percent or better seven times in an eight-game period. "They've been real supportive. It's nice to know people want to see you out there and acknowledge what you're trying to do. I think I can be effective come playoff time."

He didn't get the chance. The Blazers, who stumbled to a 7-13 record over the final 20 regular-season games, entered the postseason as the No. 7 seed and faced No. 2 seed Houston, led by center Hakeem Olajuwon.

Adelman went with Robinson, Williams, Grant, Drexler and Strickland in his starting unit. Portland lost the first two games on the road, slipped past the Rockets 118-115 in Game 3 and lost 92-89 in Game 4 for elimination in the best-of-five series. Kersey, a DNP/CD in Game 3, played a total of 38 minutes in the series, making 5 of 16 shots while scoring 11 points with nine rebounds.

IT WAS THE END of an era. Soon after the season, Geoff Petrie resigned as vice president/operations during a meeting with owner Paul Allen and right-hand man Bert Kolde. Petrie wanted clarification of the working relationship between himself, Rick Adelman and Brad Greenberg, the team's director of personnel. Petrie went to bat for Adelman and quit after losing the battle. Four days later, Adelman was fired.

Adelman and Kersey were together for all of Adelman's 10 years coaching in Portland — 4 1/2 as an assistant coach and 5 1/2 as head coach.

"Rick was always the guy helping me out," Kersey told Hoke Currie in 1998. "We were close. He was your friend, your confidante, your coach. He could talk to you more on a one-on-one level, and when he took over as head coach, he was more of a players' coach.

"Rick was a dream to play for. He wouldn't practice you too hard. He wanted you to get your work done and then get out of the gym. I guess you could say he didn't like to beat a dead horse. I really enjoyed playing for him. He was very fair — maybe even too fair, actually. He would give you the benefit of the doubt. He knew when to get on you, but he probably didn't get on us enough sometimes.

"It was funny when Rick would yell. His voice would get shallow. Nobody would laugh, but it was like, 'OK, Rick, are you really yelling at us?' But you knew the point he was trying to make. He was a coach you'd run through a wall for. We wanted him to succeed, and we did succeed when he was there."

Kersey felt Adelman was under pressure to play Harvey Grant during his final season at the Blazer helm.

"I think things were being taken out of Rick's control as coach," Kersey said. "It was disheartening for me to see it. I think (the coaches) were under pressure to play Harvey, because they gave him the starting spot."

That probably wasn't true. Adelman wouldn't have allowed interference from above to affect his decisions on playing time. He always held a soft spot in his heart for Kersey, anyway.

"I think about that team we had," Adelman says today. "Clyde and Terry (Porter) were great players, our leaders in many ways. But Jerome and Buck (Williams) — they were so tough-minded. They set the tone for everything. You always knew Jerome had your back. I can't say enough about Jerome and the player he turned into. He was totally unique, the way he played. So aggressive and so tough-minded."

Jerome with young Kiara at his Portland home. Kiara was the apple of Jerome's eye—until his granddaughter, Harley, was born. *Courtesy Anjela Stellato*

Chapter Fifteen

'Nothing Like It in the World'

ON JULY 19, 1994, Kiara Elizabeth Kersey was born, weighing a strapping 10 pounds, seven ounces, while measuring 21 1/2 inches.

"It's really overwhelming," Jerome Kersey said over lunch with a sportswriter two months after the birth of his only offspring. "Totally. Nothing like it in the world. It feels like, where has this been all my life? Some things have been missing in my life, and definitely, one of them was having a kid."

Grandmother May Kersey "was delighted," Jerome said. Unfortunately, grandfather Herman Kersey had died the previous year.

"One of my biggest regrets is he didn't get a chance to see Kiara," Jerome said. "He just loved babies. I don't know if there would have been enough of the baby to go around."

At two months, Jerome said of Kiara, "She looks around, moves her head around, is cooing … it's a new experience every day. Knowing you're responsible for how they're going to grow up … seeing her change, seeing her wiggle, every little thing they do — what a growing process, for her and for me."

Others noticed as much.

"Jerome always wanted to be a father — always," says Traci Rose, former VP/corporate communications and community relations for the Blazers. "Kiara hung the moon for him. He loved her so much. She was his everything.

"He loved babies anyway. If there were ever a baby anywhere within 50 feet of him, it would be in his arms. I have so many pictures of him with my kids after they were born. He'd take the baby and go into the locker room. When he finally had his own, it was life-changing. His life was forever changed when he became a papa."

The mother was Anjela Stellato, a graduate of Barlow High in suburban Gresham who worked as a flight attendant and had won the "Miss Santa Cruz" beauty pageant in 1989 while attending UC Santa Cruz. Kersey first laid eyes on Anjela when she sang the national anthem before a game at Memorial Coliseum during the Blazers-Lakers playoff series in 1991.

The two met at Huber's Restaurant in downtown Portland the following summer. The place was crowded and the host said he could seat Anjela and a girlfriend if they'd be willing to share a table.

"We moved past the line into Huber's and he took us to a table with eight guys," recalls Stellato, who now lives in Seattle and works for Delta Airlines. "We were getting introduced, and one of the people was Jerome. After he figured out I was the one who sang the anthem the previous year, he kept tapping me on the shoulder wanting to talk to me."

Kersey took her for a quick spin in his new red Ferrari 348 Spider and got the phone number of her parents, with whom she was staying. Within 48 hours, she had taken a yacht ride with him. Soon, they were an item.

By Christmas, she says, they were engaged.

"It was a whirlwind six months," Stellato says. "It was the equivalent of five years of stuff. It was so busy. All the places and events constantly. I was the first girl he brought home to meet his family in Virginia."

It was an on-again, off-again relationship. In late 1993, she became pregnant. Soon thereafter, she moved in with him in his home in sub-urban West Linn.

"We were so excited," she says now. "He wanted children so badly. I wasn't a big fan of living together because of my conservative back-ground. Before he asked me to marry him, I'd only been to his house a few times. I never spent the night there. I didn't want to sleep with him. I think he respected that. We weren't having sex on a regular basis. There were still checks in my heart."

They set a wedding date for the last weekend of August 1994. It was not to happen.

KERSEY WAS less than happy with his status as a reserve with the Blazers during the 1993-94 season.

After six seasons as a starter, he had averaged only 16.4 minutes in a bench role, with two DNP/CDs (did not play/coach's decision). Kersey shot a career-low .433 from the field and averaged 6.5 points — his low since his rookie year — and 4.2 rebounds a game.

"There was no rhyme nor reason to why I wasn't playing last year," Kersey said before the 1994-95 season. "We definitely needed the things I'd been bringing to the team for years. Rick (Adelman) and I never talked about it. I would have taken it better if somebody had just told me, 'You're not going to play,' rather than going into the game thinking I'd worked hard in practice, showed what I can do, and then wind up not playing.

"Rick and I had a wonderful relationship up to that point, but for whatever reason, it totally went sour last season. The frustration of it was just too much. It affected my relationship (with Stellato), my family, my friends. I wanted to be a recluse. After games, I was proba-bly rude to fans at times, and I apologize for that, but … I just wanted to be left alone. I tried not to let it get into my personal life, but I took it home with me. I couldn't leave it on the court."

Kersey felt the 1993-94 Blazers had been a selfish team.

"We didn't play together," he said. "Everybody had his personal agenda. Management takes half the blame, though. They had guys' minds all messed up about, 'Am I going to be here or not?' Three or four starters from the year before were wondering if they were going to be on the team."

There was a new sheriff in town. P.J. Carlesimo had been hired out of Seton Hall as head coach. Kersey said he had a conversation with his new coach and told him if he didn't fit into his plans, he'd like to be traded.

"I'm not going to sit back half the year and swallow it," Kersey said. "I'm not going to let that happen again. I'll be more vocal about my situation."

His first choice, Kersey said, was to stay with the Blazers.

"I'd like to start again," he said. "I'm going to go out there and break my neck — figuratively — to be the best player I can be. If that's not good enough to start, hopefully I can come in and play some significant minutes."

Kersey came to camp in good shape, in part because of working with a personal trainer 2 1/2 hours a day to prepare for a scheduled appearance on "American Gladiators," which was eventually canceled. In late September, without the Blazers' blessings, he joined a Nike team that included Alonzo Mourning and Anfernee Hardaway and visited China, South Korea and Japan. He got fined $20,000 by the Blazers, but the fine was covered by Nike.

With Cliff Robinson holding out in a contract dispute and Harvey Grant recovering from knee surgery, Kersey started most of the preseason. When the Blazers opened the regular season, though, the starting five were Robinson, Buck Williams and Chris Dudley on the front line and Clyde Drexler and Rod Strickland in the backcourt. Kersey and Grant were primed for the most back-up minutes up front, with guards Terry Porter and James Robinson also in the rotation.

"Jerome handled it professionally, but in his mind, he was still a starter," says Dudley, who would play with Kersey his final two seasons in Portland. "That's what you want in a player. He didn't go down without a battle. He'd beat the crap out of you in practice."

Dudley and Kersey shared an agent — Dan Fegan.

"I hit it off with Jerome," Dudley says today. "Got to know him well on and off the court. He was a great guy, a guy who wanted to help everybody. A teammate you wanted to go to battle with. 'Warrior' is a term that is a little overused, but in his case, it was appropriate. I loved playing with him.

"I loved watching him play on those teams that went to the Finals. I remember how hard he went after everything. If there was a loose ball, he was going at it. If there was a sliver on the break, he was going through it and exploding at the rim. He drove that team. Clyde was the best player, but Jerome was the heart."

For many years, Dudley — a diabetic — has run a week-long overnight camp for youths with diabetes.

"Jerome came out a couple of times and was great with the kids," Dudley says. "He also did other stuff for our foundation. One call to Jerome, and it was, 'Just tell me where; I'll be there.' You didn't have to ask him twice."

Dudley — who would remain a Portland resident for many years after his retirement and ran unsuccessfully as the Republican candidate for Oregon governor in 2010 — credits Kersey's upbringing for his character.

"Sometimes those who have a tougher road coming up are the guys who are humble and hungry," Dudley says. "That fits Jerome to a 'T.' He had to work his butt off and made himself into a great NBA player. He was so genuine. Roll up your sleeves and get after it. A great guy to hang out with. That team was so beloved in the community, and Jerome was a big part of that. He was the real deal."

KERSEY SPRAINED an ankle as the Blazers beat Sacramento to go 3-0, and Harvey Grant took advantage by scoring 12 points on 6-for-11 shooting in 25 minutes off the bench. When Kersey returned to action, he had lost his spot in the rotation. In late November and early December, he did not play in five of six games.

Kersey wanted a trade but understood that he was a "base-year" player. That meant he counted for only $550,000 against the Blazers' salary cap, but another team would have to fit his $3.6 million contract under its cap and give back a player who made no more than $550,000, plus 10 percent. Basically, he was untradeable.

There were flickers of success. On January 11, Kersey— who had 16 DNP/CDs in 31 games — came off the bench for 12 points in 17 minutes to help Portland beat Golden State 104-92.

"Jerome's numbers were good, but it's not the points he scored, it's the energy and good defense he played," coach P.J. Carlesimo said. "He gave us a huge lift, got his hands on balls and did what Jerome Kersey has always done — he got us going."

"I may look a bit long in the face sometimes," Kersey told reporters, "but when I hit the court, I'm going to play hard."

On February 17, two days after the Blazers traded Clyde Drexler to Houston, they beat Seattle 114-109. Kersey, playing the entire fourth quarter and 24 minutes in total, chipped in 11 points, seven rebounds, two assists and two steals.

As the season wound down, Carlesimo moved Grant to shooting guard to back up Aaron McKie, who was starting in the absence of Drexler. Kersey returned to the rotation and drew double-figure minutes every game during the last few regular-season contests.

PORTLAND FINISHED the season 44-38 and was the seventh seed in the Western Conference playoffs. That meant a date with the second-seeded Phoenix Suns, led by Charles Barkley and Kevin Johnson. With Barkley averaging 33.7 points and 13.7 rebounds, the Suns swept the Blazers 3-0 in the best-of-five series.

Kersey played well off the bench, serving as Portland's No. 4 scorer in the series with a 12.7-point average while making 16 of 28 shots from the field.

After he had left the Blazers, Kersey spoke about how difficult it had been to be a reserve his last two seasons in Portland.

"Especially the last year, I didn't keep myself in the best condition," he told Hoke Currie in 1998. "I gained to about 248 (pounds). My attitude was, 'I'm not going to do any more than I have to. I ain't playing, so why the heck do I need to be in shape?' "

Kersey didn't make it easy on Carlesimo.

"I was disgruntled the whole year," Kersey said. "It was a continuation of the same thing from the year before. It was like, 'Why should I do any more to make your job easier if you're not going to play me?' By nature, I'm not that way. I'm not vindictive in matters such as that. To be disgruntled all the time — that's not the spirit of the way I live.

"P.J. was a little confrontational. He was an in-your-face coach. And when you're not playing, you don't want to hear it. One night I came out of a game and I threw a towel at the bench. He fined me for it. The next day in practice, he said, 'I fined you only half as much as I could have. Do you want to talk about it?' I was like, 'What are we going to talk about? You've already fined me.' So I just walked away."

Today, though, Carlesimo looks back at his season coaching Kersey with fondness.

"I caught both 'Romey' and 'TP' (Terry Porter) in transition," Carlesimo says. "They were still good, but their minutes were going down. Both of them were real professional about how they treated me. Jerome was always very good to me.

"They had reason to not be happy with me. If you played Jerome 20 minutes, he wanted 25. You played him 30, he wanted 35. He was never happy to be out of a game, but you always knew what you were going to get. Jerome Kersey was a pro, for sure. On the court, he didn't back down from anybody. He represented the franchise really well. He was what the Blazers were all about for a lot of years. You could go into a grocery store or gas station in Portland, and an 85-year-old grandmother would come up and go, 'How come Jerome's not playing?' "

Carlesimo was at Seton Hall when Kersey was in his prime in the early '90s. Carlesimo followed the Blazers closely because one of the players he had coached in college — Mark Bryant — was with them.

"Such a great team," Carlesimo says. "They had Clyde (Drexler), Terry and Buck (Williams), who were all outstanding. They were so much fun to watch. But Jerome was like a highlight film. He ran the floor, he was so strong — I loved the way he played. He went at it hard. He was so good for Portland. Romey epitomized the love affair Portland has with the Blazers."

Two of Carlesimo's assistant coaches that season also held respect for Kersey.

"I considered him a great professional," says current Dallas coach Rick Carlisle, with more than 800 regular-season victories in his 19 seasons as an NBA head coach. "He never wavered in what he stood for and how he played. He always played as hard as he possibly could. He improved his shooting every year. Defensively, he was tough-minded and brought a real edge to the game. I always had great admiration for him when I was with other teams and playing against him and coaching against him.

"I watched those Portland teams when they were really good in the late '80s and early '90s," says Carlisle, who guided the Mavericks to the 2011 NBA championship. "They played with attitude. They got to the Finals those two years because of that attitude. Jerome was a big part of that. He just had a real fighting, warrior-type approach that fueled those teams when they made their run. He could have been an All-Star if (small forward) hadn't been so thick with talent during that period. He was not a good competitor — he was a great one."

Johnny Davis was another young assistant on Carlesimo's staff that season. Davis, who had been a rookie point guard on the Blazers' 1977 championship team, would coach 28 years in the NBA, including head coaching stints with Orlando and Philadelphia. He was the coach assigned to do individual workouts with Kersey.

"Jerome hadn't had a good first half in a game at Philadelphia," Davis recalls. "At halftime, he asked, 'What do you think is wrong?' I said, 'Forget about the first half. You can be the difference for us in the second half. Do everything even harder.' He was already going all out, of course, but he nodded his head and said, 'OK.' He put his head down and was just a beast the second half. He did everything he could to bring us to victory."

The 76ers won that game 86-85, despite 16 points on 7-for-11 shooting in 24 minutes from Kersey.

"You knew Jerome Kersey was going to give you full effort every single night," says Davis, now retired and living in North Carolina. "No nonsense out there. His motor was exceptional. One of the nicest guys off the court you'd want to meet, but a fierce competitor on the floor. He played the game as hard as one could play it, and he did it every night.

"He was a gracious, humble guy, but also very confident. He wasn't a shrinking violet. He did not give an inch to anyone on that floor. The opponents felt him. You better get your rest (the night before) if you're playing Jerome Kersey. If he was your assignment, buckle up. It was going to be nonstop from the opening tip to the final horn.

"I can see why he was a fan favorite in Portland. He was a favorite of mine. He was a basketball player. He did a lot of things to help you win — rebound, run the floor, block shots. He gave you the energy you needed, and he did it all the time. He was great in the locker room. His teammates loved him, and so did the coaching staff."

Carlesimo, Carlisle and Davis would be back with the Blazers for the 1995-96 season. So would Buck Williams. But Kersey would not. Williams and Kersey had played together for five years, four as the starting forwards. You could count the number of offensive plays run for them on one hand.

"We had a lot in common," Williams says today with a chuckle. "During our years together playing for Rick (Adelman), we would isolate and put Duck, Clyde and Terry in a three-man game on one side of the court and leave me and Jerome up high on the other. Jerome and I would stand over there, brooding. We would be cursing out (the coaches) in our minds — pissed off. There was a little conversation going on. Sometimes we'd get so frustrated, we'd run in and get involved in the offense on our own."

In truth, Kersey and Williams knew their roles and fulfilled them well.

"I got lots of kudos for being the final piece when we got to the Finals for the first time (in 1990)," Williams says. "Jerome deserved credit just as much as I did. He was the glue to that team. He was the unsung hero.

"If some guys are not scoring, they're not an asset. Jerome was doing so many other things to make the team better."

Williams and Kersey had similar life stories. Williams was from tiny Rocky Mount, N.C., an hour and a half southeast of Kersey's hometown of Clarksville, Va.

"Jerome and I always had the bond of growing up in the country," says Williams, who would also play 17 NBA seasons and became president of the NBA Players Association. "He'd give me a hard time about farming and growing crops. We related to each other in that way. I loved him. He was one of the greatest teammates I ever had. He was like a little brother of mine."

Williams laughs when asked about Kersey as a bachelor.

"Oh my God," he says. "Weren't too many ladies in Portland who didn't want to date Jerome. Clyde and Terry had to slow him down a little bit. He was the ultimate bachelor around Portland. It was part of his personality. He was so engaging, and the young, single girls loved him. He didn't discriminate at all. Equal opportunity all the way."

Williams loved to razz Kersey about his attire.

"It was a little suspect," Williams says, chuckling again. "One day we were on the bus. Jerome came on with one of those knee-length black leather jackets. We called him 'Shaft.' He said, 'Shut your mouth.' We had a great time kidding him about that. He didn't wear it anymore. We died laughing. I always called him 'Country,' but he was a dresser. He enjoyed trying to be debonair and smooth.

"He had some talent in a lot of areas. He loved cars. He had a little singing career. He just enjoyed life."

Williams and Kersey did have one major difference. Williams, an All-American at Maryland, had been the third selection in the 1981 NBA draft. Kersey was a mid-second-round pick out of Division II Longwood.

"He earned everything he received," Williams says. "He came up the hard way. No one gave him anything. He clawed his way into the NBA and worked his butt off to get himself established. Talk about the American dream. Jerome exemplified that."

A light moment on photo day before training camp for the 1991-92 season. *Courtesy Portland Trail Blazers*

A championship ring at last for Jerome.   *Courtesy Orlando Turner*

Chapter Sixteen

New Teams and Finally a Ring

JEROME KERSEY had spent 11 seasons in Portland. As the 1994-95 season ended, he sensed his time there was over. He was looking to move on and play somewhere else.

"I'd hoped to be able to finish my career here, but I don't think there's going to be room for me with the guys they have," he said. "I think I've been productive when I've gotten the minutes. I'm not that old (33 in June of 1995). I've got a lot of wisdom, and I have a lot of energy left.

"Once (the Blazers) let Clyde (Drexler) go, I wasn't really thinking about staying. We still had a very good team with all of us there, but they wanted to look for younger guys. They said, 'You guys are getting old. We don't want to pay you guys.'"

Having an infant daughter helped Kersey get through his last season with the Blazers.

"Kiara was like the cushion in between game time," he told Hoke

Currie in 1998. "It was nice having my own private home life. I was anguished about even going to practice the next day. I think God put her in my life at that point in time for a reason."

The Blazers were allowed to protect eight players in the June 24, 1995 expansion draft. Kersey was left exposed and the Toronto Raptors took him with the 13th of

the 27 selections. The Blazers were so anxious to get his $4.4 million salary off their books, owner Paul Allen agreed to cover all the salary if the Raptors would take him.

Initially, Kersey was excited about it.

"When Portland didn't protect me, I took it real personal," he would say later. "I thought, 'I can go (to Toronto) and make some noise again. Everything is starting fresh. I can get myself in condition and go up there and show people I can still play.' "

By this time, though, Kersey was having second thoughts about marrying fiancée Anjela Stellato.

"He had gotten a call from Isiah Thomas, who had taken over as GM of the Raptors," she says today. "I said, 'When are we going to have to move?' He looked at me and said, 'What do you mean, we?'

"It threw me for a loop. The next thing was, 'I want to postpone the wedding.' I said, 'Why would we do that? We have Kiara. We have this amazing family. Why would we postpone this?' It was a differing of opinion. I'm sure his head was spinning.

"He wasn't putting me and the baby first. It was his career over me and the baby. It was heartbreaking. It was like he wanted to have his cake and eat it, too. You can't put raising a child on hold."

Years later, Kersey would briefly address the subject with Hoke Currie.

"I had three two-year relationships before Anjela," he said. "I always said I wasn't going to get married until I finished playing basketball, but my plan (with Anjela) was to get married. When we had Kiara, I thought things were right with me and Anjela, but they turned out not to be. I'm quite sure we'd have had three or four kids if things had worked out."

Stellato took baby Kiara and moved out of Jerome's West Linn home.

"He loved me, but I didn't just need the love, I needed the commitment," she says. "His lifestyle put him into a position where every place he went, there was constant temptation. At the end of the day, he could not resist all the temptation.

"If you separate the sexual part, he was a loving, caring human being. He was the best father he could be for being away all the time. We had a workable relationship after we split up."

Kersey and close friend J.R. Harris had many discussions about Stellato.

"He fell in love with her," Harris says. "He moved her into his house. That wasn't a Jerome move right there.

"But there was a problem. (A partner) had to get by the fact that at one point before you met this guy, he was single and well-liked by the ladies. I was with them when a lot of arguments went down. You had to be very confident in who you were if you were going to be dating him. When you were out with him, the games women play — she had to deal with some of that. That was tough for Anjela. It would have been tough for anybody."

Says another of Kersey's close friends, Kevin Brandon: "Some of it was, Jerome wasn't settled in his life at the time. Anjela is a very strong-willed woman. Jerome is not going to allow anyone to show him the way to go. He absolutely did love her, but they just couldn't mesh."

Stellato stayed in Portland, and Jerome enjoyed his time with Kiara when he was in town.

"Kiara had him wrapped around her little finger," Anjela says. "She was his everything. She ruled the roost, for sure. He was more harsh with his words than his hand. He didn't like raising a hand to her. That was how both of us were raised. We both decided a pat on the butt or a timeout in the corner was all we were going to do for discipline.

"That little girl never wanted for anything. It was whatever she needed whenever she needed it, to the point where I'd have to tell Jerome, 'This is too much.' He was big on holidays and birthdays. We were very cordial and caring as far as Kiara was concerned. He always wished we would be around more, but his lifestyle was his lifestyle. He lived in a lot of different places. We stayed put in Portland."

KERSEY SPOKE with Isiah Thomas a couple of times after being chosen by the Raptors in the expansion draft.

"They didn't have much (salary) cap room," Kersey said later. "Isiah said, 'We'd like to sign a couple of more guys. You can come up to camp, but we're going to let you go. I'd rather tell you now and you can go out and choose another team.' "

Rick Adelman, meanwhile, had been hired by Golden State to coach the Warriors.

Said Kersey: "I thought, 'Oakland is close to Portland, and I can still see my daughter. I can play for a coaching staff I'm familiar with, a coach who knows what I can do. I know what the coach's philosophy is.' So I opted to go to Golden State and play for the minimum (salary)."

On his way out of Portland, Kersey was gracious.

"I've had an illustrious career here — a lot longer career with one team than I expected," he said. "I met a lot of great people working with the Blazer organization. I like our fans and it's been a wonderful city to live in. I'm not going to leave with any bitterness or hard feelings.

"This will be like a resurgence for me. I have a lot of quality time left in me. I'm going to play at least two more seasons after this year."

Kersey would play six more NBA seasons — though only one with the Warriors. Jerome started 58 games and averaged 6.7 points and 4.8 rebounds, shooting a career-low .410 from the field while playing an average of 21.3 minutes on a team that struggled to a 36-46 record.

"Rick had his hands tied a little bit," Kersey would say. "He had a lot of forwards. Donyell Marshall was playing with a big contract. Chris Mullin and Rony Seikaly were there, and Kevin Willis came in (after the trade deadline). That was probably my toughest year because we weren't winning."

Adelman, though, was glad to have him.

"The players didn't like Jerome at all," Adelman says with a chuckle. "He played too hard. He played so hard in practice. Some of those guys didn't appreciate that."

The Warriors' best player that season was guard Latrell Sprewell, who later famously would wrap his hands around P.J. Carlesimo's neck, resulting in a 68-game suspension.

"Jerome got into it with Sprewell," Adelman recalls. "He wasn't antagonizing anybody; that's the way he played. That's why I wanted him at Golden State with us. One practice, Sprewell got after a rebound and Jerome went after it, too. (Kersey) came over his back and Sprewell just went off. He couldn't believe Jerome. He didn't like it. That's just who Jerome was. He wasn't going to back down from anybody."

Adelman hadn't planned on Kersey being a starter.

"Rick didn't have any intentions of him taking anybody's position," assistant coach John Wetzel says. "He wanted him to come in and play hard and practice hard and be an example."

Marshall was ticketed to be the starter at small forward.

"Jerome did what Jerome does and took the job," Wetzel says. "He became the starter and Donyell came off the bench. We were getting ready to scrimmage one day. We had a jump ball and Jerome said to Donyell, 'I'm going to put you in 'mix' today. I'm going to kick your ass. Let's get after it.' Donyell's reaction was, 'Jerome, don't rough me up.' "

AFTER THE 1995-96 season, Kersey signed another one-year free-agent contract, this time with the Los Angeles Lakers, featuring 24-year-old center Shaquille O'Neal — in his first season with the team — and an 18-year-old rookie guard named Kobe Bryant.

"It was a chance to play for a quality organization," Kersey explained in 1998. "It was a very young team with a chance to win a title — as good a chance as anybody. We had Shaq coming in. We had Eddie Jones, Nick Van Exel, Elden Campbell, and the mystique of the Lakers. I'd played against them for all those years. People were like, 'What? You're playing for the Lakers?' I'd had some of my best games against them."

Kersey started 44 games alongside Shaq and Campbell on a big, powerful front line. Van Exel and Jones were the starting backcourt, with a deep reserve corps that included Bryant, veteran guard Byron Scott and sweet-shooting forward Robert Horry.

The Lakers finished the regular season with a 56-26 record, with Kersey averaging 6.8 points and 5.2 rebounds in 25.2 minutes per game. As the No. 4 seed in the Western Conference, they beat the fifth-seeded Trail Blazers 3-1 in a best-of-five first-round series, then lost in five games to Utah in the West semifinals. In nine playoff games, Kersey averaged 5.4 points and 5.3 rebounds in 23.3 minutes off the bench and shot .486 from the field — the latter figure second only to Shaq's .514 on the Lakers.

Kersey enjoyed playing for coach Del Harris.

"He had an old-school mentality," Kersey said in 1998. "He was fair with me, appreciated what I did on the court. He was coaching a lot of young guys. That will drive you crazy sometime."

One of them was Bryant, of whom Kersey said this: "One of the best talents I've seen at that age. He works hard."

The next stop for Kersey was Seattle, another team with a chance to win it all. The Sonics had gone 57-25 in 1996-97, losing to Houston in seven games in the West semifinals. That was a year after taking the Chicago Bulls to six games in the NBA Finals.

Like Adelman, Seattle coach George Karl savored Kersey's physicality and work ethic.

"There are certain players — and Jerome is one of them — who know how to play hard every night," Karl said upon signing him. "He's one of the tougher guys in the league. Physically and mentally, he has very little fear of any challenge. He has tremendous courage and mental toughness that will be an asset to us when the playoffs begin."

The Sonics, led by All-Stars Gary Payton and Vin Baker, finished the 1997-98 regular season 61-21 and were the No. 2 seed in the loaded Western Conference. They got by the upstart Minnesota Timberwolves 3-2 in a best-of-five first-round series but fell in five games to the Lakers in the West semis.

Kersey suffered a stress fracture to his left foot that caused him to miss half of the regular season. He came off the bench in all but two of his 37 regular-season games, averaging 6.3 points and 3.6 rebounds in 19.4 minutes while dividing time with sharpshooter Dale Ellis. Karl started Kersey, however, in all five playoff games against the Timberwolves. Jerome averaged 7.8 points and 3.4 rebounds while shooting .485 from the field in 22.2 minutes per game.

Kersey wound up defending 6-4 southpaw Anthony Peeler in Minnesota's three-guard starting lineup while Detlef Schrempf took on 7-foot Kevin Garnett.

"Detlef covered certain guys better than other guys, but he did a good job on Garnett," Karl says today. "Jerome took the 'A' assignment and Detlef took the 'B.' "

Kersey returned to a reserve role against the Lakers but played well, averaging 7.8 points and 4.6 rebounds in 20.4 minutes.

"Jerome was not the best player at remembering plays," Karl says. "It didn't matter, because he knew how to play. You wanted him to be more creative and innovative and active rather than giving him mental assignments or a detailed play.

"I loved his energy. He was a happy guy. He was good in the locker room, good with his teammates. He had lost some of his athleticism as he got bigger. He was so athletic when he was coming up. I remember writing a scouting report and thinking, 'I'm happy he is finding a jump shot, because he is going away from what he does really well, and that's going to the basket.' I loved when he played with (Clyde) Drexler and (Terry) Porter. They played smart and fast and hungry, and they were athletic as hell — top three all-time of all the teams I can remember in that department."

Karl was disappointed when Kersey got hurt that season.

"I would have wanted him to have been a larger part of our team's personality," the coach says. "He didn't meet the enthusiasm I had when we got him, but we still loved him. It was just his attitude, his daily positivity, his daily energy. Guys like Jerome are so valuable to

NBA teams. They're not flashy; just everyday, blue-collar guys who get the job done."

Karl says he enjoyed coaching Kersey.

"He was accommodating," Karl says. "I'm a guy who can be a little gritty in criticism, but I can also be funny. He made me more funny than gritty. He made you feel good even though you might be in a three-game losing streak. His presence was happy. In the same sense, he was a serious SOB."

Kersey was appreciated by Karl's assistant coaches, too.

"Jerome would be a '3 and D' in today's game — a power 3 and small 4," says Dwane Casey, now head coach of the Detroit Pistons, the reference to a 3-point shooter and defender. "We loved his competitive spirit. He'd take on one of the toughest offensive players on the other team. I don't know how many times he'd get into it with the other team's players. I remember breaking up a lot of fights on the court. Any time somebody on the other team got hot, we'd send Jerome in to cool him off. If we needed toughness and physicality, we wouldn't hesitate to put Jerome in.

"He was a mentor to our young guys, talking about being a pro and his work ethic. He'd set the tone in practice. I wish we'd had him the year we went to the (1996) Finals. It would have given us another body to go against (Michael) Jordan."

Casey was the coach tasked with doing individual workouts with Kersey.

"Being a young coach, I appreciated him having the patience to work out with me," Casey says. "He was a joy for me to work with. I probably learned more from him than he learned from me."

Casey says he enjoyed Kersey as a person, too.

"He was a beautiful guy — serious-minded on the court, but always with a quick smile off the court," Casey says. "All the guys loved him. There were so many positive things. He brought everything to the table we were looking for."

Terry Stotts was an assistant coach on two staffs that had Kersey

— in Seattle in 1997-98 and again with Milwaukee in 2000-01, Kersey's last NBA season.

"Jerome was a role player for us in those years at the end of his career," says Stotts, now coach of the Portland Trail Blazers. "He was a guy who led by example. Even at that age, he was competing for minutes, because he loved to play."

Stotts remembered Kersey well from his prime years in Portland.

"Jerome was the Blazers' Nate McMillan," Stotts says, the comparison to the longtime Sonic swing man. "The fans loved how hard he played, how hard he competed, how he defended. He excelled in that role."

Casey concurs with the comparison.

"Jerome and Nate would both get into scuffles," Casey says. "They were both tough, serious-minded guys. Both of them loved to win. Jerome was a little bigger and stronger than Nate, but they were similar type of players and shooters. I have a picture in my office at home in Seattle of Nate and Jerome walking on the court together. Love that picture."

McMillan, known as "Mr. Sonic" during his playing days in Seattle, spent all 12 of his NBA seasons with the Sonics. Does he agree with the coaches' observations?

"Absolutely," he says. "I would compare myself and my career to Kersey's. He was a glue guy. He wasn't the star on the team, but he kept the team going. He didn't put up big numbers with the Blazers, but for them to have the success that they had, he was a major part of that. You need those type of guys to have success in the NBA."

Kersey and McMillan played the one year together in Seattle. It was Nate's final NBA season. They squared off against each other for many years in the Pacific Division.

"Jerome was a hard-hat guy for the team that was our rival," says McMillan, who would go on to be an NBA head coach for 17 years with Seattle, Portland and Indiana.

"He did a lot of dirty work. He didn't say much. His play did his talking. He was fearless. He threw his body around. You had to prepare for Jerome as much as you had to prepare for Clyde (Drexler) and Terry (Porter) and the rest of those guys. He battled everybody — with us, it was mainly Xavier (McDaniel). Those guys didn't like each other.

"Jerome could be a pest out there, getting up under people's skin. He would frustrate you because of the way he played. He played reckless. If he was going to get to a spot, he wasn't going to allow you to it first. He was going to get out in transition and run hard."

McMillan was glad to get to be a teammate of Kersey's, just as he was with another former Blazer — Maurice Lucas, who played with the Sonics in 1986-87, McMillan's rookie year.

"They would become two of my closest friends in the NBA," McMillan says. "On the floor, Jerome wasn't a trash talker, but he didn't back down. He got up into your face and he played you hard. He didn't think anyone could outwork him.

"Off the floor, he was one of the nicest guys I've ever met. He was the guy who introduced me to sushi. When we'd travel, he'd invite me to go out and eat. He was a kindhearted, respectful, humble guy. Didn't have a mean streak at all in him — off the court."

Hersey Hawkins, the Sonics' starting shooting guard that season, remembers Kersey in much the same way as McMillan.

"Jerome was older and had seen a lot through his years, and he was able to teach our younger guys how things should be done," Hawkins says. "He was going to give you 110 percent, and if you were going up against him, you had to match his aggressiveness and tenacity. He was going to bring it every possession. If there was a loose ball, you better be ready, because he was going to go get it.

"He was an endearing guy to be around in the locker room. There are people who are magnets for others. People want to be around them because they're encouraging and positive. That was Jerome. He'd give it to you as well. He'd joke, he'd mess around with you, but it was always something that you could take."

As he neared the end of his playing career, Kersey rediscovered his religious roots.

"I was raised a Southern Baptist," he said. "Whether I wanted to go to church or not, my grandmother instilled that in me. Last summer, I start-ed going to a church with (friend) Kevin Brandon and his family. I enjoyed it. It's fulfilling for me. You feel so enlightened after you go to church.

"My grandmother is always praying for me. I do the same for her. I'm not a Bible thumper. I've read different versions of the Bible three times. Last summer, the first thing I would do every morning was read the Bible. It's soothing. It helped my overall day. It became a ritual. I go to chapel before games. It gives you a religious base. God has given me the skill level to play in the NBA. You have to give thanks where thanks should be given."

THE NEXT YEAR, Kersey was off to San Antonio, where he would spend two seasons — and win the only championship of his career in the lockout-shortened 1999 season. The Spurs were coached by a young Gregg Popovich and led by twin towers — the veteran David Robinson and second-year pro Tim Duncan. During that season, Kersey averaged only 3.2 points, 2.9 rebounds and 15.5 minutes in 45 regular-season games. The next season, at age 37, he had a bigger role, starting 18 games and averaging 4.5 points and 3.1 rebounds in 18.2 minutes through 72 regular-season contests.

"Jerome's role was diminished, even though his efficiency ratings were high," close friend Mitch Walker says. 'He wanted to play more. He was always a team-first guy, but he said, 'I got to get some more clock.' He was a gamer.

"Pop loved him to death. He'd talk to him on the side, and say, 'I'm going to try to get you some more minutes.' Jerome would tell him, 'Don't worry about it; I'm here to support the younger guys.' He was the best teammate you could ever have, whether a starter or coming off the bench and not playing a lot of minutes."

The first season — the first of Popovich's five title runs — Kersey proved a good role model for the Spurs' young group.

"He was consistently professional," Popovich said in 2015 after Kersey's death. "Every game he came out and laid it on the line. That infused into everybody. He was very important in the maturation and establishment of a culture. He was a warrior for us. He shot it pretty good, he was a decent scorer, but mostly he was a heck of a teammate. He was a rough-and-tumble guy on the court. He gave everybody confidence with his physicality."

Sometimes Popovich took that to an extreme.

"Pop used him as our designated enforcer," says Steve Kerr, a reserve guard in San Antonio during Kersey's two years there. "One night there was some big guy trying to get physical with David. Pop called a timeout and drew up a play where Jerome set a screen on this guy. Pop told him, 'Go ahead and take a shot at him — I'll pay the fine.' Jerome went out and knocked the guy on the ground. It was a different time back then."

Kerr, now coach of the Golden State Warriors, says Kersey had a "good way about him — always had a smile on his face. But I remember how strong he was. He got kicked out of a game one time and we came into the locker room afterward at the Alamodome and he had torn the urinal out of the stall. Imagine that — right out of the wall. Yeah, he had a temper, and he was so powerful."

Starting small forward Sean Elliott recalls the incident in a slightly different way.

"He came into the locker room and ripped one of the steel doors off the stall," Elliott says. Told of Kerr's version, Elliott laughed. "Either way, it's pretty impressive. Holy crap. We nicknamed him 'Manimal.' He was one of the strongest guys I played with or against. If there was one guy you had to have on your side in a street fight, it might have been Jerome."

But both Kerr and Elliott liked Kersey as a person.

"I enjoyed being around him," says Kerr, who has won eight NBA titles — five as a player with Chicago and San Antonio, three as coach at Golden State. "During the lockout year, we both ended up living in San Antonio without our families. We'd catch dinner together occasionally. Pop always loved having vets and guys who were super professional on the Spurs. Jerome fit right in. He was just an old pro. He'd been around for so long, he knew exactly how the NBA worked. He never did anything that surprised you. He was there every day on time, putting in the work. He was a really good influence on everybody."

Elliott had a long history of being matched up with Kersey, including the latter's heyday in Portland. Elliott was a rookie starter for the Spurs during the epic seven-game playoff series against the Blazers in 1990.

"He literally beat me to a pulp in that series," Elliott says today. "For the next couple of years, whenever we faced each other, he was really hard on me. I hated him. But after my two years playing with Jerome, he was one of my favorite teammates of all time. I loved the guy. He was incredibly supportive of me. Every day when he came to practice, he had a great attitude. He was one of the nicest guys to be around. When you're in those heated battles sometimes, it's hard to realize the guy on the other side is an actual human being instead of a monster."

Kersey was Elliott's backup during the 1999 championship season. Elliott made one of the biggest baskets in franchise history against Kersey's old team, Portland, in Game 2 of the West finals. His corner 3 in the closing seconds gave the Spurs, who had trailed by 18 points in the second half, an 86-85 victory in what was known as "the Memorial Day Miracle."

"I made shots throughout my career, but that was the biggest — a big shot for the franchise and the city," Elliott says. "That shot gave us a lot of hope and a lot of belief. Whenever I see the highlights of it, I notice the first guy hugging me when I got back to the bench was Jerome Kersey."

In 1999-2000, Elliott missed most of the season after undergoing a kidney transplant. Popovich went small forward-by-committee, using Kersey, Chucky Brown and Jaren Jackson.

"He was a gentle giant, a very considerate guy," Elliott says. "I can't say enough good things about Jerome. An imposing presence on the court. Off the court, the sweetest guy."

Will Perdue was in the last of four years as a backup center with the Spurs that season.

"Jerome and I played together on the second unit at practice and wound up spending a little more time together than I'd have thought," says Perdue, who owns four championship rings — three with the Chicago Bulls. "What stood out is, nothing seemed to bother him. You gathered from being around him he knew how fortunate he was to be playing basketball and having the career he'd had. He was always happy-go-lucky, had a smile on his face.

"During practice and during games, he brought it. He was at the point in his career where, 'Whatever you guys need me to do, I'll do it.' That's hard for guys to do at the back end of their careers. He never second-guessed it. I don't remember his complaining about anything. The ultimate compliment is, he seemed like he was centered. He had his priorities straight. He knew what was important. He felt privileged to make the type of money he made and have the career he had."

And: "Jerome was one of those guys you'd want in a foxhole with you. He'd try to do whatever was necessary to help you survive. He came across as a guy who would do anything for you. If you were a stranger and had a flat tire, he'd be the guy to pull over and help you."

Kersey and Perdue rode on the same float during the Spurs' championship parade through the Riverwalk. Kersey played sparingly in the playoffs that season. His minutes decreased in each series; he played four minutes in two games in the five-game championship series with the Knicks. At that point in his career, it didn't matter.

"I remember the joy he had to be there," Perdue says. "He was like a kid in a candy store. He proudly put on that T-shirt that said 'Spurs, NBA champions.' He was waving to people and smiling. He was having the time of his life.

"Then he made some comment to me like, 'This is what you stole from me that year (1992, when the Bulls beat the Blazers). I'm glad I got to experience this.' I laughed. I was happy for him. He never walked around like, 'I deserve this.' He felt privileged to be there."

One of Kersey's closest friends was there to celebrate with him when the Spurs closed out the Knicks in Game 5 at Madison Square Garden.

"After the game is over, I come down from my seat and Jerome is looking for me," Mitch Walker says. "Security at MSG is tight. He tells the security guys, 'He's with me,' grabs me and pulls me to the court. Suddenly I find myself standing next to Popovich. The cameras start interviewing Pop and I'm right next to him. My phone blows up. 'Mitch, you're on TV.' Jerome knew that meant a lot to me."

The moment meant a lot to Kersey, too, though perhaps not as much as it might have when he was in his heyday with the Blazers.

"He was extremely happy to get a ring," Walker recalls. "The journey was a long one. He was whooping it up, but he'd have loved to have gotten that ring in Portland because he was so close with his teammates there. The Spurs were a different team, and it was his first year with them."

Walker got to peek into the postgame locker room scene.

"It wasn't an off-the-wall type of party," Walker says. "Champagne was spraying all over the place and he got into that, but David Robinson and Avery Johnson were the team leaders. They were laid-back and had a very religious component."

After Kersey showered, he and Walker went back to the team hotel, the Four Seasons near Central Park on 57th Street.

"Normally guys would be all over the place," Walker says. "It wasn't that. We went out later to a few clubs around the city. He was celebrated everywhere he went. We got into party mode, but it was just him and me and some diehard fans who happened to be where we were."

In a quiet moment, Kersey looked his friend in the eye.

"This championship is not just for me," Kersey said. "It's for my family and all my teammates over the years. It's for the folks back at Longwood. It's been a long time coming."

That summer, Kersey got together with some former teammates to celebrate.

"I have a picture with Jerome's (championship) ring on my finger," Orlando Turner says. "He was happy, but he didn't brag about it or self-promote. I'm sure when he got by himself, he'd sit back and say, 'Job well done.' "

AFTER THE SPURS were eliminated in the first round of the playoffs in 2000, Kersey was a player without a team. Shortly after the start of the 2000-01 campaign, Kersey signed on with coach George Karl and the Milwaukee Bucks. Injuries to a wrist and foot limited him to only 22 regular-season games, however, and he was not activated for the playoffs. Finally, at age 38, after 17 fulfilling seasons in the NBA, his playing career was over.

Kersey had gone up against some great small forwards through his long career. Asked by Hoke Currie in 1998 who were the toughest to defend, Jerome offered these observations:

"Larry Bird. He's 6-9, a big body, and he used his body well. And James Worthy. Really quick, and ran the court so well. He had a quick first step that was tough — probably the best first step of all of them. Adrian Dantley was only 6-5 but about 225 and so strong in his legs and upper body. He had muscle tone and a nice base. You couldn't move him. He used his body well and made good moves, and he made his free throws. And Xavier McDaniel. We came in at the same time, played the same spot and were both physical players. Neither one of us would back down. We probably called each other everything under the sun, and the moon, too.

"Of course there was Scottie Pippen. And also Purvis Short when he was with Golden State. He gave me fits. He was quick and had that fadeaway jump shot. And Eddie Johnson in his prime. A great shooter and offensive player."

Kersey described his style of play this way:

"My whole game is predicated on my legs and being physical with you. I'm not going to out-finesse you. I'm going to make you play hard. I'm going to try to make you work every time you come down the court. You might beat me once or twice, but are you going to beat me a third, fourth and fifth time? You're not going to consistently beat me. I'm not going to let you.

"Right off the top, I'm going to put my hand on you. I'm going to put my forearm on you. Guys are always saying, 'You're holding. You're always holding!' That's the way I play. I'm going to hold you, get you complaining about me. It takes you off your game."

Kersey had piled up some great individual statistics along the way. He scored 11,825 points and grabbed 6,339 rebounds in 1,153 regular-season games. He scored 36 points in one game. He twice grabbed 20 rebounds. He had single-game highs of 10 assists, six steals and five blocked shots and once played 52 minutes in a game.

The postseason is where he really made his impact felt. Kersey participated in 126 playoff games — more than a season and a half of extra contests — and averaged 12.4 points and 5.7 rebounds, better than his regular-season marks of 10.3 and 5.5. He was a gamer, a player who rose up to play his best ball when it mattered most.

Stats, though, never told the story about Jerome Kersey. He provided intangibles that can't be measured in a statistical column. He commanded respect from his coaches and teammates as well as his opponents for the way he went about his business. He loved to play the game of basketball, and he was able to do it at the highest level for longer than just about any second-round draft pick in history. (Only one player drafted lower played more games. Kersey was taken with the 46th pick in the 1984 draft. Kyle Korver, who played in 1,232 regular-season games, was chosen with the 51st pick in the 2003 draft. Korver played in 145 playoff games in his career.)

Now, though, it was time to get going on the rest of his life.

Jerome performing with Blazer
Dancers. *Courtesy Portland
Trail Blazers*

Teri and Jerome. *Courtesy Teri
Kersey Valentine*

Chapter Seventeen

'Someone You Truly Fall in Love With'

JEROME KERSEY had been playing organized basketball for a quarter-century. Now that part of his life was over. For many former NBA players, moving on to the next phase of life can be difficult.

It was certainly that way with Jerome in 2001 after the last of his 17 years in an NBA uniform. At 39 years of age, he had plenty of life left to live.

But what to do? Kersey went through a withdrawal of sorts for a spell.

"He didn't really know what to do," close friend J.R. Harris says. "He was in mortgage broking for a while. There was a time I was trying to get him to set up a boutique car shop. He knew a lot about cars. In 2008, he and I were involved with (Portland auto dealer) Joe Khorasani in a sports agency. We represented a few NBA players, but we didn't last long. He went through a time where he just didn't know what direction to go."

"Jerome didn't miss the limelight, but he missed the basketball action," says Ron Sloy, another good friend. "He missed the physical part of it. He needed structure. A lot of those guys are lost after they retire. There's nowhere to go."

Kersey returned to his home in suburban West Linn. He did some traveling. He joined Columbia Edgewater Country Club in Portland and got more serious with golf.

"He started out about 25-handicapper," Sloy says. "He eventually got down to about a seven. He grew to love the game. He was quite a player."

Jerome got to spend more time with his daughter, Kiara, who was now in elementary school and growing like a weed.

"I have a lifetime to spend with my daughter," Kersey said shortly after his retirement as a player. "I want to try to be the best father I can be. That entails being the best person I can be. With age comes wisdom. Your kids are your legacy, so you are trying to leave the best kind of legacy you can for them."

Kersey had more time to reflect on life.

"My philosophy is you have to work hard for everything you get," he said. "If you possess this attitude, you can attain most things. You have to set goals for yourself. Setting goals is about knowing what you want to be and where you want to go in life.

"You can't set unrealistic goals. Competitive goals are important. Whatever you want, go work hard for it. Don't let anybody think they can tell you what goals you can't reach as long as they are attainable. When you reach that goal, you move on to other things. You have to keep setting goals for yourself, places you want to go, the type of people you want to be around."

In 2003, Kersey was hired to help with a public-relations and internal problem with the Trail Blazers. Behavior of such players as Rasheed Wallace, Bonzi Wells, Ruben Patterson, Qyntel Woods and Zach Randolph was exacerbating a problem that had been brewing within the team for about eight years. Wallace was setting NBA records for technical fouls. Woods faced dog-fighting charges. Wells had several publicized incidents involving opposing players and fans. Four players were arrested on marijuana charges in a 12-month period. The "Jail Blazers" image of the team was running rampant.

Kersey was hired as "director of player programs," a position designed to work with the players and soften the team's image amid growing discontent from the fan base.

"Judging by the redundancy, there is definitely some kind of problem here, and probably has been since the J.R. Rider days," Kersey told the Portland Tribune when he was hired. "When I was a young player with the Blazers, we had guys to keep us in line, players like Jim Paxson, Kenny Carr, Mychal Thompson and Caldwell Jones. Then when Clyde (Drexler), Terry (Porter) and Buck (Williams) were with us as veteran players, we policed the young guys. We probably have a shortage of veteran leadership on this team."

By the end of the 2003-04 season, general manager Bob Whitsitt was fired and the remake of the franchise brand was ready to begin. Kersey was off, too, to Milwaukee to serve as an assistant coach for Porter, who was beginning his second season (2004-05) as coach of the Bucks.

In an interview with the Portland Tribune the previous summer, Kersey had expressed reservations about coaching in the changing landscape of the NBA.

"The approach to the game has changed so much," he said. "It's like you have to be hands-off with the players now. You can't say anything to them; you have to baby them. But if you can't offer constructive criticism, what's the use of being a coach? Maybe I'm just too old-school."

Kersey didn't let that affect the way he worked with Bucks players through the 2004-05 campaign.

"One day I put him in charge of a box-out drill," Porter says. "You could see the players weren't putting out the effort. Jerome finally got in there and said, 'This is not the way to do it.' And he got in there and showed them how. They were not doing it with the determination that Jerome Kersey did."

Kersey enjoyed working with Porter and the players but the role was short-lived. The Bucks floundered to a 30-52 record and last place in the Central Division, and Porter and his staff were fired at season's end. In one respect, that was OK with Kersey. He wanted to spend more time with daughter Kiara, who was 11.

"I saw her three times last year," Jerome said. "(Coaching) was a real unsatisfying time in my life. I'm not into ego-massaging. It was definitely an eye-opener for me."

In 2005, Jerome was honored as a member of Longwood University's inaugural Sports Hall of Fame class, joining a group of six that included major league baseball's Michael Tucker and LPGA pro Tina Barrett.

By then, Kersey had moved from West Linn to a home in Happy Valley, a little further northeast in the Portland suburban area. And he had met someone who would become the most important person in his life.

TERI FOLSOM was a native Oregonian of sorts. Born in Los Angeles, the third of four children to Ken and Evelyn Folsom, she moved to Medford, Ore., in the southern edges of the state while in junior high. Her parents manufactured notebooks and leather products. Teri graduated from North Medford High in 1991, attended Linn-Benton Community College in Albany and earned her certification as a dental assistant at Portland Community College. She married George Donnerberg in 1993, with whom she got her introduction to the Trail Blazers.

"George's family had season tickets to the Blazers," Teri says today. "In high school, he had posters of Jerome on the wall of his bedroom. Our first date was a Blazer game. My family were all Laker fans. I paid no attention to the Blazers at all. I don't remember seeing Jerome on the floor because we were playing Phoenix and I was watching Charles Barkley."

Teri worked as a dental assistant as she raised three children

— Makenzie (born in 1993), Brendan (1998) and Madison (called "Maddie," 2000). In 2004, Teri and George divorced. The next year, she met Jerome while having drinks and dinner at Huber's Restaurant in downtown Portland. Ironically, they'd already met — sort of — when their daughters faced each other in YMCA basketball. Kiara and Makenzie were 11.

"Jerome would be at a lot of the games," Teri recalls. "One time, Makenzie got fouled hard by Kiara and I got mad. Everyone was saying, 'Well, she plays like her dad.' "

On the night fate intervened at Huber's, Jerome recognized Teri and bought her a drink. They talked for a spell, he got a phone number, and soon they were dating.

"Jerome was very kind and thoughtful," she says of the things she first noticed about him. "He loved to take care of his family. They were very important to him. He always talked about his daughter and his grandma. He called her "grandma mom." I'm very close to my family, too. That was important to me that he talked about his family that way.

"When we first got together, he was always inviting my family to his house. He grew very close to my parents. He never spoke badly about anybody. He really was a good guy."

Shortly before Teri met Jerome, she was diagnosed with multiple sclerosis. Through the years they were together before marriage, he was more open about her condition than she was.

"She'd get upset with me," Jerome told the Portland Tribune. "She'd say, 'Why do you have to tell people I have MS?' I was like, 'Well, you have it.' But she didn't want people to pity her."

Jerome, says Teri, was always "a huge support. He was with me through most of it. There were days where he literally picked me up and carried me. He was a nurturer. When I wasn't feeling well, he was at his best."

Teri and Jerome dated "off and on" for the next eight years. He was mindful that she had three young children to help raise, and he had a daughter as well.

"He was good with my kids," Teri says. "A little more strict than what they were used to. He was raised with a strict hand by his grandpa."

During the times it was just the two of them, there was rarely a dull moment. They would sometimes go to dinner, and to listen to music, or to sing.

"Jerome was a great singer," Teri says. "He sang a lot. He made sure I could hear him singing. He liked to do karaoke. I'm not the greatest singer. He believed he was a really good dancer. He enjoyed dancing.

"What he really enjoyed doing was driving. He loved his cars. I know more about cars than I ever cared to, but it's kind of fun now. We'd get in the car and he'd just drive all around — not fast, but just go. Sometimes we'd go sightseeing through the state of Oregon. We'd go out in the country, to the beach, (to a vineyard) for wine tasting. We drove to British Columbia three times."

By that time, Kersey owned only two automobiles — a Jaguar and a 1969 Ford Fairlane "muscle car."

"He had seen (the Fairlane) in Virginia when he was younger," Teri recalls. "It was broken down in the owner's yard. He told the guy when he made enough money, he was going to come back and buy it. Eventually, he did. He fixed it up himself. He spent lots of hours working on that car. He liked to dink around with that stuff."

While Jerome played 18 holes at Columbia Edgewater, Teri would sun herself at the pool. When they'd go out, she grew used to being somewhat of an accessory.

"If people approached us while we were eating and asked for an autograph, he'd say, 'When we're done eating,' " Teri says. "And when we finished, he'd go find them and sign. He would always stop and talk to people. He didn't make you feel dumb for coming and talking to him. He was very receiving of his fans.

"I knew what I'd gotten myself into. I would sometimes get a little annoyed when I was handed the camera, but no, I was proud of him. I was proud of the man I married. He deserved that attention, to be recognized."

Kersey believed in chivalry.

"One time, we were getting into an elevator at a game at the Rose Garden," Teri recalls. "A young couple got in, and the guy entered before the girl. Jerome grabbed the guy's shoulder and pulled him back out and said, 'You need to let her go in before you.' The guy just looked at him. The girl walked in, and Jerome asked, 'Are you guys married?' She said, 'No.' And he said, 'Well, you probably should think about that.'

"Only he could do that. He always opened doors for me. He was absolutely a gentleman. That's what Jerome's real story was about."

MEANWHILE, grass wasn't growing under Kersey's feet. After his senior year at Longwood, Jerome was two courses short of graduation. He made good on a promise to his grandmother that he would get his degree, completing the courses online. On May 13, 2006, with May Kersey proudly in attendance, Jerome walked with a bachelor of science degree in social work.

Kersey also returned to the Trail Blazers' organization as an ambassador.

"When he finished his career, he had a strong desire to stay connected to the team," says Traci Rose, former VP/corporate communications and community relations for the Blazers. "He had the exact same dedication to the community. Portland was his home. It was in his heart. To be able to come back and connect with the team and the fans was important."

As an ambassador, Kersey would visit suites at the Rose Garden before games and at halftime, shaking hands, signing autographs and taking photos with team sponsors. It was more than two decades since he had arrived in Portland, a raw rookie out of Longwood College.

The ambassador role was a natural for Kersey, who was a popular figure with Blazer fans, so good at mingling with those who remembered him as an important member of a team in one of the most revered eras in franchise history.

"Jerome worked so well in community engagement," says Tom Fletcher, who served on the business side of the Blazers' organization for nearly 10 years (from 2002-11), finishing his tenure as the club's vice president/corporate sponsorships. "When we had functions in the arena, he'd do a meet-and-greet and/or chalk talk with our partners. It was amazing to have guys like Terry Porter, Kevin Duckworth and Bobby Gross in those roles, too, but Jerome was just fantastic."

Kersey, Porter and Duckworth were among former players who participated in summer caravans throughout Oregon in the 2000s, staging basketball clinics, playing golf, attending dinners and spreading the good word about the Blazers in towns such as Pendleton, Bend, Hood River, Grants Pass, Medford, Roseburg, Tillamook and Lincoln City.

"They were beloved as much then as when they were on the team," Rose says. "For those communities to see those guys, it was really magical."

"It was a way to reach out to the outlying markets and make a con- nection with the entire state of Oregon," says Fletcher, now senior VP/ global partnerships with the Phoenix Suns. "We'd hit different towns each year. Clinic, appearance, golf event, dinner."

Kersey was also a regular on the Blazers' annual "sponsor trips," in which 50 to 100 corporate partners would convene in Palm Springs or Phoenix.

"He would play golf and be there for the dinners," Fletcher says. "You'd show up with Jerome and watch people's eyes light up. Jerome appreciated it. You could see the warmth in his eyes when they reacted like that. The relationship he'd build with our partners was something. They felt like they were friends with Jerome. And they were, because that's how he was. We got so lucky with him and Terry. They made you feel like they were your good buddies. Being around a larger-than-life guy like Jerome made their day.

"In my job, sometimes you run into entitlement with former players. Jerome was humble. He loved being in front of our partners.

He never gloated about his history and what he had done on the floor. He loved the fact that fans still acknowledged his contributions to the organization. He had a connection with the people of Portland. I loved the way he handled it."

Kersey continued to make appearances at charitable events, including for the Boys and Girls Club.

"Throughout my career, people have asked me about my favorite players," says Rose, who worked for the Blazers for 27 years (1986-2013). "They were Terry and Jerome, and not because they were great players. It was the kind of human beings they were — how they treated people, how they engaged in the community. They set the bar. I was so blessed to be able to work with them. It was a very different organization back then. Much smaller. The NBA was not quite the big business it is today. We were all real close.

"I don't think Jerome ever forgot where he came from and how blessed he was. He recognized the privilege he had. He had an extraordinary way of understanding his responsibility to give back."

KERSEY was inducted into two state sports halls of fame in 2008 — Virginia, his birth state, and Oregon, his adopted state.

"This is a tremendous honor," Kersey told emcee Bill Schonely during the induction ceremony in Portland. "The people in this community, the incredible embracing (Blazers players) get as people aside from being basketball players. … It's been a lovefest with the city for me. I guess I'm a transplanted Oregonian."

Schonely asked about the success Kersey's teams enjoyed during his time in Portland. The Blazers made the playoffs in each of his 11 seasons, reaching the NBA Finals in 1990 and '92.

"We quickly came together as a family," Kersey said. "That included everybody right down to the ball boys. We honored each other, we spoke to each other with kindness, we cared about each other off the court. That culminated with the success we had on the court."

Kersey mentioned that players in his era didn't make the same kind of salaries players did even a few years after his retirement from the game.

"But I would never change the era" (in which he played), he said. "I got to play against some of the greatest basketball players who ever played this game. No money in the world is worth (changing) that.

"With our team, we all shared in one another's glory. Just like (the Hall of Fame selection). I share this award with everybody I ever played with, and especially everybody I played with for the Trail Blazers. It's a team sport. You don't do anything individually. You do it as a team. You win. You lose. You laugh. You cry. In the end, you enjoy your life and savor the memories."

In May of 2009, Kersey returned to Longwood to serve as the keynote speaker for graduation. He delivered a 10-minute prepared speech in which he combined humor with an inspirational message.

"I hope you remember the joy and great sense of accomplishment that you feel right now," Kersey told the graduates as he stood on the stage upon which he'd walked only three years earlier to receive his diploma. "Hold on to that feeling as you go forward into this very challenging world."

Kersey emphasized the need for hard work to attain goals and achieve success in a career.

"I spent 17 years facing off against some of the most famous and accomplished basketball players in NBA history," he said. "I left the NBA a different man than when I entered. What did I learn along the way that allowed me to succeed after I left Longwood? That when you stop working on your game, you stop succeeding. Put as much time and effort into your craft or your major as you may do on your Facebook or MySpace page. You should be just fine if you do that.

"My work ethic was derived from my grandparents. I was a guy who was in the gym early and late. I was on the court, in the weight room, running — trying to not only get better at my craft, but also to become a leader for every team I played for, or whatever I do in life. Be aware of where you are on the court of life and business at all times.

Learn how the rule-makers and enforcers think. Your sense of what is right is irrelevant if you can't adapt to the rules.

"Your success is going to be a function of listening to your coaches and doing exactly what needs to be done and knowing how the referees are going to call the game. The companies and organizations for jobs you apply for need role players more than prima donnas. Rookies are at the mercy of the veterans. You most likely will do work that you think is beneath you. It is not. You aren't the first person to get that assignment or react with indignation. You will not enter the game as MVP, and veterans won't treat you like one until you earn that through hard work and sacrifice. Your commitment to winning within the organization's values has to be rock solid."

Kersey implored the graduates to be team players — and to thank those who have supported them along the way.

"In this life, you won't do it alone," he said. "You can't do it alone. You don't need to do it alone. Life's success is a team effort. Most of you have had the help of at least one person whose presence or support at a critical moment helped you arrive at this very special moment. Most of them are sitting right behind you or beside you. Take a minute to turn around and wave at those people and show that you love what they did for you. That's your team for life. Always look to return the favor."

JEROME CONTINUED to serve as an ambassador for the Blazers and also served as a regular studio guest on Comcast Sports Northwest's weekly "Talking Ball" television show. In 2012, Chris McGowan was hired as president/CEO of the organization.

"Jerome was one of the first people I met with when I took the job," McGowan recalls. "I had lunch with him at Jake's Crawfish, which was his favorite restaurant, and we discussed a wide variety of subjects. It was an incredible opportunity for me. It's nice when you can draw ideas from someone who is such a big part of your history."

In 2013, McGowan hired Kersey as the organization's director of alumni relations.

"He managed our group of former players, particularly on game nights," McGowan says. "He oversaw those relationships, scheduled appearances and filled in where we needed him. In the offseason, he would join our group going to various sections of the state as part of our 'Rip City Relay.' He would help us with sponsor presentations. He worked with multiple departments.

"I had the opportunity to work with him a lot. He was in the office every day. His desk was right next to mine. We spent a lot of time talking about the team. He was an ex-player who worked hard on a daily basis. I know why he was such a good player. He was diligent. He filled a role for us that a lot of professional sports organizations don't have. He was so well-liked. He knew everyone in the community. He was very plugged in."

During this time, Kersey began to notice how much food went to waste from the suites at games at the Rose Garden (which was re-named Moda Center in 2013).

"The servers would bring containers for us to take leftover food and bring it home at the end of games," Teri Kersey Valentine says. "One night Jerome said, 'I'm going to take them down to some home-less people downtown on my way home.' We put the leftover food in boxes and he dropped them off to people living on the streets."

Jerome began to make a regular practice of it.

"He would go to other suites and load up all the food," Teri says. "I don't know that he was supposed to be doing it, but I don't think he cared. We often took separate cars because he was working the games and had to be there early. There were a few times, though, when I was with him, and sometimes the kids were with us, too. On some nights, it was freezing outside. He'd park the car downtown and tell us, 'Don't get out.' He's making sure I'm safe in the car, but he's out walking around making sure the people are getting food.

"We called him 'the Napkin Policeman.' He'd have napkins and plastic forks for these people on the streets. He'd bring them food and say, 'I just came from the Blazer games. This is good food,' just so they

276

knew. And he'd tell them, 'God bless you.' He wouldn't make just one stop. It was several stops to pass out food to different groups of people."

Why was Kersey possessed to do such a thing? Does it go back to his childhood, growing up in a poor family?

"Absolutely," Teri says. "It is also a reflection of the kindness in his heart. You just don't meet people like that every day."

Jerome was always glad to go back to his roots for a special occasion. The last time he returned to Longwood was for "Jerome Kersey Bobblehead Day" on Feb. 16, 2013, as the Lancers played in-state rival Radford during their first season in the Big South Conference. Several of his teammates showed for the festivities. A pickup game featuring former Longwood players was organized earlier in the day. Jerome was the only one from his era to participate.

"After the game, we rented a huge area away from campus, where we could be by ourselves, talking politics and sports, drinking and just hanging out," Orlando Turner says. "Any time we had an excuse to get together and hang out, we took it, especially when Jerome was involved."

JEROME HAD ALWAYS gotten cold feet when contemplating marriage. It happened again with Teri.

"He was scared of getting married," she says. "Part of it was his upbringing. He told me that he was afraid of being 'left,' like his (biological) mother had left him. He felt abandoned by her because she left him to be raised by his grandma.

"He told me he didn't feel like he could love me the way I deserved to be loved. I don't think he felt like he deserved to be loved sometimes. He wasn't ready to commit. I wasn't going to push it. We had never lived together. I had three kids, and if we were just dating, I wasn't going to move him in and out. He had to make a choice."

Jerome's close friend Kevin Brandon offers some perspective:

"He fell in love with a couple of women — Anjela and Teri — but there were other women who came and went in his life who were incredible. I'd ask him, 'How do you not fall in love with this woman?' It didn't faze him. He'd always tell me there was something wrong with them. I'd think, 'There's something wrong with everybody.' But it wasn't just women. Jerome couldn't submit to almost anyone — even with friends. He wouldn't let very many people get really close. That's just the way he was."

"Teri was the one, someone you truly fall in love with," says another close friend, J.R. Harris. "There was something about Teri that Jerome could not shake. There was a different love there with Teri. They had their issues, too. I'd get Teri's side of it and his side of it. But he loved that girl."

Nick Hodel was another good friend in which Jerome confided.

"He and Teri were on and off quite a bit," Hodel says. "It's safe to say she was a little controlling, but there was no controlling that guy. He was going to do what he wanted to do. … he was a tough guy for any woman to put a thumb on."

Teri gave Jerome an ultimatum. He waffled. He hashed things out with close friends such as Brandon and Harris.

"We broke up for about four or five months," she says. "I was moving on. He had a hard time with that. I told him I needed him to make some changes and show me he was truly ready to commit. Like, going to church was important to me. He started going back to church on his own.

"He talked a lot to Huggy (Brandon) and J.R. He did a lot of praying with Huggy and his grandma. He knocked on my door one day and said, 'I'm ready to give you everything you want.' I said, 'OK, I'm ready, too.' "

Teri and Jerome became engaged in April and were married on September 21, 2013, at Columbia Edgewater Country Club. Ron Sloy was his best man. His groomsmen were Brandon, Harris, Eddie Bynum, Mitch Walker and Teri's brother-in-law, Nolwenn Mandrou.

The newlyweds honeymooned in Kauai for a week.

"It was the first time either of us had gone there," Teri says. "It was a wedding gift from the Sloys."

The Kerseys settled into home life in the Lake Oswego house Jerome had purchased in 2011. Makenzie was then a sophomore at Oregon State, so she was only there on occasional weekends, holidays and the summer. Brendan, 15, and Maddie, 13, were at home.

"Jerome wasn't used to having three kids around all the time," Teri says. "He was very particular about things. If you left a fork out, then it was a mess. That was something he had to get through getting married. It's not just me; I come with three kids, and they're all moving in. That's a big deal."

But Jerome loved Teri's children and treated them like his own. He had one of his own — Kiara, who by now was a young adult.

"Jerome struggled some when Kiara got into her teenage years, but he loved being a dad," says close friend Kevin Brandon. "He wasn't with her mother, and he couldn't be with her all of the time. He was on the road a lot. That was hard. But that was his soft spot, for real."

Jerome had challenges in his marriage, too, much his own doing.

"I never knew him to love a woman like he loved Teri," Brandon says. "Part of it was because she didn't just bow to everything he said. She challenged him more than other women. He adored her. But even with that, he still couldn't do what he really needed to do. He couldn't totally submit to her. He was devoted to her, he was committed to make it work, but there was something within him. … that was a challenge within him to submit to another person. He just couldn't."

Well, at least until he became a grandfather.

"Jerome expected a lot of Kiara," Teri says, "but she was his world, for sure — until Harley came along."

On March 27, 2014, Harley Kersey was born into the world. Suddenly, Jerome's priorities changed.

"Once Harley came, she was all he could talk about," Teri says. "When he was with her, he just lit up."

"One of the best times in our relationship was when I had Harley," Kiara says. "You love your parents, but it's different seeing them as grandparents. You see them in a totally different light."

279

Kiara says she'll never forget the look on Jerome's face when she told him he was going to be a grandpa.

"The look of shock and awe was absolutely priceless," she says. "I've never seen his mouth open so wide or smile so big. Harley had my dad wrapped around every single one of her fingers. They were pretty much inseparable. We'd meet at the games and he'd be the only one holding her in the suite. That was his duty. He was an amazing grandfather.

"You can never get the image of a 6-7 man changing a tiny baby's diaper — and doing the 'goo-goo, ga-ga' talk — out of your head. I will cherish those memories together."

Jerome and Kiara's mother, Anjela Stellato, split up when Kiara was just an infant.

Today, Kiara is 27 and the mother of three children — Harley, now seven, and three-year-old twins Tristan and Zayden. Kiara looks back at her father with much fondness. But it wasn't easy growing up under parents who weren't together.

Kiara was born while Jerome was still with the Blazers and was seven when he retired from playing in the NBA in 2001. During those years, as she was living with her mother in suburban Gresham, she saw Jerome irregularly — mostly during the summers.

"When he was with the Spurs, I stayed with him for a while (in San Antonio)," Kiara says. "When he was in Milwaukee, I had Thanksgiving with him there. It was a little bit touch-and-go getting to see each other. He saw me as much as he could."

After Jerome's retirement as a player, his visitation rights gave him Kiara every other weekend. She was an active girl who loved sports and music and played bass clarinet in the school band.

"Mom and Dad did a fantastic job," she says. "There wasn't a lot of fighting. My mom wanted my dad to be a part of my life just as much as he did. After he retired, he went to most of my basketball and volleyball games and to my band and choir performances."

Today, Kiara finally grasps the impact her father had on the Portland community.

"To me, my dad was just my dad," she says. "But I saw what he did for other people and for the community and how much it meant to him. He reached out and connected with complete strangers. I didn't completely understand it then. But now in a world where I see how many people aren't that way, I understand how well-respected he was.

"I always admired him. He had such a strong work ethic. He was a 100 percent guy in everything he did. I grew to appreciate it more as I got older. I was thinking the other day about how at different points in your life you go, 'Oh, I get it.' Another moment comes, and those moments keep happening as you grow older. I had a lot of great moments with my dad."

When Kiara was 11, Teri entered her father's life.

"We've gotten along well," Kiara says. "Teri has always treated me as if I were one of her own."

Kiara has a younger half-sister, Milan, by her mother.

"My dad treated her like another daughter," Kiara says. "Milan would stay at my dad's house with us. It doesn't matter if it's (his) blood. He was at the hospital the day she was born. He loved that girl just like his own."

Kiara witnessed firsthand many of the transitional stages Jerome experienced through his adult life.

"I saw him change from dad to husband, and eventually to grandpa," she says. "People handle change in different ways. I wasn't sure how my dad would do in these new roles, but in God's hands, I felt everything would work out. And it did."

Alas, but for far too short a time.

Jerome and close friend J.R. Harris. *Courtesy J.R. Harris*

Chapter Eighteen

Relationships

FROM THE TIME he was in college through his post-playing years living in Portland, Jerome Kersey attracted friends like sports aficionados collect trading cards — by the droves.

Jerome's life was about relationships, and he was an expert at it.

"I considered Jerome one of my best friends," says Ira DeGrood, a former teammate at Longwood. "But he made everybody feel that way when you're with him."

"I never knew anybody else who, every person he interacted with, could make you feel like you were his best friend," says one of his best friends, Kevin Brandon. "It could be a stranger on the street he'd just met. That's who Jerome was."

Many of Jerome's genuine friendships have been mentioned in previous chapters. What follows is a closer look at a few of those who gained entrance into his inner circle (in alphabetical order — no playing favorites here).

HIS GIVEN NAME is Kevin Brandon, but everybody calls him "Huggy." That's short for "Huggy Bear," a nickname he picked up at Longwood.

"If you asked anyone at Longwood during the years I went there if they know Kevin Brandon, they would say no," Brandon says with a laugh. Why Huggy Bear? "I'm lovable," he says. "An easy guy to get along with."

Brandon was two years ahead of Kersey at Longwood. They became friends during Jerome's freshman year. Jerome would become the godfather of Kevin's son, Myles. Myles and Jerome's daughter, Kiara, were born a week apart.

Jerome and Kevin got acquainted through a fraternity on campus, Omega Psi Phi. Jerome wasn't a member, but Kevin was, and so were a half-dozen of Jerome's basketball teammates — Mitch Walker, Orlando Turner, Dalany Brown, Mike McCroey, Kenny Ford and Troy Littles.

"We called Jerome 'The Freshman,'" says Brandon, a Richmond native now retired and living in Durham, N.C., after a career in social services. "There was such a small number of black students, we were all good friends. But Jerome and I did not really jell until two or three years after he left Longwood. Over time, we became incredibly good friends."

Brandon didn't play basketball at Longwood. He was involved in a pair of club sports — rugby and wrestling — "but I never was really into the sports part of it," he says today. "I was the outside person, a person with whom Jerome could get away from that part of his life. As the years went on, I was someone who remembered him when we had to pitch a dollar together to buy a Coke."

After Kersey departed for Portland and the NBA, Brandon kept in contact with him. The friendship grew. Aside from a year and a half in the late 1980s — when Brandon, ironically, worked at Oregon Health & Science University and lived in Portland — he lived mostly in the Washington, D.C., area through his professional career.

"Whenever the Blazers would come out to play the Bullets, we'd get together," Brandon says. "I flew out to Portland to see him several times over the years. And we met at other places, too. We'd talk on the phone two or three times a week. We'd talk about everything."

Kevin and his wife, Rhonda, have been married for 36 years. Jerome was a bachelor through most of that time. He made the most of it, Kevin says.

"Jerome could party, but it was very conservative," Brandon says. "Give him a cold beer or a Jack (Daniel) and Coke, he was a happy man. He could stay up late. Everything he did, he did it hard. He ate hard. He partied hard. But if we were smoking weed, he wouldn't do it. He didn't need that. Jerome would try just about anything, but he wouldn't do drugs. Don't bring it around him. I'd challenge anybody who said that wasn't true.

"He was very popular with the women. When we'd go places, they just loved him. I was a big teddy bear sitting in the corner. The whole time I was hanging with Jerome, I was a married man and he was single. He was used to that lifestyle. I had to draw the line. But I had fun."

A few times, Brandon and another Longwood friend, Mitch Walker, flew out to see Jerome in Portland.

"When he went places, he had to wear a certain outfit," Brandon says. "We didn't have the money to dress like he did. He'd sometimes tell Mitch to change his clothes when we were going out. If you really needed something, he'd take you to the store to buy you something. He always had something going, from the time you woke up until the time you fell asleep. It did not stop."

Jerome had eclectic tastes in food. Sushi was at the top of the list.

"That was his thing," Brandon says. "He'd make you try it. He made me try alligator once, and it was good. He would never let us take leftovers home. He'd say, 'We don't do that.'

"He also loved chitlins (pig intestines). That was one of his favorite meals. My mother-in-law would cook them for him sometimes. Once we'd been out all night drinking and having a good time. We got in at 2 or 3 in the morning, and he decided he wanted some chitlins. He sat there and ate them, and then he got sick. He had an incredible appetite — not just for food, but for life."

Kersey had an appetite for fast cars, too.

"He bought quite a few of them," Kevin says. "We'd be getting ready to go somewhere and he'd be out there cleaning his rims. He loved speed and was a good driver. Sometimes he'd be going pretty fast and I'd be scared to death. He laughed and thought it was the funniest thing in the world. He'd let us drive his cars. One Ferrari he bought was a lemon. It wouldn't start a lot of the time. He got it back to the dealer pretty soon after he bought it."

Kersey could be stubborn. But he was loyal.

"Jerome had an opinion about anything and you couldn't change it," Kevin says. "He thought everything he was doing was the best. Because he had such a high level of contacts, he thought he was always at the top of the game. Sometimes you'd try to tell him things and he wouldn't listen. He had his way of doing things.

"But he was someone you could trust. No matter what was going on in Jerome's personal world, he was there for you. He would drop things and do what you needed him to do."

For 10 years, Brandon worked at the Hospital for Sick Children in Washington, D.C.

"We had babies to kids age 21," Kevin says. "Some had birth defects. Some were abused. Some had been shot or overdosed on drugs. It was like a rehab hospital. Every single time Jerome came to D.C., he visited the kids at the hospital. He always made a point to come over.

"Through the years, he probably gave us about $20,000 to buy things for recreation and activities. But he also gave us his time. The kids, as well as the staff, loved him. When Jerome would come through, it would be uplifting that someone that important cared that much that he would come in and share that time. Never did he act rushed. He would sign autographs. Anything they needed, he was there to do for them."

Kersey was generous on a personal basis, too. When Brandon and his wife were discussing how they'd come up with enough money for a down payment on a house after they moved to Portland, Kersey gave them $25,000.

"It was a loan, but he never asked me about that money," Kevin says. "If I hadn't given him a penny back, he'd have never said anything."

In tribute, the Brandons have started a scholarship fund in Jerome's name at Longwood. They made an initial donation of $25,000.

"We're still putting more of our own money into it when we can," Kevin says. "We've done fundraisers, too. The goal is to raise $100,000 and endow the fund. I will make that happen. The scholarship will go to a player on the basketball team. Jerome was not an A-and-B student, but he worked hard at his grades. The coach can decide which player works the hardest on and off the court and deserves it each year."

(Donations to the fund can be made at give.longwood.edu/athletics.)

SOME 40 YEARS after they were in the basketball program together at Longwood, Ira DeGrood still carries strong memories of Jerome Kersey.

"Jerome meant a lot to me," says DeGrood, now a teacher and athletic director at Osbourn High in Manassas, Va. "I have a poster of him, Terry Porter and Buck Williams on the wall in my office. I have pictures with him in it all through the house. He was in my wedding. I was at his bachelor party. I think about him daily."

Kersey is the greatest player ever to come out of Longwood. DeGrood, who came to Longwood in the same class as Jerome, wasn't even a member of the team during his four years there.

"Basketball was my first love," he says. "I was a 6-1 white guy who went to Longwood thinking I was going to a small school and would walk on and play right away as a freshman. I found that was tougher than I thought."

DeGrood participated in preseason pickup games with Kersey and other varsity players. They were in another league.

"I wasn't going to make the varsity squad," DeGrood says. "I decided to play intramurals instead. It was more fun for me to watch Jerome play and hang out with him."

Kersey didn't act like a big shot during his time at Longwood. In most ways, he was just one of the guys.

"He treated me and everybody else the same all the time," Ira says. "We played flag football and softball together. We'd get some guys together and scrimmage the (varsity) volleyball team. He'd sometimes come home with me on weekends and hang out with me and my mom and dad. He loved my parents.

"Jerome was a genuine, down-to-earth person. He always found time for you. Everybody loved the man."

In the summer of 1988, Kersey spent some time at DeGrood's house in Manassas, about 30 miles from Washington, D.C. Steve Bianco — who had played a year of JV ball at Longwood — was also there. One day, the house phone rang.

"I answered and a deep voice asked, 'Is Mr. Jerome Kersey there?' " DeGrood says. "I gave him the phone. He was on it for a good 15 minutes. Steve and I were listening. Jerome kept saying, 'I'm not coming unless I can bring my friends.' After he hung up, we said, 'Who was that?' "

The caller was John Thompson, who was coaching the U.S. Olympic team that year.

"He was asking me to be part of a bunch of pros from the area who would come practice against the Olympians on the Georgetown campus," Kersey told them. "I told him no unless you can come."

"We went, and it was one of the most unbelievable experiences I've ever had," DeGrood recalls. "We got to meet a lot of players — David Robinson and that group. I think we were the only two people other than the players in McDonough Arena that day."

One year, DeGrood and Bianco flew to Portland to visit Kersey. He picked them up at Portland International Airport. On the way into town that night, they drove by a building in downtown Portland that had a huge Nike mural of him plastered on the wall.

"Isn't that ridiculous?" Kersey said.

"We laughed and said, 'Yeah, it is,' " DeGrood says. "He was almost embarrassed about his stardom at times."

Kersey was a groomsman in DeGrood's wedding. After the reception, Kersey asked Ira and his wife Tammy, "Do you guys want to go back to your hotel? Or if you'd like to continue (partying), I'll be your chauffeur."

"We went to a place in town where we danced and had more fun there," DeGrood says. "He paid for everything and drove us so we weren't drinking and driving. It was like the ultimate wedding gift. He was very caring of other people. Every time we talked on the phone after that, he'd ask, 'How's Tammy? How's your sister? How are your kids?' He was like part of our family."

In 2013, DeGrood flew to Portland for the wedding of Jerome and Teri Kersey.

"We played golf and smoked cigars at his bachelor party," he says. "I have a picture of him sitting in his black Ferrari convertible. I had so much fun with that guy."

SOME MIGHT CONSIDER Doug Gorman an unlikely friend of Jerome Kersey. Gorman, now 80, was a cattle rancher in Central Oregon for many years who is now retired and living in Longview, Wash.

In 2003, while Jerome was serving as the Trail Blazers' director of player programs, Gorman called the team's practice facility in Tualatin.

"I was involved in some stuff I thought he might have an interest in," Gorman says. "I told the receptionist, 'I'd like to talk to Jerome Kersey.' She said, 'They're on the court.' I said, 'May I leave my name and number? I don't want anything from him.' He called me right back. We had dinner and became friends right from the get-go."

The next year, Kersey served as an assistant in Milwaukee under former teammate Terry Porter.

"I shipped him out a half a steer, cut and wrapped," Gorman says. "He lorded it over Terry. Terry asked, 'Why can't I get some of that?' When Jerome told me, I said, 'I'm happy to send some to Terry, too.' But Jerome was having too much fun busting Terry's chops about it."

Doug and wife Karyn attended both of Jerome's Hall of Fame banquets in 2008 — one in Virginia and one in Oregon.

"He used to introduce us as his 'West Coast parents,' " Doug says. "Karyn and Jerome played some golf tournaments together. One of my daughters used to call herself and Jerome 'twins.' Their birthday is the same date. Karyn and Teri spent time together at the ranch. We'd stay at their home when we'd come to Portland for a Blazer game."

Once, when Jerome and Karyn were playing a golf event in Warm Springs, Ore., he got pulled over for speeding by a member of the reservation's police force.

"The officer looks at Jerome's driver's license, and he calls it in," Doug says. "My wife and Jerome are sitting in the car and they hear his supervisor say, 'You will not give Jerome Kersey a ticket on this reservation.' "

Gorman gets emotional.

"It's hard to talk about Jerome — it really is," he says. "He's one of those rare human beings. He did not have an exaggerated sense of his own self in Portland. I don't get along with those kind of people. I loved him to death. There isn't a thing I wouldn't have done for him. He'd have said the same for me. He was caring, giving — a marvelous human being."

BRIAN GRANT and Jerome Kersey were never teammates, but they felt a brotherhood through the NBA and shared a kinship as former Trail Blazers who lived in Portland. Grant entered the NBA in 1994 and didn't come to Portland until 1997, after Kersey had departed. They faced each other for seven seasons.

"When I played against Jerome, I always respected him," says Grant, retired and living in West Linn. "He was the kind of guy I didn't like to play against -- a hustler and a banger, like me. And once we both retired, my respect for him went through the roof.

"When I moved back to Portland, I would see him at events, both of us representing the Blazers. I'd see him every time I came to Moda Center. We'd gotten real cool with each other, become closer friends.

Right before he died, we were hanging out a lot. We were there for each other. We talked about a lot of things each of us were going through."

In 2005, Grant learned he had early onset Parkinson's disease. "Jerome was the first person I came out to," Grant says.

It was at a Blazer game shortly after the death of another ex-Blazer, Kevin Duckworth. The team honored Grant, Kersey and Chris Dudley in a halftime ceremony.

"I was nervous because I was afraid people would recognize my hand was shaking," Grant says. "Before we went out to center court, Jerome asked me what was wrong. I told him I hadn't told anybody, but I had come down with Parkinson's disease. He said, 'Really? So what?' I said, 'I'm nervous.' He said, 'Can't even tell. Go on out there. You'll be all right. I got you.' We've been fast friends ever since. That's when I really got to know him and love him."

Through his foundation, which benefits Parkinson's research, Grant conducted an annual auction and charity gala. Kersey got on the phone to enlist players and former players to help. He volunteered to be part of an auction item that featured a fishing trip in Alaska.

"He went even though he had a real problem with motion sickness," says Grant, chuckling at the memory. "We went together two years and had a great time. The year after that, I couldn't make it, and he stood in for me. The years we both went, we got to do a lot of fishing, which I love to do. He had a pretty good time, too, once we started catching fish. He caught a halibut two inches too long to keep, and we were like, 'No!' It was a big one.

"At night, we'd come back to a small lodge, eat great seafood — salmon and halibut — and have glasses of nice wine. He's a bit of a wine connoisseur. He's one of the finest guys I've ever known, well-loved within the Portland community for no better reason than he was a great guy."

BEGINNING IN 1985, Franklin Grant worked at Longwood as a chief fundraiser. In the early years, he also was involved with athletic fundraising. He missed by a year of being at Longwood at the same time as Jerome Kersey.

"But I thought it was important that we recognize a former athlete of his caliber playing in the NBA," said Grant, who passed away at 69 on June 11, 2021.

For five or six years in a row as a fundraiser for the athletic department, Grant put together bus trips for Lancer fans to cover the three-hour drive from Farmville to Landover, Md., to watch Kersey and the Blazers face the Washington Bullets.

"They were hugely successful," Grant says. "We raised a fair amount of money and the people really enjoyed getting a chance to see Jerome play again. One year, Jerome scored 29 points, and all the local people were over-the-moon happy. After the games, we'd stick around. After he'd showered and left the locker room, Jerome would get as close as he could and say hello to everybody. He was so accessible."

In 1989, Grant put together a fundraiser at a local bowling alley. Jerome was the featured guest.

"A nice crowd showed up," Grant says. "Everyone had a great time. We drank some beer, bowled and had some fun. My wife invited Jerome and his friends over for breakfast the next morning — and they came. It was a delight for my sons, who were about 18 and 19 years old at the time and invited some of their buddies over. Jerome loved my wife's cooking."

Through the fundraiser, Grant got to know Kersey on a personal basis. In 1991, Grant was scheduled to be in San Francisco on business. Kersey invited him to detour to Portland to spend some time there.

"I spent about a week there and stayed at Jerome's house," Grant says. "He got me a ticket for a couple of Blazer games. I was sitting in the players' section, and people were asking me where I was from. I told them I was with Longwood, and I became kind of a celebrity. It was comical and fun at the same time.

"I was there when he had his Ferrari. He said, 'I know you want to drive this thing.' I said, 'Damn right I do.' But he said you had to go to driver's school to be able to drive it. I didn't get to drive it, but he took me for a drive. We did 130 (mph) from one stoplight to the next."

Kersey took Grant to a Blazer practice and introduced him to teammate Buck Williams as "my friend Franklin from Longwood."

"Before one of the Blazer games, he took me into the souvenir shop and bought something for me and my wife," Grant says. "He also got something for my kids and for all their friends who had been at our place when he was there a couple of years earlier. He picked something out for each of them personally. After I got back (to Farmville), I realized there was one young African-American man who didn't get something. I mentioned it to Jerome, and he sent something out for him, too."

One summer several years later, the Grants were eating pizza on the back deck of their home when Kersey called.

"He told me he was in town and asked if we wanted to meet him at Perini Pizza," Franklin says. "We ate pizza twice that night."

Grant was one of many friends who spent the day with Kersey when he graduated from Longwood in 2006.

"He got a standing ovation," Grant says. "It was a sweet moment."

Grant was asked to speak at a memorial service in Clarksville after Kersey's death in 2015.

"It was truly one of the great honors of my life to stand up there and make my remarks with his grandmother and family in attendance," he says.

J.R. HARRIS met Jerome while working as a hotel doorman in Seattle in 1984. A relationship that started there grew into one of Jerome's closest over the next three decades.

"We knew we would be best friends for the rest of our lives, no matter what," says Harris, now retired and living in Seattle. "It was a natural fit for us. We both had a bunch of stories about our grandmothers. We talked on the phone three or four days a week and saw each other pretty regularly.

"Jerome had many good friends. He used all of us differently.

Any time he struggled, he'd come and stay with me, just to get out of Portland. Jerome was really a country guy — a small-town guy with a big heart. He would do anything for his friends. He fell in love with Portland. The people there just loved him."

Harris was privy to Jerome's sometimes unusual eating habits.

"He was fixing some eggs and grits one morning and he brought out some sugar," Harris says. "I started to laugh at him about it. He said, 'If I can't be myself in front of you, I can't in front of anybody. I just like sugar on my grits.'

"He loved his sushi. He introduced me to it. He said, 'I'm going to get you to eat some octopus.' I said, 'No, you're not.' I don't like the idea of eating rice with seaweed in it, either. He never got me there."

Harris saw Kersey in nearly every public setting possible over the years. He has never forgotten how well he handled his celebrity status.

"To understand Jerome, you had to spend time with him," Harris says. "You had to see what he was all about when people walked up to him and asked for an autograph. He had one of the most beautiful smiles in the world. He had a great knack for making people feel good about themselves."

NICK HODEL shared a couple of passions with Jerome Kersey — cars and golf.

When he met Kersey early in his career with the Blazers, Hodel owned a tire store in North Portland. Kersey came into the store one day to purchase some tires and wheels.

"I didn't know who he was," says Hodel, now retired and living in Portland. "I wasn't a big basketball guy. After he left, my manager said, 'You know who that was, don't you?' "

A couple of days later, Kersey called to ask Hodel to place an order.

"He offered to take me to lunch, and we hit it off," Hodel says. "We talked about lots of things. He ended up being a very good friend. We spent a lot of time together over the years. We did a little bit of every-thing together. I'm 71 now; I was almost like a father figure to him. I'd do anything for him; he'd do anything for me.

"He loved being around my house. It was like we were family. I had three small kids when we first met. When he'd come over for dinner, he would spend time with the kids. He was like their 'Uncle Jerome.' He'd meet one of their friends and ask them questions. A month or two later, he'd be over again, and my wife would mention how he remembered all the kids' names. My daughter used to love watching him eat half a dozen eggs and half a pound of bacon for breakfast. The only complaint he ever had was sleeping. His feet would hang over the edge of our bed in the guest room. But he was a real pleasant person."

A giving one, too.

"NBA players wear a new pair of shoes for almost every game," Hodel says. "Jerome would either give his shoes to kids in a parking lot or give them away for charity auctions."

Once he got to high school, Nick's son, Adam, wore the same size shoes as Jerome.

"Jerome was over at the house one time and Adam asked him, 'What kind of shoes should I get for basketball this year?' " Hodel recalls. "Jerome said to me, 'Hodie, bring Adam to my house; I'll give him some shoes.' Jerome was a shoe freak. He had hundreds of pairs of dress shoes in his closet. He just loved shoes. When he bought some nice loafer dress shoes, he'd get two or three pairs in different colors.

"So I took Adam there and Jerome told him, 'Go up in my closet and get some shoes.' Adam was up there for 10 minutes and came back with a brand new pair and asked, 'Could I take these?' Jerome said, 'I told you to get some shoes. I want you to go fill up the trunk of your dad's car.' He must have had 30 pairs of shoes in there when we left. My son put them in his bedroom and lined them up and had his buddies over and gave them some."

Nick was sometimes the recipient of Jerome's generosity.

"One day he said, 'Hodie, I'm going to get rid of a bunch of suits; you need any?' " Hodel says. "I said, 'I'd take a suit.' He brought me into his closet and said, 'Take this one, that one.' He may not have worn those suits two or three times. It was not strange for him to hand me an Armani. Those cost money. I'm 6-3. We had the same waist and shoulder size. Only thing I had to do was taper the sleeves of the jacket and the length of the pants."

The Hodels lived west of Portland, not far from the Hillsboro Airport, from which the Blazers chartered flights beginning in the early '90s.

"Jerome would get a new car and wouldn't want to leave it at the airport," Hodel says. "Our house was on the way, so he'd store it in my garage. I'd take him out there and drop him off and would pick up him when he got back. I got to know most of the Blazers through him.

"He went through cars like I went through clothes. He had Mercedes, Porsches, a few Ferraris. The nicest one was a Testarossa. (NBA players) were able to get whatever car they got anxious for. That's part of the life they got to enjoy."

After Kersey left the Blazers, Hodel visited him for a week in both Los Angeles (when he was playing with the Lakers) and San Antonio (when he was with the Spurs).

"Stayed with him and got to go to practices and games," Hodel says. "Got to meet Shaq (Shaquille O'Neal) and Kobe (Bryant). It was really fun."

Hodel and Kersey were members of Columbia Edgewater Country Club.

"He was a pretty good golfer," Hodel says. "Wasn't when he started, though. I was a member at Rock Creek then. Rock Creek had out-of-bounds stakes to the left all around the course because there are homes along the course. He'd pull out a driver and knock it over a fence. He'd jump over the fence and get his golf ball from someone's yard. I told him, 'Some of the homeowners might see a big black guy jump over their fence and get worried.' We'd laugh about it.

"He was a pretty bad golfer to start, but he got down to an 8, 9, 10 handicap. Like most tall guys, he had good leverage and he'd hit it a long way. He loved golf as much as he loved cars at the end. The members (at Columbia Edgewater) still say how much fun and how nice he was. Even if they just met him one time, they considered him a friend. He was an easy guy to get to know. He made everybody feel like a friend."

WHILE WASHING HIS CAR in the driveway of his West Linn home in 1988, Ron Sloy met Jerome Kersey.

"He had moved across the street from me, about four houses down," says Sloy, who played baseball at Mt. Hood Community College and University of Oregon and was a fourth-round draft pick of the St. Louis Cardinals in 1979. "He drove by my place, got out of the car and said, 'So, you like white cars?' "

Sloy owned two white cars at the time; Kersey had several black cars.

"Hey, white is fine with me," Sloy responded. "I don't have a problem with black, either."

Both men laughed, and a conversation followed that led to a friendship that lasted nearly three decades.

"Jerome came across as shy at first," says Sloy, who served as Kersey's financial advisor for 25 years. "He was soft-spoken and very down to earth."

They became close friends. Sloy served as best man in Kersey's wedding in 2013.

"We had a lot of the same interests," Ron says. "We lifted weights together. Jerome was disciplined with the way he trained. He carried it through life, the way he treated his family and friends. He had his own regimen and stuck with it. He was pretty structured. He didn't get off track too much. We played a lot of golf together. When we started, he was just learning the game."

Sloy put Kersey on an allowance to ensure that he wasn't spending too freely.

"In the early days, we would butt heads on a couple of things," Sloy says. "But I listened to him as much as he listened to me. I didn't try to run his life, nor did he ask me to. He was always concerned about his family — his grandma, his aunts, his (birth mother) and how they were taken care of."

Sloy once attended a Boys & Girls Clubs function with Kersey.

"I had never heard Jerome speak publicly," Sloy says. "He was so articulate, so at ease with the audience. Jerome had the ability to make people feel very comfortable. You quickly figured out he didn't think he was any better than you. And he was a great motivator."

Sloy became involved in helping Kersey with charitable causes.

"I got calls all the time, like, 'This kid is sick and in the hospital. Can Jerome come see him?' " Sloy says. "I can count on one hand the number of times he didn't follow through with a visit."

Sloy had friends whose son, Cori Ferris, acquired leukemia.

"Cori had been a Jerome Kersey fan since he was little," Sloy says. "He had heart surgery when he was six; Jerome drove to his house and put a letter (of encouragement) in his mailbox. Then he got sick again. His parents asked if it would be possible for Jerome to meet with him. So they brought Cori over to (Kersey's) house. Jerome gave him a pair of Shaq's tennis shoes, then showed up at the end of the summer and gave the family $2,500 for a trip to Vegas. Two days later, the mother, Karen, called me and said, 'Ron, we've never known anybody like him.'

"I saw Jerome do so many things like that, but he didn't want to be recognized for it. He'd read about somebody and call me and say, 'Can you look into this and see if there is something we can do for them?' "

There was a woman in her mid-90s who lived in a Salem, Ore., care center. She was a huge fan of the Blazers.

"Somebody from the care center called and asked if there were any way he could visit her, that she's all about Jerome Kersey," Sloy recalls. "When he showed up, one of the news stations had TV cameras there. He asked that the station not film it. He didn't want any recognition. He spent three hours visiting with her. There were thousands of incidents like that."

A couple in Idaho who followed the Blazers avidly named their newborn daughter "Kersey." Jerome heard about it and said he'd like the chance to one day meet her.

"Eighteen years later, Jerome drove to Boise for her high school graduation," Sloy says. "He was sitting in her living room and surprised her when she got home."

Sloy went on a few pleasure trips with Kersey. Once, they went fishing in British Columbia with Ron's father and Jerome's teammate, Kevin Duckworth.

"We drive to Vancouver, where we get on a floatplane to Port Alberni," Sloy says. "Jerome catches about a 45-pound king salmon. He fights the fish for about 45 minutes. I'd never seen him more excited in my life. He turns to my dad and says, 'Big Ron, that was exhilarating!'

"That night, Jerome and Duck are at my dad's cabin in Port Alberni. The generator goes off and it's pitch black. We're heading to bed and I look over at Duck and see him with a flashlight pointing at his face with his eyes closed. The next morning, I tell Jerome, 'Duck sleeps with a flashlight.' Jerome says to him, 'Big fella, why did you have the flashlight on?' Duck said, 'In case a bear or something breaks into the cabin.' My dad goes, 'Duck, you're bigger than any bear. What are you afraid of?' "

Sloy says Kersey would have an Oreo cookie or two nearly every morning.

"One day Ahmad Rashad is in town and he sets up an interview with Jerome," Sloy says. "Rashad and a camera crew are with him and they're coming down Highway 43 in Jerome's blue BMW. Jerome pulls over next to me, rolls the window down and says, 'Hey dude. I brought you a present.' He flips me an Oreo. That was his favorite cookie."

Sloy smiles at his many memories of Kersey.

"Jerome had great taste in clothes," he says. "He turned out to be a sharp dresser. Loved his shoes, loved his watches. He had a beautiful voice. I have video of him singing happy birthday to several people.

"The world would be so much better today with Jerome Kersey in it. He's the kindest man I've ever met."

MITCH WALKER had one of the longest-standing relationships with Kersey. They came to Longwood together as freshmen in 1980 and were amigos for 35 years.

A New York native, Walker settled in the Big Apple after college but kept in close touch with Jerome through the years.

"Jerome would come back east for games about five times a year," Walker says. "When he'd play against the Knicks or Nets or 76ers, I'd go to the games."

Walker would often serve as Kersey's entertainment guide on his forays to Gotham. Fame can have its benefits.

"We would go out the night before games, or after games," Walker says. "Sean 'Puffy' Combs had a club called 'Justin's.' It would have a line to get in. When you're a celebrity like Jerome, you don't wait in lines.

"We would pull up to the curb and I'd say, 'Jerome, go to the front of the line.' He'd lay back and I'd be the mouthpiece and go to the bouncer and say, 'I got my boy Kersey of the Blazers here; we got friends inside.' He'd say, 'Jerome, my man,' and bring us in behind the velvet ropes. Jerome was never super comfortable with that early on. I said, 'Jerome, this is New York. This is how it works.' "

Jerome would often meet up with friends at the clubs.

"There were certain guys like Patrick Ewing he was cool with," Walker says. "Whenever he came in town, Patrick was part of things that we did. Derrick Coleman was another guy he was cool with. We always caught up with Charles Oakley. Sometimes Jerome would bring teammates, like Terry (Porter) or Duck (Kevin Duckworth) or Mario Elie or Robert Pack."

There were plenty of opportunities for female companionship.

"Oh, my goodness," Walker says. "It was a slugfest. He did extremely well. There were a lot of crumbs that fell into my lap. Jerome was a night person. He loved nightlife. We always did things. He hadn't been to places like Harlem. Whenever I got with him, I always showed him the rest of the city, not just Midtown, the touristy stuff. We did things at the Apollo. This was before Harlem was gentrified.

"We had a lot of interesting nights at some of the most prominent nightclubs in New York. We were no strangers to the gentlemen's clubs. He had an opportunity to take advantage of his fame, and we had our fun, but he wasn't looking to take advantage of people. That's not how he was wired."

Walker and another Longwood alumnus, Kevin Brandon, often went out on the town on Kersey.

"Jerome was extremely generous," Walker says. "He'd pay for everything. If the bill were $6,000 or $7,000, Kevin and I would be heading for the bathroom when the check came. There were times, though, when we would pick up the tab. If he found that we paid, he would get angry with us. 'I'm not letting you guys pay for anything,' he'd say."

When Kersey was with the Bucks at the end of his career, they played in Philadelphia. Walker drove in to watch the game. Afterward, Mitch and Jerome hit the town for a couple of hours, then retired to his room at the Ritz-Carlton.

"He's knocked out on the bed, so I crashed in a chair," Walker says. "Middle of the night, I get up to go to the bathroom, and Jerome is on the floor, sleeping with a comforter over him. Later, he told me I'd been snoring so loud, the bathroom was the only place he could get any sleep."

"Mitch, I knew you had a two-hour drive back home in the morning," Kersey told Walker. "I wasn't going to wake you up. I was going to let you sleep in peace."

"That's just how that guy was," Walker says.

After Kersey retired, he would often meet Walker and other friends for the festivities at NBA All-Star Weekend.

"Once we went to a Jordan Brands party that Michael Jordan was hosting," Walker says. "He grabbed Michael and we talked to him for a minute. In L.A., there was a party at one of Michael Jackson's homes. It was an amazing property."

When Walker would fly out for a visit to Portland, he'd get a whiff of Kersey's taste for his wheels.

"He had a red Porsche," Walker says. "He had a black Ferrari. One day Kevin (Brandon) and I were with him when he was driving either his black AMG or gold Benz S500. Jerome never had a problem putting his foot down to see how fast his car would go. I'm here to tell you — fast."

When living by himself, Kersey owned a Rottweiler named "Butkus."

"Probably weighed 130 pounds," Walker says. "We had to enter the house through the back door. You'd have to open the back gate and you'd hear the dog coming. You were half-scared, thinking, 'I hope it's not my day to get eaten alive by that damn dog.'"

Walker says Kersey had friends from many walks of life.

"Each of us had a different kind of box that we checked for Jerome," Walker says. "We all miss him."

RICK ZIEBELL met Jerome Kersey during the 1992 NBA playoffs. Rick and his wife, Linda, were season ticket-holders and had courtside seats at Memorial Coliseum for the Trail Blazers. They flew to Los Angeles for Game 3 of the Blazers' first-round playoff matchup with the Lakers. Ziebell knew Portland center Wayne Cooper. In the bar at the Ritz-Carlton Hotel in Marina del Rey the night before the game, the Ziebells saw Cooper, Kersey and Cliff Robinson. Wayne introduced them to his teammates.

That summer, the Ziebells went on a Blazer-organized cruise of the Caribbean. Among those also on the cruise was Kersey, who was with then-girlfriend Anjela Stellato.

"We played some craps and hung out quite a bit," says Ziebell, who owns Salem Door & Supply Company. "They sang karaoke. Jerome had a great voice. That's how our relationship jelled."

Ziebell and Kersey kept in close touch over the next 20-plus years.

"He'd come to our house at Thanksgiving," Ziebell says. "He came to our kids' high school graduations. We played golf together. I loved being around him. When you first meet Jerome, you're in awe. He made everybody smile. He brought out the best in everybody."

Ziebell once flew to L.A. with Kersey so he could accompany Jerome on the drive back to Portland.

"We went to Beverly Hills to pick up the Ferrari he had ordered," Ziebell says.

Another time, Ziebell flew to the Bay Area and made the drive with Jerome to L.A. after Kersey had signed a free-agent contract with the Lakers. "Spent six days hanging out with him," Rick says.

"If Jerome asked me to do something, I did it," he says. "If I asked Jerome for a favor, he did it. A co-worker of my brother-in-law was dying of cancer. They did a fundraiser so she could take the kids to Disneyland. I asked Jerome, 'Would you mind bringing a basketball, or make an appearance?' He brought a Brandon Roy jersey, an auto-graphed team basketball and set up a stand to do autographs. He put out a tip jar and personally raised almost 3 grand."

Ziebell says his admiration for Kersey grew throughout the years.

"I could tell stories for a day of people whose lives he touched," Ziebell says. "People who go to the games might not remember who we played or the score of the game, but they remember (Bill) Schonely or Jerome signing an autograph or doing something special. That made their night. I would hear that from a lot of people.

"I can't say enough positive things about him. He touched every-one's heart."

Kiara Kersey at the memorial service for her father in Memorial Coliseum.
Courtesy Portland Trail Blazers

Chapter Nineteen

Gone Far Too Soon

THE ARTHROSCOPIC SURGERY to repair a meniscus tear in Jerome Kersey's left knee seemed to have gone well. Six days later, Kersey was moving around, and though the knee was still a little swollen and felt stiff, that was to be expected.

The date was Wednesday, February 18, 2015. It was the 15th birthday of Jerome's stepdaughter, Maddie Donnerberg. Jerome and his wife, Teri, had reservations to take Maddie to dinner at Benihana's that evening.

Jerome spent time that day at the Trail Blazer offices in Portland's Rose Quarter, taking care of some business in his position as the team's director of player programs and alumni. He told co-workers he wasn't feeling well, hopped in his Jaguar and headed early to his Lake Oswego home. Once there, he mentioned nothing about how he felt to Teri.

Jerome sipped on a Heineken and Teri sat on the couch in the living room, chatting and watching a basketball game with her husband. Late in the afternoon, Jerome headed upstairs to get ready for dinner.

Moments later, Jerome called down to his wife. "Teri!"

"That was odd," Teri says. "He didn't normally call me Teri. He usually said, 'Honey.' "

Maddie, who was also upstairs dressing, answered Jerome with "she's downstairs."

Jerome yelled again for Teri. She rushed upstairs. He told her he was having a hard time breathing. Jerome tried lying on the floor, but every time he lied on his back, it made it harder to breathe. Maddie brought the phone to her mother as the 9-1-1 dispatcher answered.

"He's having difficulty breathing," Teri told the dispatcher. "He just had knee surgery."

Teri, for years a dental assistant, suspected it could be the result of a blood clot, "but I didn't know."

Moments later, an ambulance arrived with emergency medical technicians, who immediately administered oxygen "in case it was a heart attack," Teri says, and hooked him up to an IV.

When the EMTs placed Jerome in the ambulance, his body started shaking.

"I turned to a fireman and said, 'Oh, no, I think he's dying,' " Teri says. "He said, 'No, he's just in pain.' "

Once Jerome had been laid down, though, the blood clot went fully to his lungs.

Teri rode with the fireman — driving behind the ambulance — to Legacy Meridian Park Medical Center in Tualatin. On the 20-minute drive, she placed three calls — to her mother, to Jerome's close friend, J.R. Harris, and to his daughter, Kiara.

Once Teri got to the hospital, she was met by a chaplain.

"That's never a good sign," she says.

An EMT driver told her they were still working to save Jerome, but it didn't look good. The doctor came into the waiting room when she was sitting with the chaplain.

"Jerome died," he told her. "He didn't make it."

Teri was in shock. It was 6:30 p.m. They were supposed to be having dinner within the hour, celebrating a special occasion. Now, she had been told her husband had succumbed to a pulmonary embolism.

"I was like, 'This can't be happening. Go fix this,' " Teri says.

Soon, Kiara and her mother, Anjela Stellato, showed up in the emergency room. Teri hardly knew what to say. Her parents arrived and brought her home.

"You know the craziest part?" Teri says today. "There on the table in the living room, Jerome's beer was still cold. Everything happened so quickly. One minute, we're watching TV and everything is fine. The next thing you know, he's gone."

WHEN TERI got to her house, Pam Lucas — the widow of ex-Blazer Maurice Lucas, who had died of cancer nearly five years earlier — was already there to provide support. Soon, J.R. Harris — one of Jerome's closest friends — showed up. He had driven from his house in Seattle almost immediately after getting a call from Teri.

A week earlier, Harris' first grandchild had been born at Portland's Oregon Health & Science University. Jerome had visited J.R.'s daughter, Taylor, in the hospital for about an hour. Jerome's granddaughter, Harley, was less than a year old. Soon, J.R. and Jerome drove downtown to buy gifts for their grandchildren.

"We were at a red light and I looked at Jerome for a couple of seconds and had an epiphany," Harris says today. "We'd known each other for 31 years. Now we're shopping together to get our grandkids' clothes."

The next day, Kersey went in for knee surgery. He was home within hours. That night, while watching the Duke-North Carolina basketball game, he had a phone conversation with Harris.

"We talked on the phone every day after that," Harris says.

A little after 6 p.m. on February 18, Harris missed a couple of calls. When he got to his phone on a third attempt, the caller ID said "Jerome Kersey."

"I pick up the phone," Harris recalls. "Teri says, 'J.R., I've been trying to call you. Not good news. They're working on Jerome's heart."

"It didn't even register," Harris says. "I'd just talked to him. I hung up the phone, then called her back."

"It doesn't look good," Teri said.

"I'm on my way," Harris said.

Once he hit Interstate-5 headed for Portland, Harris called Teri again.

"He's gone," she said.

"I just lost it," Harris says. "I'm driving down I-5, sometimes going 40 miles an hour and sometimes 90. I can't believe I'm going to go to Jerome's house in Lake Oswego and he's not going to be there."

Over the next three hours, Harris makes some calls, gets some more.

"My phone is flooding," he says. "I can't pick it up. I'm crying too hard. I call my daughter, Taylor, and a few other people. I didn't know what to say. Nobody does."

Harris pulls up in front of the Kersey home at 9:45 p.m.

"The only light on is the master bedroom upstairs," Harris says. "I'm thinking, 'Is he not going to be in there?' I text Teri and say I'm in front of the house, but I'm not ready to come in. I finally gather myself and get strong enough to go into the house. I get inside the door and smell his cologne. I don't get the, 'What's up, Harris?' greeting I always get. And I break down. I'm there to comfort Teri. She's the one who has to hold me."

Brian Grant was at a jazz music show at a theater in downtown Portland when he got word of Kersey's death that night.

"My phone kept ringing," says Grant, the ex-Blazer forward. "I finally walked out and answered. It was my son, Jaydon. He was crying. He said, 'Dad, Jerome just died.' I was like, 'What?' I got shaky and called Terry (Porter). He couldn't even talk. It crushed us. I knew Jerome, but my heart went out to Terry and people who knew him much longer than I did. I still get a little choked up thinking about it."

WHEELS SPUN into motion in the hours after Jerome Kersey's death.

Jerome had pre-arranged to be an organ, eye and tissue donor. Over the ensuing 48 hours, his donations gave the gift of life to eight children at a burn center through the Shriners Hospital in Galveston, Texas. Three patients received his skin grafts. The cornea donation enhanced the lives of four people who received a groundbreaking eye surgery, according to Donate Life Northwest.

"It further solidifies who my dad was a person," Kiara Kersey says. "Giving, giving, giving, even after he passed away. That's what he was about."

"I think back to the children at the pediatric burn center and the eye donations and I'm grateful to be a part of it," Teri says today. "But that phone call (from donation center officials) — I don't wish that on anybody. "That was like talking to somebody two days after your loved one dies and dissecting them on the phone. I didn't even know which way was up at that point. The lives that were saved and helped — that's awesome. Of course I want to be a donor. But the questions you have to answer — it was difficult."

Teri wasn't the only person in disbelief over Jerome's death.

"I was shocked — as shocked as I've been in my professional career," says Chris McGowan, the Blazers' president and CEO. "Jerome was so full of life and health and raring to go."

Thousands of Blazer fans felt the same way. Few players in franchise history were as revered as was Kersey. It was a terrible blow to those who loved to watch him play and had grown to consider him as one of the important faces of the franchise.

Michael Lewellen had seen Jerome in the Blazer offices on the day of his death. That night, the team's vice president/corporate communications was charged with writing the official press release that announced his death.

"That may have been the most difficult press release I ever wrote," says Lewellen, who worked for the Blazers from 2012-19. "I was at New Seasons Market to get some food with the intention of going back to the office to do some work that night. My phone started going crazy. Chris McGowan called to say the news was spreading that Jerome had passed away. I scrambled back to the office. We were trying to confirm it was true before we sent anything out. Finally, we got that information from Teri."

Lewellen coordinated the press conference that night in which McGowan and former Blazer teammate Porter were among the speakers.

"I woke up and thought it was a bad dream," Porter said at the gathering. "Maybe God figured he was missing an energy guy. Maybe he needs an intangible guy on his team."

"If you needed something, he was the first one to do it," McGowan told reporters. "He never really said no. … our organization is still in shock. His legacy is never going to be forgotten."

Long-time team president Harry Glickman said he knew of only one person whom Kersey ever disappointed: "My nine-year-old granddaughter, who got very upset when he got married instead of waiting for her."

Added Glickman: "When I think of Jerome, I don't think of his rebounds or his defense or his scoring. I think of the way he related to a loose ball. He was the best we ever had."

Lewellen also played a large role in handling the media logistics for a memorial service held at Memorial Coliseum five days later.

"Those were a difficult 48 hours, not only in breaking news of his death but in being witness to the conversation the media had with Terry, one of Jerome's best friends," Lewellen says. "It was tough for our employees. Jerome was one of us.

"He was always a guy for a smile and a kind word. Despite being so physically imposing, when he was around small children at some of our events he was always relatable. He was kind to people and had a smile for them. I'll always remember him for that."

Lewellen had worked for Nike during Kersey's heyday with the Blazers in the 1990s.

"I didn't know him personally then, but was a fan of his game," Lewellen says. "He came from an unknown university (Longwood). I was from a small school, too (Arkansas State), so I felt an affinity there. Then to come to work for the Blazers so many years later and be around him on a regular basis was fantastic. That added to the affection I had for him — I got to enjoy him as a player first, then as a fellow employee, a man and a father. That could not have been better."

Wrote Ben Golliver of Sports Illustrated: "Grief counseling was made available to all (Blazer) employees and it was decided that Kersey's office would remain untouched. … So many flowers piled up from fans that the organization decided to construct a makeshift memorial in front of Moda Center's main fountain. Kersey's jersey and a large, framed photo were put up next to the organization's 'Rip City' sign."

(Kersey's office in the Rose Quarter remained untouched "for at least three years," according to McGowan.)

A pair of memorial services were held — a personal service on Saturday, February 22, at Athey Creek Christian Fellowship in Wilsonville, Ore., and a public ceremony two days later at Memorial Coliseum.

About 500 friends and family attended the personal service. Among the attendees were former Blazers and teammates Porter, Clyde Drexler, Buck Williams, Kiki VanDeWeghe, Cliff Robinson, Mark Bryant, Robert Pack, Steve Johnson, Wayne Cooper, Bob Gross, Tracy Murray, Darnell Valentine, Kenny Carr, Greg Smith, Michael Harper, Antonio Harvey, Michael Holton, Chris Dudley, Steve Colter and Darrell Imhoff.

A crowd of nearly 2,000 paid homage to Kersey two days later in the arena in which he performed as a hometown hero for 11 seasons. Many of the same former players were on hand along with ex-front office executives Glickman, Geoff Petrie and Bucky Buckwalter, coach Rick Adelman and long-time team chaplain Al Egg, who spoke at both services. Also attending the public service were members of the current Blazer team and their coaching staff, including head coach Terry Stotts and players Damian Lillard, Robin Lopez, Steve Blake and Nicolas Batum.

At each service, there were video presentations of Kersey in action on the court. The Saturday service included a slide show of his more personal side with family and friends, including his grandmother, Teri, Kiara and granddaughter Harley. Andy Stokes sang at both services. Monday's service concluded with the music video "Bust a Bucket," which was performed by Dan Reed in 1992, accompanied by Kersey, Duckworth, Porter and Williams, among others.

Broadcasting legend Bill Schonely emceed on Monday and led those in attendance in a rousing "Mercy, Mercy, Jerome Kersey," a catch phrase of the Schonz during his years calling Kersey's games.

"Schonely said it perfectly at the service," J.R. Harris says. "There were other great Blazers, other players who were popular, but this was the guy the city really loved. He became very visible. He was the only one who stayed the whole time. He never left."

"The true measure of a man is the impact he had on those he touched," Porter told the audience. "Jerome had a lot of people in his life in that category."

"He was about lifting the human spirit," close friend Mitch Walker said. "Jerome lived a life of giving, not taking. Let's honor him by continuing to give to our communities."

"He relished being an ordinary guy, even though he was anything but ordinary," said Kevin Brandon, another good friend. "It's not how many years you have on earth; it's what you do during your life."

"They say the true character of a man is judged by how he treats those who can do nothing for him," Ron Sloy, best man in Kersey's wedding, told the crowd. "It didn't matter who you were, Jerome treated you well. He was a big man who never looked down on anybody. He loved people. He loved kids. He loved his family. If love could have saved Jerome Kersey, he'd have lived forever."

Porter, Kersey and Brian Grant had spent the day before Jerome died together, speaking with students at Madison High.

"I'm so glad God gave me last Tuesday with Jerome," Porter told the audience. "Two old warriors, broken-down bodies, talking to kids about a brighter future, about appreciating those who blazed the trails before them."

Like Kersey, Porter came from a small school (Wisconsin-Stevens Point). Porter was a late first-round draft pick while Jerome went with the 46th pick overall, in the second round of the draft.

"God has called you, but you don't have to worry about being a second-round pick in his draft," Porter said. "You are a guaranteed lottery pick."

Schonely read a poem written by Helen Marshall about happy

memories living on after a loved one is gone:

"I'd like the memory of me to be a happy one,
I'd like to leave an afterglow of smiles when life is done
I'd like to leave an echo whispering softly down the way,
of happy times and laughing times and bright and sunny days.
I'd like the tears of those who grieve to dry before the sun,
of happy memories that I leave now that my life is done."

Kiara thanked Blake for giving up his uniform number (25, which was also Jerome's) for the rest of the season in honor of her father. She thanked owner Paul Allen for taking care of travel accommodations from Virginia for members of Jerome's family. She spoke of the way her father had embraced being a grandfather. She spoke lovingly of Teri, who "knew how to love him strong and give him a kick in the butt when he needed it."

"We are the only ones besides my mom who had that relationship with my dad," Kiara would say later. "We really bonded through the time after my dad passed away. Harley was such a healing presence for both of us through that time. She has always loved Harley the same as any of her kids."

At one point in the public service, Kiara spoke directly to her father.

"It would be really easy for me to be angry right now for so many reasons," she said. "Harley's first birthday is right around the corner, and we were in the middle of planning the whole thing. What about Harley's first day of school, or giving me away at my wedding some-day? I don't understand God's timing, but I know you'd want me to appreciate the time we had together and not dwell on this moment. I choose to imagine there is one of two things right now. You're either dunking on Jesus or riding a Harley Davidson while singing with my grandpa in heaven.

"Dad, I'm devastated and grieving. However, I'm overwhelmingly grateful and celebrating the 21 years I've had to see the many dimen-sions of your character. I know you would challenge me to fill the shoes you wore through your multiple walks of life. I'm going to give my all to continue to fulfill the Kersey legacy you started."

There was a touching moment few were aware of during the public ceremony.

Harley Kersey was in attendance with her mother, Kiara, and grandmother, Anjela Stellato. The baby — she wasn't yet one — looked up at the Jumbotron and saw Jerome's photo. Her face was one of wonderment.

"Papa!" She said. "Papa!"

Teri spoke bravely, with composure and poise, at both services. She received a standing ovation twice during Monday's ceremony — when she took the stage and when she finished her talk.

She noted attending memorial services with Jerome at the Coliseum for former Blazers Kevin Duckworth, Maurice Lucas and Dale Schlueter.

"I held his hand and looked at him and said, 'Don't you ever do this to me,' " she said. "Amazing to think I'm standing here today."

Kersey's widow thanked everyone for the "outpouring of love and support for the family."

"My story with Jerome had nothing to do with basketball," she told the audience. "It was a complete love story. The man I knew was loving, caring, thoughtful, kindhearted, husband, father, grandpa. Jerome along with our four children and granddaughter led a very simple life. If he didn't have a Blazer game or event to attend, most nights we spent at home. He was very much a family man and enjoyed dinner with our kids, where we sat every night and had dinner together. He made sure we prayed at every meal, whether at home or a restaurant. We loved that about him. He took care of his family. It was important to him that we were always OK."

Teri said she often spoke with Jerome about growing old together — "me getting older; he was already there," she joked.

Teri said Jerome could be a procrastinator.

"If he said he'd do something, he'd do it, but on his own time," she said. "It took him nearly nine years to marry me. During that time, I would always remind myself that God's timing is perfect. When we got married, it was all that — the perfect day. So beautiful. It was the happiest day of my life. I will never forget the look on his face when he saw me walk down the aisle. He had tears in his eyes. I had finally become one with my best friend, my soul mate.

"I no longer feel like God's timing is perfect. This doesn't feel perfect at all. What I do know is, God's timing is God's timing. Not once have I questioned why. I may never understand. I just pray that God gives me peace. I believe in the Lord Jesus Christ, and so did Jerome. Although my plan was to spend the rest of my life with Jerome, I am so thankful and so blessed that he loved me enough … (voice breaking) and chose to spend the rest of his life with me. His very last words to me were, 'Baby, I love you.' He was my dream come true."

Later, when asked how she was able to hold it together during her two speeches, Teri would shake her head and say, "It was divine intervention. That was 100 percent the Lord speaking through me. I'd never spoken in front of people in my life."

REACTION TO JEROME'S DEATH hit hard throughout the league. TNT studio analyst Shaquille O'Neal, who had played with Kersey with the Lakers for one season (1996-97), said, "What I admired about Jerome was he just played so hard. He was a professional. He taught me a lot."

The Portland Tribune reached out to many who had played with Kersey for the Trail Blazers, along with several other ex-Blazers.

"My whole family is devastated," said Buck Williams, the power forward alongside Kersey on the great Blazer teams of the early '90s. "We're just heartbroken."

"I saw him (Wednesday) morning in the office," said Schonely, the radio play-by-play voice for every game Kersey played as a Blazer. "I was giving him a hard time about walking around without crutches. He said, 'Have a great day, Schonz.' I had a great day — for a while.

"Jerome might be the most popular Blazer player we've ever had. He was admired for everything he stood for, and had such great visibility in the public after he retired. Everybody loved the guy."

Kersey's death left his friends and former teammates searching for answers.

"It's like you don't know how to process it," said Clyde Drexler, the greatest Blazer of them all, who spent 10 1/2 seasons alongside Kersey in a Portland uniform. "I feel very sad for his wife Teri, his kids, the fans, for the city of Portland. It's a terrible loss for the community."

"Blazer Nation is going through a tough time right now with the loss of Duck, Luke and now Jerome," said Chris Dudley, who played two seasons in Portland with Kersey.

"I don't have an answer for this gone-too-soon thing," said Geoff Petrie, the Blazers' vice president/operations during Kersey's heyday. "It's just terrible to lose a guy like this, so young in the scheme of things. Jerome was just full of life."

The Blazers unloaded Kiki VanDeWeghe — Drexler's best friend on the team — in 1988 to make room for Kersey in the starting lineup. But Clyde understood it was a business decision.

"From the day he arrived, Jerome had the best attitude of any player I've ever been around," Drexler said. "He was willing to do whatever it took to get onto the court and help us win. I don't think I ever heard him complain about anything. He was a guy who worked for every inch of what he got.

"If he had a problem with anything or anyone, he'd face it the same day. I loved that about him. He was the kind of teammate you'd go to war with. He'd show up and give you everything he had. I had the utmost respect for him as a teammate. He didn't take days off. He was one of the most important pieces on a deep and talented team.

"I played with Jerome longer than any other teammate. We were like brothers, trust me. We played together, we battled together, we went against all odds together. I can't believe we've lost him."

The Blazers' next home game was Sunday, February 22, against Memphis at Moda Center. Black and white placards that read "JK25" on one side and "Mercy Mercy" on the other, were placed on each of the 20,000 seats. Black patches with "JK25" in white letters inside a red ring were added to the players' jerseys and worn for the rest of the season. For the game against the Grizzlies, commemorative T-shirts were worn by the players and coaches during warmups; the players all wore black socks.

During the game, a video tribute was shown, featuring Kersey's playing career and his post-retirement involvement with the organization and the community.

"The stuff on the court was only a small part of what he did," director of production Billie Olson told Golliver. "We wanted a mix of basketball and community. It was really important for us to convey how important he was to Rip City … how he was so much bigger than just the player."

Before pregame introductions, there was a 25-second moment of silence for Jerome. The fans — many clad in Kersey throwback jerseys and carrying signs that read "Win it 4 Jerome" or "Mercy Mercy, there's no one like Kersey" — erupted in cheers when it ended.

There was a video tribute, with highlights of his career, including a post-retirement Kersey dancing along with cheerleaders and interacting with fans. The video ended with "Jerome Kersey 1962-2015," remaining on the screen for an extra beat as Puff Daddy's "I'll Be Missing You" played at low volume on the sound system.

IN THE MONTHS following Kersey's death, his widow struggled to keep her life together. She was helped immeasurably by her sister, Alanna Mandrou.

"All of a sudden, I had to face everything," Teri says. "She stayed with me for a month. Having her around was like my security blanket, my comfort. At first, I told her husband he couldn't have her back."

Teri was forced to go through Jerome's substantial wardrobe.

"Jerome was a clothes hoarder," she says. "Oh my God — six closets full. He had 280 pairs of shoes. I never should have felt bad about bringing home a new pair of shoes. Dozens of suits and hundreds of ties."

Teri and J.R. Harris gathered much of the clothing and donated it to "Best Foot Forward," an organization that provides professional apparel for low-income men.

Teri received many letters, cards, emails, calls and texts. Hundreds of people reached out via social media.

"Our mailman was delivering something one day and saw my last name and asked if I were related to Jerome," she says. "I told him, and he had three stories to tell me. It's enduring. It makes my heart feel good. I love hearing all the stories. I still hear them all the time. People tell me what Jerome did for them, that he 'came and talked to my child who was in the hospital.' He did that often. He didn't tell people about his hospital visits.

"There were times when I had no idea what he was up to. He'd be on his way to work and would stop at the children's hospital and see some kids, or he'd heard about someone who had cancer and was dying and he'd hang out with them for a little while. It wasn't something that somebody asked him to do. He did those things out of the kindness of his heart."

Teri's religious convictions have helped her deal with her loss.

"We weren't even married for a year and a half," she says today. "For Jerome to be taken from me that soon … but I'll never question, 'God, why did you take Jerome from me?' There's always a reason. I know Jerome believed in God, and I believe he's in heaven."

Today, Teri Kersey is Teri Kersey Valentine. She married her family dentist, Kyle Valentine, on March 11, 2016. They live in West Linn. Teri had worked as a dental assistant for Kyle for about five years.

"Kyle was Jerome's dentist, too, and Kiara's," Teri says. "Kyle and Jerome were friends. They went to a Blazer game together once."

The Valentines own and operate the Valentine Clinic — specializing in non-surgical anti-aging options — in

Vancouver, Wash. Kyle also serves as director of programs for the nonprofit Jerome Kersey Foundation, with the primary initiative to provide pediatric dental care for the underserved. The foundation was established shortly after Jerome's death by Teri and her sister.

"But Kyle IS the foundation," Teri says. "I'm just the face. He does all the hard work. He does everything in the background."

At Longwood University, Kersey's name has hardly been forgotten. In 2016, the playing surface at Willett Hall was named "Jerome Kersey Court." A mural of Kersey is on the wall inside the Lancers' locker room. His retired No. 54 jersey hangs from the rafters.

MORE THAN six years after his death, the people who knew Jerome Kersey best still lament their loss.

Every year on the anniversary of his death (February 18) and his birthday (June 26), several of his closest friends — including Mitch Walker, J.R. Harris, Ron Sloy and Kevin "Huggy" Brandon — drink a Jack Daniel and Coke in his memory.

"His passing remains very painful for me," Geoff Petrie says. "When it happened, it just absolutely floored me. I always saw him as an indestructible guy and spirit.

"I was in Portland for a benefit at an art gallery about a week before he died. Jerome was there. We sat down at a table and talked for some time. I met his wife. He was so frigging happy and upbeat about everything — his life, his job. It was so great to see him like that. Then a few days later — gone. It's one of those things in life that doesn't seem fair."

"I still struggle with the loss of him," Harris says. "I miss the calls from him saying, 'I'm driving up from Portland.' I have worn something of his every day since he died. We used to switch watches, shoes, bracelets. I didn't like his clothes — well, he got better through the years — but I wear one piece of jewelry every day.

"Jerome brought a lot of guys together. I have not let those relationships die because he's gone. I've put an effort into communicating with every guy Jerome brought into my life, every person that I enjoyed with Jerome when he was around."

"I was devastated when he died," Brandon says. "I still haven't accepted it. I still feel like he's alive. I dream at night that we're doing things. In my dreams, I know he's dead, but he doesn't know it. He's still living. It's weird. I still have his number in my phone. When my mom died, it took a chunk out of me. The only other person like that is

Jerome. It took a part of me away."

"When Jerome died, I was in federal prison," close friend Eddie Bynum says. "I was incarcerated from June 4, 2014, through June 5, 2015. The IRS did a sting on my car lot, and got me for money laundering. To show our friendship, Jerome was there from beginning to end. He and Ron Sloy spoke on my behalf at my sentencing. I learned of his death in the prison yard. I spoke with his wife, and she gave me the word on what happened.

"You've probably heard what a good person Jerome was. Whatever you've been told, you can multiply that times 10. I went to charity auctions with him. There was so much stuff he did that people don't know about. Whatever stories you hear from people, there are 10 others you haven't heard.

"I'm happy about one thing. When God calls me home, I get to see him again."

Buck Williams gets emotional talking about his fallen teammate.

"I miss Jerome a lot," he says. "We talked often on the phone. Every time we talked, even if we hadn't seen each other in a long time, it was like we'd been together the day before.

"I would love to see the organization retire his jersey — not only for what he did on the court, but what he did off of it in Portland. He was Mr. Trail Blazer just as much as Terry and Clyde. He gave his all to the community. He left nothing undone. He always had time to try to make the fans happy. He loved the Portland area and made it his home.

"I tell my wife often how much I miss him. The memories, they'll go on forever. I hope that organization will remember him in a significant way."

Index

E

Earl "The Pearl" Monroe 24
Eaton, Mark 99
Edwards, James 172
Elie, Mario 218, 226, 300
Elliott, Sean xx, 168, 227, 258, 259
Ely, Bruce xx
English, Alex 142
Erving, Julius "Dr. J" 13, 97, 177
Eubank, Justin 21

F

Fegan, Dan 239
Fitch, Bill 124
Fitzsimmons, Cotton 181, 199, 203
Fletcher, Tom xx, 272
Florence, Thomas 3
Ford, Kenny xx, 38-40, 42, 43, 49, 284
Fratello, Mike 139

G

Gaines, Clarence "Big House" 24, 34
Garnett, Kevin 253
Golden State Warriors 95, 137, 140, 151, 152, 155, 165, 179, 180, 183, 186, 198-200, 220, 224, 240, 250, 251, 258, 262
Gorman, Doug xxi, xxii, 289, 290
Grant, Brian xiv, xx, 215, 290, 291, 308, 312
Grant, Franklin xx, 291-293
Grant, Harvey 228, 233, 238, 239

Green, A.C. 213
Greenberg, Brad 232
Gupton, Ms. Weston xx, 56

H

Hansen, Bobby 206
Hardaway, Tim 180
Hargrove, John xxi, 1, 6, 130-132, 133-136
Hargrove, Tommy xx, 6, 7
Harper, Derek 168
Harper, Michael 38, 311
Harris, Del 165, 252
Harris, J.R. xiii, xxi, 105, 176, 177, 210, 249, 265, 278, 282, 293, 294, 306, 307, 312, 317, 319
Hawkins, Hersey xx, 256
Hillcrest Elementary School 11
Hite, Dale xx, 5, 6, 8, 25, 29, 32
Hodel, Nick 278
Holton, Michael xx, 121, 140, 311
Hornacek, Jeff 171, 179, 202
Houston Rockets 124, 178, 187, 221, 226, 232, 240, 252
Howerton, Bob 16, 22

I

Indiana Pacers 110, 119, 129, 179, 255
Inman, Stu xix, 71, 102

J

Jackson, Jaren 259
James, LeBron x, xxii
Jensen, Jay xv

M

Madison Square Garden 62, 74, 155, 260

Magann, Rick 18, 64

Majerle, Dan 202

Malone, Karl 145, 183, 189, 198

Marshall, Donyell 250

Mason-Dixon Athletic Conference v, 39, 53

McCroey, Michael xx, xxiii, 39, 40, 41, 43, 49, 50, 284

McDaniel, Xavier 151, 162, 166, 181, 262

McGowan, Chris xx, 275, 309

McKie, Aaron 240

McMillan, Nate xx, 255

Mecklenburg County 6

Mecklenburg County Public Schools xix, 17

Mecklenburg Sun 3, 7, 16, 22

Memorial Coliseum x, 96, 110, 115, 125, 145, 150, 152, 162, 169, 171, 178, 203, 236, 302, 304, 310, 311

Miami Heat 153, 154, 229

Miller, Reggie 179

Milwaukee Bucks xii, 102, 111, 112, 152, 153, 164, 165, 184, 231, 255, 262, 267, 268, 280, 289, 301

Minnesota Timberwolves 180, 187, 230, 252, 253

Mitchell, Fannie 9

Moda Center xiv, 276, 290, 311, 316

Moe, Doug 167

Mosely, Mike xx, 7, 10, 26, 29

Mullin, Chris 41, 183, 250

Murray, Tracy 222, 226, 228, 311

N

Neal, Ernie xx, 50, 69, 74, 85

Nelson, Don 151

Newell, Pete 71

New Jersey Nets 129, 151, 159, 167, 182, 225, 226, 300

News-Progress 18, 64

New York Knicks 62, 96, 130, 142, 150, 154, 155, 166, 167, 170, 179, 220, 260, 300

Norman, Ken 153

Norris, Audie 77, 78, 95, 97

North Carolina Central University 28

O

Oakley, Charles 39, 53, 300

Ogilvie, Bruce xix, 76, 80

Olajuwon, Hakeem 75, 124, 204, 221, 228, 232

Omega Psi Phi 49, 284

O'Neal, Shaquille 251, 296, 315

Oregonian, The iv, 76, 96, 97, 106, 115, 134, 180, 183

Oregon State University iv

Orlando Magic 187, 242

Orr, Ron xx, 49, 53

Ossey, Bud v